PEOPLE AND LAND
IN THE HOLINESS CODE

SUPPLEMENTS

TO

VETUS TESTAMENTUM

EDITED BY
THE BOARD OF THE QUARTERLY

J.A. EMERTON – PHYLLIS A. BIRD – W.L. HOLLADAY
A. VAN DER KOOIJ – A. LEMAIRE – B. OTZEN – R. SMEND
J.A. SOGGIN – J.C. VANDERKAM – M. WEINFELD
H.G.M. WILLIAMSON

VOLUME LXVII

PEOPLE AND LAND
IN THE HOLINESS CODE

AN EXEGETICAL STUDY OF THE IDEATIONAL FRAMEWORK

OF THE LAW IN LEVITICUS 17–26

BY

J. JOOSTEN

E.J. BRILL
LEIDEN · NEW YORK · KÖLN
1996

The paper in this book meets the guidelines for permanence and durability of the Committee on Production Guidelines for Book Longevity of the Council on Library Resources.

Library of Congress Cataloging-in-Publication Data

Joosten, Jan.
    People and land in the holiness code : an exegetical study of the
ideational framework of the law in Leviticus 17–26 / by J. Joosten.
        p.   cm. — (Supplements to Vetus Testamentum, ISSN 0083–5889 ;
    v. 67)
    Includes bibliographical references and index.
    ISBN 9004105573 (cloth : alk. paper)
    1. Bible.   O.T.   Leviticus XVII–XXVI—Criticism, interpretation,
etc.   I. Title.   II. Series.
BS1255.2.J66   1996
222'.1306—dc20   96–41882
                                                                            CIP

Die Deutsche Bibliothek – CIP-Einheitsaufnahme

[Vetus testamentum / Supplements]
Supplements to Vetus testamentum – Leiden ; New York ;
Köln : Brill, 1996
    Früher Schriftenreihe
    Reihe Supplements zu: Vetus Testamentum
    ISSN 0083-5889
    ISBN 9004105573
NE: HST
Vol. 67. Joosten, Jan: People and land in the holiness code. -
1996
Joosten, Jan:
People and land in the holiness code : an exegetical study of
the ideational framework of the law in Leviticus 17-26 / by J.
Joosten. – Leiden ; New York ; Köln: Brill, 1996
    (Supplements to Vetus testamentum ; Vol. 67)
    ISNBN 90-04-10557-3

ISSN   0083-5889
ISBN   90 04 10557 3

PRINTED IN THE NETHERLANDS

CONTENTS

PREFACE

The continuing theological and ethical relevance of Biblical law is again a burning subject of debate today. The present work is intended as a preliminary to such questions with regard to one well defined corpus of laws. Basic to this underlying intention is the understanding that a correct assessment of the authority of these laws for the Christian Church today will be possible only if their original context is first taken into account. This means we must pay close attention to questions like: who is addressed in these laws, and in what capacity? Who is speaking? What are the unspoken presuppositions underlying the discourse? What is the aim of the laws? It is only when these, and many other, questions are addressed, that the further problem of the relevance of the law in a contemporary historical context can be properly assessed. It is my prayer that the academic study of biblical law, to which the following chapters it is to be hoped may make a modest contribution, will ultimately bear fruit in the teaching and the practice of the Christian Church.

The origins of the present work lie in a doctoral dissertation, defended in May 1994 at the Faculty of Protestant Theology in Brussels. My thanks are due to H. Jagersma and K. A. D. Smelik who acted as advisers for the original dissertation. I am grateful also for remarks of M. Weinfeld, who accepted to act as an opponent at the public defense. The present version owes much to subsequent observations made by J. Milgrom, G. Braulik, B. Schwartz, K. Grünwaldt and J. Lund. A special word of thanks goes to A. Lemaire, who accepted the work for publication in the SVT series and who has contributed much to a clear and dependable presentation of the research. My thanks are due also to my friend, Stephen Fairhurst, who has been of crucial help in improving the English style of the original draft.

My father, Marius Joosten, has followed the development of the research from its inception; his criticisms considerably sharpened the argument in several places. To Martine I express a different kind of thanks: our courtship and marriage ran parallel with the writing of the original dissertation, which means she listened to hours of theorizing on the Holiness Code when she might have wished to hear a more romantic discourse. Finally, I wish to thank the "paroisse du Champ de Mars"

who in 1993 granted their pastor six months' study leave and thus allowed me to complete the dissertation.

Jan Joosten
Strasbourg

ABBREVIATIONS

AJT	*Asian Journal of theology*
AnBib	Analecta Biblica
ANE	Ancient Near East(ern)
ANET	J. B. Pritchard, *Ancient Near Eastern Texts Relating to the Old Testament* (3rd edition, Princeton, 1969)
AOAT	Alter Orient und Altes Testament
ASTI	*Annual of the Swedish Theological Institute*
ATD	Das Alte Testament Deutsch
BA	*Biblical Archaeologist*
BBB	Bonner Biblische Beiträge
BC	Book of the Covenant
BDB	F. Brown, S. R. Driver, C. A Briggs, *A Hebrew and English Lexicon of the Old Testament* (Oxford, 1907)
BEATAJ	Beiträge zur Erforschung des Alten Testaments und des Antiken Judentums
BEThL	Bibliotheca Ephemeridum Theologicarum Lovaniensium
BHS	Biblia Hebraica Stuttgartensia
BiOr	*Bibliotheca Orientalis*
BJPES	*Bulletin of the Jewish Palestine Exploration Society*
BKAT	Biblische Kommentar Altes Testament
BN	*Biblische Notizen*
BOT	De Boeken van het Oude Testament
BWANT	Beiträge zur Wissenschaft vom Alten und Neuen Testament
BZ	*Biblische Zeitschrift*
BZAW	Beihefte zur Zeitschrift für die Alttestamentliche Wissenschaft
CAT	Commentaire de l'Ancien Testament
CBQ	*Catholic Biblical Quarterly*
COT	Commentaar op het Oude Testament
EM	*Encyclopedia Miqra'it*
EThL	Ephemerides Theologicae Lovanienses
ETR	*Etudes Théologiques et Religieuses*
EvTh	*Evangelische Theologie*
Exp	*The Expositor*
FRLANT	Forschungen zur Religion und Literatur des Alten und Neuen Testaments
H	Holiness Code
HAL	L. Koehler, W. Baumgartner, *Hebräisches und Aramäisches Lexikon zum Alten Testament* (3rd edition)
HAR	*Hebrew Annual Review*
HAT	Handbuch zum Alten Testament
HBS	Herders Biblische Studien
HSM	Harvard Semitic Monographs
HTR	*Harvard Theological Review*
HUCA	*Hebrew Union College Annual*
ICC	International Critical Commentary

IEJ	*Israel Exploration Journal*
JANES	*Journal of the Ancient Near Eastern Society*
JAOS	*Journal of the American Oriental Society*
JBL	*Journal of Biblical Literature*
JBTh	*Jahrbücher für Biblische Theologie*
JCS	*Journal of Cuneiform Studies*
JETS	*Journal of the Evangelical Theological Society*
JQR	*Jewish Quarterly Review*
JSNTS	Journal for the Study of the New Testament, Supplement Series
JSOT	*Journal for the Study of the Old Testament*
JSOTS	Journal for the Study of the Old Testament, Supplement Series
JSS	*Journal of Semitic Studies*
KAI	H. Donner, W Röllig, *Kanaanäische und Aramäische Inschriften* (Wiesbaden, 1962)
KEH	Kurzgefasstes Exegetisches Handbuch
KHCAT	Kurzer Hand-Commentar zum Alten Testament
König, *Syntax*	F. E. König, *Historisch-kritisches Lehrgebaüde der hebräischen Sprache*, Bd III (Leipzig 1897)
MT	Masoretic Text
NICOT	New International Commentary on the Old Testament
NIV	New International Version
NRT	*Nouvelle Revue Théologique*
OBO	Orbus Biblicus et Orientalis
OLA	Orientalia Lovaniensia Analecta
OTS	Oudtestamentische Studiën
RA	*Revue d'Assyriologie et d'Archéologie Orientale*
RB	*Revue Biblique*
RHPR	*Revue d'Histoire et de Philosophie Religieuses*
RHR	*Revue de l'Histoire des Religions*
RivBib	*Rivista Biblica*
RSV	Revised Standard Version
SBAB	Stuttgarter Biblische Aufsatzbände
SBL	Society of Biblical Literature
SBLDS	Society of Biblical Literature, Dissertation Series
SBS	Stuttgarter Bibelstudien
SJOT	Scandinavian Journal of the Old Testament
SR	Sciences Religieuses/Studies in Religion
SVT	Supplements to Vetus Testamentum
THAT	Theologisches Handwörterbuch zum Alten Testament, ed. E. Jenni, C. Westermann
ThLZ	*Theologische Literaturzeitung*
ThZ	*Theologische Zeitschrift*
TRE	Theologische Realenzyklopädie
TUAT	Texte aus der Umwelt des Alten Testaments
TWAT	Theologisches Wörterbuch zum Alten Testament, ed. G. J. Botterweck, H. Ringgren
TWNT	Theologisches Wörterbuch zum Neuen Testament, ed. G. Kittel, G. Friedrich
UF	*Ugarit-Forschungen*
VF	*Verkündigung und Forschung*

VT	*Vetus Testamentum*
WMANT	Wissenschaftliche Monographien zum Alten und Neuen Testament
ZA	*Zeitschrift für Assyriologie*
ZAW	*Zeitschrift für die Alttestamentliche Wissenschaft*
ZDMG	*Zeitschrift der Deutschen Morgenländischen Gesellschaft*
ZDPV	*Zeitschrift des Deutschen Palästinavereins*
ZKW	*Zeitschrift für Kirchliche Wissenschaft*
ZThK	*Zeitschrift für Theologie und Kirche*

English translations

English translations are from the Revised Standard Version unless indicated otherwise.

INTRODUCTION

The interpretation of ancient texts needs to take account of the interactive frame presupposed, though not usually explicitly stated, in the discourse. Indeed, one of the most fundamental rules of hermeneutics is that the proper horizon of a text must be taken into account if one is to understand it correctly. In plain terms, it is important to know who is speaking (or writing), to whom, under what circumstances and with which presuppositions.[1] The aim of the present work is to contribute to the study of these questions with regard to the so-called Holiness Code (Lev 17-26).

THE IDEATIONAL FRAMEWORK OF THE LAW

The attached work, particularly in Chapters 3 to 6, may be viewed as an inquiry into the interactive frame of the law contained in the Holiness Code. The research focuses on the notions of people and land: the people of Israel are the designated addressees of the law, whereas the land is depicted as the space within which the law must be put into practice. As will become increasingly clear throughout this study, the notions of people and land can be properly understood only in reference to a set of conceptions underlying the discourse: a coherent structure of ideas, which may be termed the conceptual universe of the Holiness Code. It is this conceptual universe—the ideational framework of the text—which lends the notions of people and land their meaning and thus defines the scope and significance of the corpus as a whole.

The investigation of the ideational framework of a text should begin on the literary level.[2] Every text carries at least some markers as to the

---

[1] For a lucid defense of this basic hermeneutic scheme against different varieties of new literary criticism, see M. Sternberg, *The Poetics of Biblical Narrative* (Bloomington, 1985), 8-21.

[2] The literary frame of the laws of the Old Testament has, in contemporary research, been neglected in favour of an historical frame reconstructed in a highly speculative manner. In particular the priestly laws, such as the ones contained in the Book of Leviticus, have often been projected into the reconstructed historical realities of the Second Temple period and interpreted in terms of those realities. However, the reconstruction of the historical background of an undated text must, in my opinion, be preceded by attentive study of the text as it stands. In light of this stricture, the contemporary approach seems to be precipitate. Cf. Note 4, below.

interactive frame in which it purports to function,[3] and the law texts contained in the Pentateuch are no exception: they number many indications defining this frame, some of which are very explicit[4]—although, of course, their value needs to be critically appraised. Thus the approach of the present study will be primarily exegetical, taking as its point of departure expressions, phrases and literary motifs occurring in Lev 17-26. The objective, however, will always be to arrive at the structure of ideas, the ideational framework underlying the discourse.[5]

Once the literary questions have received due consideration, historical questions may be and indeed need to be asked, since the exegesis itself often points to connections in the historical reality outside the text. Nevertheless, such historical questions are to be approached with an entirely different methodological apparatus not necessarily at the command of the exegete. In the present work, historical problems are treated with the greatest circumspection, and the answers proposed are intended to be provisional.

The Holiness Code

The limitation of the research to one set of laws or, rather, to one stretch of text, is justified on several grounds. To begin with, the restriction to a relatively short and homogeneous corpus makes it possible to scrutinize the different literary indications in detail. The research presented in Chapters 3 to 6, without presuming to be exhaustive, attempts at least to cover all the data with regard to the themes of the people and the land. The coherence and unity of Lev 17-26, and the justification of the title Holiness Code, together with other introductory questions, will be considered in some detail in Chapters 1 and 2. Secondly, by placing our point of departure in this particular corpus, we allow for the possibility that other corpora of law presuppose a different framework. Although

---

[3] Cf. Sternberg, *Poetics*, 8-11.

[4] In the historical-critical approach, these indications are usually bracketed out as secondary additions to the law text. This procedure poses a methodological problem: what the text says explicitly about its frame is judged to be irrelevant, whereas the frame presumed to be relevant is not even alluded to in the text. In contrast, the methodological line of the present study is first to take the indications of the text seriously, while leaving their historical evaluation to a later stage.

[5] Tradition history is therefore not central to the present study, although tradition-historical considerations will often point the way to a better understanding of the data in Lev 17-26.

this aspect cannot be elaborated in the present work, it will be pointed out time and again that that possibility is to be taken very seriously. In particular, the Deuteronomic laws seem to operate on suppositions different from those underlying H. The divergence of the different codes in these matters may of course be exaggerated by the microscopic nature of the present investigation; a more global approach would certainly reveal a number of important convergencies as well.[6] Nevertheless, each corpus must also be studied in its individuality.

The selection of the Holiness Code as the domain of inquiry has partly been conditioned by a consideration of the relative amounts of secondary literature devoted to the law codes in the Old Testament. Studies on the Book of the Covenant (Ex 20:22-23:33) and on Deuteronomy are legion, and investigations of the ideational framework of the law with regard to these corpora are already available.[7] The modern scholarly literature on the Holiness Code is much less abundant, and a thorough study taking account of its conceptual universe is still outstanding.

---

[6] For a global approach to the pentateuchal laws, see the articles by M. Greenberg, "Some Postulates of Biblical Criminal Law", in M. Haran, ed., *Yehezkel Kaufmann Jubilee Volume* (Jerusalem, 1960), 5-28; idem, "More Reflections on Biblical Criminal Law", in *Scripta Hierosolymitana* 31 (Jerusalem, 1986), 1-17; idem, "Biblical Attitudes toward Power: Ideal and Reality in Law and Prophets", in E. B. Firmage et al., eds., *Religion and Law. Biblical-Judaic and Islamic Perspectives* (Winona Lake, 1990), 101-112.

[7] For the Book of the Covenant, see particularly S. M. Paul, *Studies in the Book of the Covenant in Light of Cuneiform and Biblical Law*, SVT 18 (Leiden, 1970); a more critical, and more hypothetical, approach to the question is found in E. Otto, *Wandel der Rechtsbegründungen in der Gesellschafts-geschichte des antiken Israel*, Studia Biblica 3 (Brill, 1988). For Deuteronomy, much information is provided in N. Lohfink, *Das Hauptgebot. Eine Untersuchung literarischer Einleitungsfragen zu Dtn 5-11*, AnBib 20 (Rome, 1963); see also the early study of G. von Rad, *Das Gottesvolk im Deuteronomium*, BWANT 47 (Stuttgart, 1929).

CHAPTER ONE

HISTORY OF RESEARCH ON THE HOLINESS CODE

The distinct character of the collection of laws in Leviticus 17-26 was first recognized in the 19th century.[1] In 1877 it was given the name "Holiness Code" (*Heiligkeitsgesetz)* by Klostermann, and this fitting appellation has stuck ever since. Early critical scholars concurred in seeing in the Holiness Code (henceforth H) an older stratum of priestly material, that was later incorporated into P (the priestly source). On other points, however, their views diverged radically. The questions raised by 19th-century scholarship have continued to dominate the discussion. They concern the integrity, composition, authorship and date of H, and the occurrence of fragments in the style of H elsewhere in the Pentateuch.

THE INTEGRITY OF H

From early on in the historical critical study of the OT, Lev 17-26 has been viewed as a relatively independent corpus, and most scholars have shared this view. However, there have always been opponents who see these chapters as either a disorderly collection of earlier laws appended to the laws of P,[2] or a continuation of the preceding priestly legislation.[3]

An argument often made against taking Lev 17-26 as an independent corpus is that these chapters show a lack of order in the subjects treated. Several laws are given twice,[4] sometimes in identical form,[5] whereas

---

[1] For the early history of research on H see J. Wellhausen, *Die Composition des Hexateuchs und der historischen Bücher des Alten Testaments* (Berlin, 1899³), 149, and F. Delitzsch, "Pentateuch-kritische Studien. XII. Das Heiligkeitsgesetz", *ZKW* 1 (1880), 619f.

[2] See in the bibliography the publications of Dillmann, Hoffmann, Eerdmans, Küchler, Gispen and Rendtorff.

[3] See V. Wagner, "Zur Existenz des sogenannten »Heiligkeitsgesetzes«", *ZAW* 86 (1974), 307-316; E. Blum, *Studien zur Komposition des Pentateuch*, BZAW 189 (Berlin, 1990), 318ff; E. S. Gerstenberger, *Das 3. Buch Mose. Leviticus*, ATD (1993), 16f.

[4] The most striking phenomenon in this regard is the relationship between c 18 and c 20: in different formulations the very same prescriptions are given.

[5] Compare 19:9f with 23:22.

other juridical questions are not even touched upon.[6] Could such a disorderly agglomerate, it is asked, be the work of one author or editor? However, the apparent lack of a system is also typical of other law collections in the OT. Recent research on the Book of the Covenant and Deuteronomy tends to indicate that a certain measure of order is nevertheless present in what at first sight seems disorderly.[7] Similar studies on H are still in an initial stage.[8]

The most important arguments in favour of taking H as a distinct corpus are the following:

1) Like other law codes (the Book of the Covenant, Deuteronomy, the laws of P, Ezekiel 40-48), H begins with prescriptions concerning the place of sacrifice (Lev 17). Though Lev 17 does not speak of holiness and does not contain the expressions "I am the LORD" and "I am the LORD your God",[9] it shares so many characteristics with the following chapters that it must be counted as part of H.[10]

2) Like other law codes (the Book of the Covenant, Deuteronomy), H closes with a chapter of blessings and curses (Lev 26).[11]

3) Throughout H we meet with so-called paraenetic elements: laws are explained and motivated. Although it must be admitted that this paraenesis varies qualitatively and quantitatively in the different chapters, the whole phenomenon is so alien to the other priestly legislation that we must put a break between Lev 17-26 and the laws that precede and follow.[12]

---

[6] For a systematic overview of the contents of H in comparison with the other law codes of the Pentateuch, see the table in C. F. Kent, *Israel's Laws and Legal Precedents* (London, 1907), vii-xxvii.

[7] See, e.g., for the Book of the Covenant E. Otto, *Wandel der Rechtsbegründungen in der Gesellschaftsgeschichte des antiken Israel*, Studia Biblica 3 (Leiden, 1988); for Deuteronomy A. Rofé, *Introduction to Deuteronomy* (Jerusalem, 1988), 159-177.

[8] See F. Crüsemann, *Die Tora. Theologie und Sozialgeschichte des alttestamentlichen Gesetzes* (München, 1992), 379; E. Otto, *Theologische Ethik des Alten Testaments* (Stuttgart, 1994), 237-240.

[9] This has led scholars like C. Feucht, *Untersuchungen zum Heiligkeitsgesetz*, Theologische Arbeiten 20 (Berlin, 1964), 63f, and R. Kilian, *Literarkritische und formgeschichtliche Untersuchung des Heiligkeitsgesetzes*, BBB 19 (Bonn, 1963), 176-179, to deny that Lev 17 belongs with the chapters which follow it.

[10] See L. B. Paton, "The Original Form of Leviticus xvii.-xix.", *JBL* 16 (1897), 31-77, pp. 32-34 and more recently B. Schwartz, *Selected Chapters of the Holiness Code*, PhD dissertation, Hebrew University, Jerusalem 1987, 189f.

[11] Some limit the law code of which c 26 is the conclusion to Lev 25f, see B. D. Eerdmans, *Alttestamentliche Studien IV. Das Buch Leviticus* (Gießen, 1912), 121; Feucht, *Untersuchungen*, 64-66. Others extend it to all the preceding priestly laws, see E. Blum, *Studien zur Komposition des Pentateuch*, BZAW 189 (Berlin, 1990), 323, n. 136.

[12] Cf. A. Cholewinski, *Heiligkeitsgesetz und Deuteronomium*, AnBib 66 (Rome, 1976), 31, n. 60. Blum, *Studien*, 322, points to the fact that paraenesis is not totally alien

4) H is distinguished from the rest of the priestly material in the Pentateuch by its vocabulary,[13] style and theology.[14]

THE COMPOSITION OF H

Even though it is meaningful to speak of H as a distinct corpus, this does not imply it is a homogeneous literary whole. It is a matter of consensus that H contains "building blocks" of older material,[15] that have been ordered and edited by a later redaction. Difficulties arise, however, when one attempts to trace the genesis of the text-form we possess today.

From its inception in the second half of the 19th century until recently, research on H as a distinct entity has been characterized by a growing complexity in the reconstruction of its redaction history. The basic rules of the analysis were quite simple.[16] Its underlying tenets were a) that the original Holiness Code has been edited by, or in the spirit of, P;[17] and b) that the P-redaction had been preceded by the redactional activity of the author(s) of the original Holiness Code. Consequently, the first literary-critical operation consisted in separating the P-additions from the original Holiness Code.[18] The second step was to distinguish between the older laws and the (mostly paraenetic) redactional framework added by the authors of the original work. Further complexity was introduced when two, three or even four different hands were distinguished in the redactional elements.[19]

---

to P, since it appears also in Lev 11:44f and elsewhere. However, these fragments, which are similar to H in several respects, are probably to be viewed as later additions to the priestly code. See the discussion below, pp. 15-16.

[13] See S. R. Driver, *An Introduction to the Literature of the Old Testament* (New York, 1956), 49f; Milgrom, *Leviticus 1-16*, Anchor Bible (1991), 35-38.

[14] See W. Zimmerli, "Sinaibund und Abrahambund. Ein Beitrag zum Verständnis der Priesterschrift", *ThZ* 16 (1960), 268-80, and I. Knohl, *The Sanctuary of Silence. The Priestly Torah and the Holiness School* (Minneapolis, 1995).

[15] On this point there is general agreement. A comparison between H and the Book of the Covenant actually allows it to be proven in a few cases. See below, p. 10.

[16] The whole procedure is described explicitly by W. Thiel, "Erwägungen zum Alter des Heiligkeitsgesetzes", *ZAW* 81 (1969), 40-73, pp. 44f.

[17] The older view was that P wrote the chapters on the basis of older material in a different style. See e.g. T. Nöldeke, *Untersuchungen zur Kritik des Alten Testaments* (Kiel, 1869), 64. Still different is the position of Horst, who thinks P-materials and H-materials were combined by a later redactor, see L. Horst, *Leviticus XVII-XXVI und Hezekiel. Ein Beitrag zur Pentateuchkritik* (Colmar, 1881), 13-36.

[18] See in particular the articles by Paton in *JBL* 16 (1897), 31-77; *JBL* 17 (1898), 149-175; *JBL* 18 (1899), 35-60.

[19] See the analyses of B. Baentsch, *Das Heiligkeits-Gesetz* (Erfurt, 1893); Kilian, *Untersuchung* ; K. Elliger, *Leviticus*, HAT (1966); Cholewinski, *Heiligkeitsgesetz*.

In recent years this historical critical approach has come under considerable critical fire.[20] Scholars have pointed to the subjectivity of the
"literary stratigraphy" it involves. Results cannot be tested in any way,
and no two analyses correspond exactly.[21] More specifically, the underlying suppositions have themselves been attacked. In several quarters,
the hypothesis has been advanced that H is not an older corpus of laws
incorporated in P, but on the contrary, a later piece of legislation, written
as a correction of P.[22] In this case, the "P" elements in H can be ascribed
to the original author(s) of H, who could freely draw on elements of the
earlier priestly style and diction.[23] It has also been questioned whether it
is permissible to separate laws and paraenesis as if they had at some
stage existed independently. Both philological considerations and historical study of the *Sitz im Leben* of the law corpora indicate that law
and paraenesis may have been intertwined from the start.[24] An extreme
exponent of this last view is H. Graf Reventlow, who derives the whole
of H from the preaching of the law in the pre-exilic Covenant Feast.[25]

In response to these criticisms, the last decade or so has produced a
different approach to H.[26] The text is taken more seriously in its
synchronic dimension with its structural and esthetic aspects receiving
more attention.[27] This approach does not deny that the present text has a

---

[20] It is a general trend in recent biblical scholarship to take the final form of the
biblical text (its *Endgestalt)* more seriously. See, for the Pentateuch, A. de Pury et T.
Römer, "Le Pentateuque en question: Position du problème et brève histoire de la recherche" in A. de Pury éd., *Le Pentateuque en question* (Genève, 1989), 9-80, esp. 48-
80.

[21] See E. Cortese, "L'esegesi di H (Lev. 17-26)", *RivBib* 29 (1981), 129-146;
Schwartz, *Chapters*, 110f; Blum, *Studien*, 321, n. 131.

[22] See below, pp. 13-14.

[23] Knohl, *Sanctuary*, 111-123, shows that there is no P-redaction in Lev 17-26. The
words and phrases typical of P are used in a way that corresponds rather to the ideas of
H. See also Cholewinski, *Heiligkeitsgesetz*, 14, n. 13.

[24] For the Book of the Covenant, this has been argued by W. Beyerlin, "Die Paränese
im Bundesbuch und ihre Herkunft", in H. Graf Reventlow, Hsg., *Gottes Werden und
Gottes Land*, Fs H.-W. Hertzberg (Göttingen, 1965), 9-29. The same point had already
been made, more generally and with reference to all the law codes of the OT, by B.
Gemser, "The Importance of the Motive Clause in Old Testament Law", in G. W.
Anderson et al., eds., *Congress Volume. Copenhagen 1953*, SVT 1 (Leiden, 1953), 50-
66. Against this view, see H. Rücker, *Die Begründungen der Weisungen Jahwes im Pentateuch*, Erfurter Theologische Studien 30 (Leipzig, 1973), 28-37.

[25] H. Graf Reventlow, *Das Heiligkeitsgesetz* (Neukirchen, 1961).

[26] However, literary critical analysis continues to be practised by some, see, e.g. J.
Aloni, "The Place of Worship and the Place of Slaughter According to Leviticus 17:3-
9", *Shnaton* 7-8 (1983-84), 21-49.

[27] Mathys, Barbiero, Schwartz and Blum are notable exponents of this new approach
(see the bibliography). See also B. S. Childs, *Introduction to the Old Testament as Scripture* (London, 1979), 185f.

history behind it; it is merely more pessimistic as to the possibility of reconstructing that history in the majority of cases.

DATE AND AUTHOR

Determining the historical background of H is problematic. It relates words and events from the period after the Exodus when Israel was camping at Mount Sinai. It is not, however, an eye-witness report, and the text itself gives indications of being written when the people of Israel were already well established in the land.[28] Moreover, comparison between H and the other legal corpora in the OT reveals differences that make it clear that they cannot all be ascribed to one person; all the laws of the Pentateuch have a long tradition behind them.[29] However, once we have eliminated the Mosaic age as a possible historical background for our text, very few indices remain for an exact dating.[30] This has not deterred scholars from placing H in the pre-exilic,[31] exilic,[32] or post-

---

[28] See particularly 18:25. In 25:32-34 the Levitical cities are mentioned, a notion which according to the narrative framework of the text was introduced years later, cf. Num 35:1-8. The threat in 26:39 "Those of you that are left (...) because of the iniquities of their fathers they shall pine away like them" also presupposes an audience of a generation with fathers who have already had the opportunity to sin against YHWH's commandments. See also 26:45. Some of these verses give the impression that the fiction of Israel in the desert is explicitly acknowledged as such (cf. such texts as Deut 5:3).

[29] For an exposition of the differences between the different law codes in the Pentateuch, see Y. Kaufmann, *Toledot ha-Emunah ha-Yisra'elit*, vol. 1(Jerusalem, 1937), 47-65.

[30] Many scholars find an unambiguous indication in 26:33-45: surely if the exile is predicted, the verses must date from the exile. On reflection, the argument is not watertight. The prediction might be genuine—Amos predicted the exile of the 10 tribes (Am 5:27; 6:7). Exile, especially after the rise of Assyria in the 8th century, was not an unknown concept to Israel. Similar threats are found in Ancient Near Eastern treaties, see M. Weinfeld, *Deuteronomy and the Deuteronomic School* (Oxford, 1972), 133. It must be noted, too, that Lev 26 contains all sorts of threats, of which exile is only one—albeit the most terrible. Cf. the considerations of Y. Kaufmann, *Toledot*, vol. 1, 198-201. Another much-cited criterion of lateness is the anointed high priest in 21:10; nothing whatsoever should be made of this, however, as is conceded by Kilian, *Untersuchung*, 185f. For the use of exact dating and the numbering of months in Lev 23, see now B. R. Goldstein and A. Cooper, "The Festivals of Israel and Juda and the Literary History of the Pentateuch", *JAOS* 110 (1990), 19-31. Haran finds an indication of an early date in the Molech-texts 18:21; 20:2-5; however, it is not impossible that this particular sin was singled out by an exilic writer in order to exemplify the things that should not be done upon returning to the land, see H.-P. Mathys, *Liebe deinen Nächsten wie dich selbst. Untersuchungen zum alttestamentlichen Gebot der Nächstenliebe (Lev 19, 18)*, OBO 71 (Freiburg, 1986), 87f. Less plausibly, the Molech-cult was revived by Jews during or after the exile.

[31] Dillmann, Klostermann, Eerdmans, Kaufmann, Haran.

[32] Cortese, Lohfink, Smend.

exilic era,[33] and some assign it to a much more narrowly defined period.[34] The most important approach to the dating of H has been to compare it to other writings of the OT in order to attain at least a relative
chronology. The entities with which H is to be compared are: the Book
of the Covenant, Deuteronomy, Ezekiel and P.[35]

The Book of the Covenant (BC)

To all appearances, the law code we find in Ex 20:22-23:33 is the oldest
collection of laws of the OT.[36] At certain places, H seems to be based on
the very text of BC.[37] However, it is by no means certain that the author
of H had the whole Book of the Covenant available to him in the form in
which we know it today.[38] In any case, since the date of BC is itself a
highly contentious issue, it cannot be used to date H with any accuracy.[39]

Deuteronomy

Earlier scholars have usually assessed the relationship between H and
Deuteronomy on the basis of very general considerations.[40] On the one
hand, H appears to presuppose several places of worship and was there-

---

[33] Vink, Blum.

[34] See, e.g., G. Bettenzoli, *Geist der Heiligkeit. Traditionsgeschichtliche
Untersuchung des* QDS-*Begriffes im Buch Ezekiel*, Quaderni di Semitistica 8 (Firenze,
1979), 102; C. F. Kent, *Israel's Laws and Legal Precedents* (London, 1907), 36-42, J.
Morgenstern, "The Decalogue of the Holiness Code", *HUCA* 26 (1955), 1-27, p. 18.

[35] As to other points of literary contact, Reventlow has sought to show that Am 4:6-
11 is dependent on Lev 26, see H. Graf Reventlow, *Das Amt des Propheten bei Amos*,
FRLANT 80 (Göttingen, 1962), 83-90. He is followed by W. Brueggeman, "Amos iv 4-
13 and Israel's Covenant Worship", *VT* 15 (1965), 1-15. Knohl, *Sanctuary*, 212-214,
argues for mutual influence between H and Isaiah.

[36] See, e.g., M. Weinfeld, "Literary Creativity", in A. Malamat, ed., *The World History of the Jewish People, Vol. 4,2. The Age of the Monarchies: Culture and Society*
(Jerusalem, 1979), 27-70, 36f.

[37] Cf. M. Paran, *Forms of the Priestly Style in the Pentateuch. Patterns, Linguistic
Usages, Syntactic Structures.* (Jerusalem, 1989), 29-34.

[38] Kaufmann has shown convincingly that H is not as such based on the Book of the
Covenant, see Kaufmann, *Toledot* , vol. 1, 58-61.

[39] Whereas most scholars date the Book of the Covenant to the time of the Judges,
the more recent tendency is to date it in the late monarchical period. See, e.g., F.
Crüsemann, "Das Bundesbuch—Historischer Ort und Institutioneller Hintergrund", in
J. A. Emerton, ed., *Congress Volume. Jerusalem 1986*, SVT 40 (1988), 27-41.

[40] An exception is Baentsch who made a detailed comparison between H and Deuteronomy and concluded that H is dependent on Deuteronomy. See Baentsch, *Heiligkeits-
Gesetz*, 76-80. His method is criticized by Feucht, *Untersuchungen*, 169. Feucht himself
dates Lev 18-23 before Deuteronomy and Lev 25-26 after Deuteronomy, but his arguments are no more convincing than those of Baentsch.

fore said by some to antedate Deuteronomy.[41] To others, on the other hand, Deuteronomy seemed more primitive, more natural, and therefore earlier than H.[42]

The question has been the subject of a detailed study by Cholewinski.[43] He concludes that H is later than Deuteronomy and dependent on it: H was composed in priestly circles on the model of Deuteronomy as a complement to the main strand of the priestly code (P).[44] It must be said, however, that his argumentation is rather a-prioristic. Alternative models, e.g. with Deuteronomy dependent on H, both dependent on a third source that has been lost to us, or with Deuteronomy and H simply standing in the same legislative tradition, are not taken into consideration.[45] It is striking that Cholewinski in his study has been able to produce very few convincing arguments—such as instances of verbal correspondence—in support of his thesis.[46] The recent attempt of Braulik to reverse the theory with regard to Deut 19-26, which chapters he views as having been composed under the influence of the Decalogue and H, does not bring any methodological progress: he merely argues, on the basis of the same texts as Cholewinski, that the dependence runs in the opposite direction.[47]

---

[41] Dillmann, Kaufmann, Schneider. Others, like Van Hoonacker and Berry place H in the time of Josiah, before Deuteronomy which they date in the exilic or post-exilic period (see the bibliography for the studies of Van Hoonacker and Berry).

[42] Wellhausen, Kuenen.

[43] Cholewinski, *Heiligkeitsgesetz*.

[44] This thesis is accepted by Thiel in his review. Blum, *Studien*, 335ff agrees that H is a priestly reaction to Deuteronomy; in his view, the same is true not only for H but for the whole priestly composition.

[45] However, he was of course aware that these alternative models exist. See Cholewinski, *Heiligkeitsgesetz*, 7f.

[46] Later contributions are equally inconclusive. Priority of H over Deuteronomy is argued by S. Japhet, "The Relationship between the Legal Corpora in the Pentateuch in light of Manumission Laws", *Scripta Hierosolymitana* 31 (Jerusalem, 1986), 63-89. The inverse relationship is defended by L. Perlitt, "»Ein einzig Volk von Brüdern.« Zur deuteronomischen Herkunft der biblischen Bezeichnung »Bruder«" in D. Lührmann und G. Strecker, Hsg., *Kirche*, Fs G. Bornkamm (Tübingen, 1980), 27-52, and S. A. Kaufman, "A Reconstruction of Social Welfare Systems of Ancient Israel", in B. Barrick and J. R. Spencer, eds., *In the Shelter of Elyon*, Fs G. W. Ahlström, JSOTS 31 (Sheffield, 1984), 277-286; id., "Deuteronomy 15 and Recent Research on the Dating of P", in N. Lohfink, Hsg., *Das Deuteronomium. Entstehung, Gestalt und Botschaft*, BEThL 68 (Leuven, 1985), 273-276; Otto, *Ethik*, 240-242. A more complicated theory of mutual influence is developed by G. Bettenzoli, "Deuteronomium und Heiligkeitsgesetz" *VT* 34 (1984), 385-398.

[47] Cf. G. Braulik, "Die dekalogische Redaktion der deuteronomischen Gesetze. Ihre Abhängigkeit von Leviticus 19 am Beispiel von Deuteronomium 22,1-12; 24,10-22; 25,13-16" in idem, Hsg., *Bundesdokument und Gesetz. Studien zum Deuteronomium*, HBS 4 (Freiburg, 1995), 1-25; idem, "Weitere Beobachtungen zur Beziehung zwischen dem Heiligkeitsgesetz und Deuteronomium 19-25", in T. Veijola, Hsg. *Das Deuteronomium und seine Querbeziehungen*, Schriften der Finnischen Exegetischen Gesellschaft 62 (Helsinki & Göttingen, 1996), 23-55.

Until new evidence is presented, therefore, it will be better to hold on to the older view that Deuteronomy and H are not directly dependent on one another but are based partly on the same legislative material.[48]

A related question has been raised by Thiel.[49] He finds Deuteronomistic ideas and expressions in H, on the basis of which he derives H from the Deuteronomistic preaching practice.[50] Though his observation is important, his conclusions are not entirely convincing.[51]

Ezekiel

In view of many similarities in ideas and expression,[52] a connection between H and Ezekiel must be postulated. For this reason, and because Ezekiel's activity—if not the book named after him—can be dated with some accuracy, the relationship between H and Ezekiel has received much attention.

In the early days of research on H as a distinct corpus, the idea that Ezekiel was the author or the editor of H enjoyed some currency.[53] The differences between the law code and the prophet proved too important, however, for this thesis to be maintained. Klostermann interpreted similarities and differences to mean that Ezekiel knew and used H almost in the form in which we have it today.[54] Later studies show a much greater

---

[48] See already A. Kayser, *Das vorexilische Buch der Urgeschichte Israels und seine Erweiterungen. Ein Beitrag zur Pentateuch-Kritik* (Strassburg, 1874), 139f; Driver, *Introduction*, 151f; Kaufmann, *Toledot*, 61-65; Schwartz, *Chapters*, 192; C. Houtman, *Der Pentateuch. Die Geschichte seiner Erforschung neben eine Auswertung*, Biblical Exegesis and Theology 9 (Kampen, 1994), 288-289.

[49] Thiel, "Erwägungen".

[50] Thiel, "Erwägungen", 70.

[51] He rejects out of hand the view according to which the said Deuteronomistic expressions derive from pre-exilic times, perhaps from the Levitical preaching of the law (Elliger, *Leviticus*, 270f). In addition, he is forced to submit that the book of Ezekiel, which contains the same elements, has also undergone Deuteronomistic editing. This seems unlikely, see D. Vieweger, *Die literarischen Beziehungen zwischen den Büchern Jeremia und Ezekiel*, BEATAJ 26 (Frankfurt a. M., 1993), 12-15, 166-170.

[52] See Driver, *Introduction*, 147f.

[53] It seems that Graf was the first to formulate this hypothesis. He is followed by Kayser, *Das vorexilische Buch*, and by Horst, *Leviticus XVII-XXVI*, 69-96. See also J. Herrmann, *Ezekiel*, KAT (Leipzig & Erlangen, 1924), XIX.

[54] A. Klostermann, "Ezekiel und das Heiligkeitsgesetz" in idem, *Der Pentateuch. Beiträge zu seinem Verständnis und seiner Entstehehungsgeschichte* (Leipzig, 1893), 368-419. The same position is taken by Driver, *Introduction*, 147-151. On the other hand, Wellhausen, *Composition*, 168f, 172; id., *Prolegomena zur Geschichte Israels* (Berlin, 1886³), 395-402, argues that H is later than Ezekiel; but his arguments are insufficient.

sophistication in the approach to the question: H is divided into parts that antedate and parts that postdate Ezekiel,[55] or Ezekiel is divided into parts that antedate and parts that postdate H.[56] The most recent study of the question is by Zimmerli.[57] He convincingly demonstrates that Ezekiel knew legislation of the exact type which we find in H, and adapted it to his needs. Yet, though without explicit argumentation, he dates the final form of H much later than Ezekiel.[58] The anteriority of H with respect to Ezekiel has been endorsed by those who see in the book of Ezekiel a pseudepigraph from post-exilic times.[59] For the linguistic aspect of the question, see the excursus below.

The Priestly Code

Although in its present form, H shares much of its language and ideas with P,[60] it still exhibits a number of characteristics that set it apart. As was stated above, the relationship between H and P has usually been seen in terms of the priority of the original H and its subsequent incorporation into P.[61] More recently, however, a different view seems to be gaining ground. Elliger was probably the first to broach the possibility that H had never existed before P, but was from the outset conceived as an addition to it.[62] This idea has received support from various quarters

---

[55] Baentsch, Kilian. Also G. Fohrer, *Hauptprobleme des Buches Ezekiel* (Berlin, 1952), 144-148. Fohrer ascribes the similarities between H and Ezekiel to their dependence on a common source; however, since this source corresponds to the laws contained in H, his theory amounts to a division of H into two parts (laws and paraenesis).

[56] H. Schulz, *Das Todesrecht im Alten Testament. Studien zur Rechtsform der Mot-Jumat-Sätze*, BZAW 114 (Berlin, 1969), 163-183.

[57] W. Zimmerli, "Die Eigenart der prophetischen Rede des Ezekiel. Ein Beitrag zum Problem an Hand von Ez. 14 1-11", *ZAW* 66 (1954), 1-26.

[58] Zimmerli, "Eigenart", 20, n. 1. In his commentary on Ezekiel, Zimmerli adopts a position that is very close to that of Fohrer: H is substantially older than Ezekiel, but Ezekiel has influenced the later redactional history of H. See W. Zimmerli, *Ezekiel*, BKAT (Neukirchen-Vluyn, 1969), 70-79.

[59] Burrows, Torrey (cf. L. Zunz, "Bibelkritisches", *ZDMG* 27 [1873], 669-689). A review of the criticisms levelled at this theory is given by M. Greenberg, in his Prolegomenon to the reprint of C. C. Torrey, *Pseudo-Ezekiel and the Original Prophecy* (New York, 1970), XI-XXXV. The theory has found a latter-day defendant in J. Becker.

[60] It is impossible here to go into the problems of the layering of P, the extent of the original 'Grundschrift' and whether there ever was an independent narrative source P. In the following, the siglum P refers to the so-called Grundschrift (Pg) including its older annexes (like the priestly *toroth* in Lev 1-7, 11-15).

[61] See above, p. 7.

[62] Elliger, *Leviticus*, 16.

and has been developed in different ways.[63] The most important recent contribution to this debate is that of Knohl, who views H as the priestly response to prophetic criticisms directed against the Temple.[64] The "Holiness School" not only composed H as a complement to P, but made various additions to P in other places (see below, pp. 15-16).

It may be too early to speak of a new consensus. The old view of the priority of H still has its adherents.[65] For those scholars who do not recognize H as a distinct corpus the question of its relationship to P does not arise in the same terms.[66] In any case, since the date of P is once again the subject of vehement discussion,[67] the determination of its relationship to H will not automatically assist us in dating the latter.

EXCURSUS: THE LINGUISTIC APPROACH TO THE DATING OF H

Determining the date of H on the basis of its literary relationship to Deuteronomy, Ezekiel or P involves a considerable degree of subjectivity. Nor has it proved possible to decide the matter on the basis of internal arguments.[68] It is understandable, therefore, that scholars should have attempted to find a more secure foundation for the dating of this text in the study of its language. For this purpose, H and P have usually been taken together.

The 19th century did not provide any firm conclusions on the linguistic profile of P/H.[69] The problem is in large part one of methodology. In order to prove the antiquity of P/H it is not sufficient simply to give examples of archaic language.[70] These may be indicative of older mate-

---

[63] N. Lohfink, "Die Abänderung der Theologie des priesterlichen Geschichtswerk im Segen des Heiligkeitsgesetzes. Zu Lev. 26,9.11-13", in idem, *Studien zum Pentateuch*, SBAB 4 (1988), 157-168; Cholewinski, *Heiligkeitsgesetz*, 334-338; W. Thiel, review of Cholewinski, Heiligkeitsgesetz, *ThLZ* 103 (1978), 258-260; Schwartz, *Chapters*, 191; E. Otto, "Das Heiligkeitsgesetz Leviticus 17-26 in der Pentateuchredaktion" in P. Mommer, W. Thiel, Hsg., *Altes Testament. Forschung und Wirkung*, Fs H. Graf Reventlow (Frankfurt a. M., 1994), 65-80.
[64] Knohl, *Sanctuary*, and other publications (see bibliography).
[65] R. Smend, *Die Entstehung des Alten Testaments* (Stuttgart, 1978; 1984³), 59-62.
[66] Wagner, Blum, Crüsemann, Gerstenberger.
[67] See Z. Zevit, "Converging Lines of Evidence Bearing on the Date of P", *ZAW* 94 (1982), 481-511.
[68] See above n. 30.
[69] See the review of earlier linguistic research in S. R. Külling, *Zur Datiering der "Genesis-P-Stücke". Namentlich des Kapitels Genesis XVII* (Kampen, 1964), 166-189.
[70] This is the approach of Y. M. Grintz, "Archaic Terms in the Priestly Code", *Leshonenu* 39 (1974-75), 5-20, 163-181; *Leshonenu* 40 (1975-76), 5-32.

rial incorporated into P/H, or they may be the result of conscious archaizing on the part of the author.[71] On the other hand, late linguistic forms may simply be indicative of later redactional additions.[72] An extensive study by Polzin has allowed real progress to be made,[73] although it is especially the work of Hurvitz which has led to usable results. In a first contribution, Hurvitz shows with regard to a number of linguistic pairs consisting of an early and a late mode of expression, that P/H consistently uses the older form exclusively.[74] In a second study, he compares the language of P with that of the book of Ezekiel and demonstrates that the former is older.[75] The debate is not over yet.[76] And even though Hurvitz' methodology is watertight, his results do not automatically decide the matter, since a talented exilic author may well have written good pre-exilic Hebrew.[77] Nevertheless, this type of linguistic research certainly is something modern OT scholarship needs to come to terms with.

FRAGMENTS SIMILAR TO H OUTSIDE LEV 17-26

When H was isolated as a distinct corpus, it became clear that other passages in the priestly literature of the Pentateuch exhibited the same style and ideas as Lev 17-26.[78] Important passages are Ex 6:6-8; 31:13-

---

[71] Archaizing language is detected in P by F. M. Cross, *Canaanite Myth and Hebrew Epic. Essays in the History of the Religion of Israel* (Cambridge MA, 1973), 293-325.

[72] A. Dillmann, *Numeri, Deuteronomium und Josua*, KEH (Leipzig, 1886), 665.

[73] R. Polzin, *Late Biblical Hebrew. Toward an Historical Typology of Biblical Hebrew Prose*, HSM 12 (Missoula, 1976). Polzin concludes that the language of P is younger than that of the other pentateuchal sources, but older than exilic and post-exilic Hebrew.

[74] A. Hurvitz, "The Evidence of Language in Dating the Priestly Code. A Linguistic Study in Technical Idioms and Terminology", *RB* 81 (1974), 24-56.

[75] A. Hurvitz, *A Linguistic Study of the Relationship between the Priestly Source and the Book of Ezekiel*, Cahiers de la Revue Biblique 20 (Paris, 1982). Ezekiel's use of later vocabulary than that of H was already pointed out by D. Hoffmann, *Die wichtigsten Instanzen gegen die Graf-Wellhausensche Hypothese* (Berlin, 1904), 24-30.

[76] For an early date of the language of P/H, see the other publications of Hurvitz, Rendsburg, Rooker, Paran listed in the bibliography. For a late date, see Levine, "The Language in the Priestly Source. Some Literary and Historical Observations" *Proceedings of the Eighth World Congress of Jewish Studies—Jerusalem 1981* (1983), 69-82, and his earlier study quoted there.

[77] This is admitted by Hurvitz, "Evidence", 55. Cf. N. Lohfink, "Die Priesterschrift und die Geschichte", in J. A. Emerton, et al., *Congress Volume. Göttingen 1977*, SVT 29 (1978), 189-225, p. 201, n. 33; Kaufman, "Deuteronomy 15".

[78] Similarities between H and these passages concern in particular the emphasis on the idea of holiness and the use of the expression "I am YHWH (your God)."

17; Lev 11:44f; Num 10:8-10; 15:38-41. This phenomenon was explained by the supposition that H was a collection of laws older than P. Klostermann held that these fragments were originally part of H (or an older form of H). A priestly redactor took them out of their original context and inserted them in different places in the priestly laws.[79] The lacunar remainder of H was then attached *en bloc* to Lev 16. For Baentsch, on the other hand, most of these fragments never were part of the original H. He posits a later redactor who composed them in the style of H and added them to the priestly prescriptions.[80]

The view that H as a whole is more recent than P sets the whole question in a new light. Knohl has ascribed both Lev 17-26 and the fragments similar to it to a "Holiness School" which set out to modify the theological mould of P.[81] The precise extent of the literary activity of this Holiness School is not entirely clear.[82]

---

[79] Klostermann, *Heiligkeitsgesetz*, 377, argues, for instance, that Lev 11:43-45 formerly constituted the conclusion to a list of unclean animals introduced in Lev 20:22-25. When P made his own list of unclean animals, he excised from H the conclusion of its list. He also omitted the original list (but not its introduction) from H, since P now already contained one.

[80] Baentsch, *Heiligkeits-Gesetz*, 4-12. This is essentially the view of Grelot, though he applies it to a different set of texts. See P. Grelot, "La dernière étape de la rédaction sacerdotale", *VT* 6 (1956), 174-189, p. 176: "On est donc en présence d'un véritable *code pénal* aux articles dispersés, élaborés sous l'influence et dans l'esprit du code de sainteté."

[81] Knohl, *Sanctuary*. According to Knohl, P is based on the idea of the numinous presence of YHWH in the Temple of Jerusalem; P's cult is supra-rational, not related to the ideas of morality and divine recompense. H tries to build a bridge between P's elitist theology and popular religion; it also takes into account prophetic criticism that accused the priestly system of immorality.

[82] Knohl ascribes much of Numbers to his Holiness School, as well as the priestly chapters in Joshua. In his view, the "Holiness School" was active over a period of several hundreds of years; it is responsible for the final redaction of the Pentateuch. In my opinion, this means an over-stretching of the hypothesis, which renders it less effective.

CHAPTER TWO

WHAT IS THE HOLINESS CODE?

A question not treated fully in the preceding chapter is that of the nature of H. What is it? And what is it for? Is it a code of positive law? A programme? A sermon? In what way is it anchored in the reality of Israel's society? Does it go back to oral traditions? Or is it purely a literary creation? It is easier to ask these questions than to answer them with any certainty. Nevertheless, a discussion of various approaches that have been essayed will allow us to draw some methodological conclusions for the study of H.[1]

In the literature, these questions have seldom been addressed specifically with regard to H; usually the Deuteronomic Code and the Book of the Covenant have been included in the discussion (sometimes even to the exclusion of H). Indeed, these three corpora share a number of characteristics: they are collections of laws, they are said to have been given by YHWH to his people at mount Sinai as part of the covenant he concluded with them.[2] They also contain some of the same prescriptions—though often differently formulated—and even, partly, the same paraenesis. We will therefore discuss H in conjunction with the two other corpora, although, it is to be hoped, without losing sight of its specificity.[3]

---

[1] Many studies of H leave themselves open to criticism because they naively ascribe to H a function which it may not have. To give only one very recent example, it appears that Blum has not circumvented this pitfall when he writes: "Wenn es um die Ausrichtung konkreter Rechts-, Kult-, und Lebenspraxis geht..." Blum, *Studien*, 334. See criticism of earlier scholars in R. P. Knierim, "The Problem of Ancient Israel's Prescriptive Legal Traditions", *Semeia* 45 (1989), 7-25.

[2] For the relationship between law and covenant, see below.

[3] The fact that H, as opposed to Deuteronomy and BC, stands in the priestly tradition has become clear from the preceding chapter. Most of the differences between H and Deuteronomy are probably due to the fact that these corpora originated in different milieux, see chapter 1, n. 48. BC is older than both.

LAW CODE

Traditionally, the laws of the Pentateuch have been understood as positive law, meant for use in the courts of law.[4] For a number of reasons, however, the law codes of the Pentateuch cannot be regarded as collections of positive law comparable to the Roman or Napoleonic codes. To begin with, none of the former codes lays down exhaustive and systematic legislation, and even when taken together, they leave open many legal questions that must certainly have been important in OT times.[5] Moreover, it is striking that the codes contain no specific instructions for judges.[6] Finally, it has been remarked that in none of the court cases that are recounted in biblical narratives is recourse had to a "book of the law" or to "the law of YHWH" or the like.[7] That this is no accident is confirmed by a unique epigraphic find: the judicial plea from Metsad Hashavyahu (Yavneh-Yam).[8]

Now, in every one of these characteristics, the biblical law codes resemble the Ancient Near Eastern (ANE) law codes unearthed in the course of the present century.[9] These cuneiform codes legislate in the same apparently haphazard fashion as the OT codes. They contain no

---

[4] See, e.g., A. Menes, *Die vorexilischen Gesetze Israels*, BZAW 50 (Gießen, 1928), 20.

[5] See S. E. Loewenstamm, "Law", in B. Mazar, ed., *The World History of the Jewish People, Vol. 3. Judges* (Tel Aviv, 1971), 231-267. Loewenstamm deduces from this that the positive law in biblical times consisted of customary law. Compare M. Noth, "Die Gesetze im Pentateuch", in idem, *Gesammelte Studien zum Alten Testament*, Theologische Bücherei AT 6 (München, 1966³), 9-141, pp. 8f; K. Galling, "Das Gemeindegesetz in Deuteronomium 23", in W. Baumgartner et al., Hsg., Fs A. Bertholet (Tübingen 1950), 176-191, p. 178.

[6] The codes are addressed, in the 2nd person singular or plural, to the people collectively or to each individual.

[7] See the remarks of C. van Houten, *The Alien in Israelite Law*, JSOTS 107 (Sheffield, 1991), 30f. One may object that the silence of the sources on this point does not mean that law-books could not have played a part in court cases. However, non-forensic contexts state on several occasions that individuals did (Jos 8:31; 2 Ki 14:6; 2 Ki 22f) or did not (2 Ki 10:31; 2 Ki 17:34-37; 2 Ki 21:8) follow the stipulations of a law-book. This indicates that if the authors of the historical books thought that in court cases a law-book should be used, they might have said something about it. Note also that the prophets vituperate against abuses in legal practice, but never mention a law-book in this context.

[8] See K. A. D. Smelik, "The Literary Structure of the Yavneh-Yam Ostracon", *IEJ* 42 (1992), 55-61, with a selection of earlier literature. As Smelik remarks, it seems that the writer of the ostracon would have had occasion to appeal to the provisions in Ex 22:25f or Deut 24:10-13 prohibiting the keeping of a garment taken in pledge overnight. Yet he does not do so.

[9] See R. Westbrook, "Biblical and Cuneiform Law Codes", *RB* 92 (1985), 247-264, with earlier literature. A translation of the ANE codes can be found in TUAT I, 1 and in ANET.

instructions for judges. And in the numerous private documents pertaining to law suits that have been recovered from the same area and period as the ANE law codes, there is not a single reference to a written code. Since, on top of all this, the pentateuchal laws and the ANE laws stem at least partly from the same tradition[10]—a fact that has been known since the day the ANE codes were translated—the temptation has been strong to see the biblical codes in the light of the ANE codes and to ascribe the same function to them all.[11]

Westbrook has defended the view that the cuneiform and biblical codes are in fact to be viewed as scientific treatises designed to illustrate the wisdom of their authors.[12] Famous precedents in law or even purely theoretical cases were studied and discussed in scribal schools and the result of the discussions is what we find in the codes. However, though the codes are not collections of positive law, neither are they monuments of pure science. They functioned as a reference work for consultation by judges when deciding difficult cases.[13] This was the primary purpose of the codes. Once they had acquired a certain status, they might be used for secondary purposes, one of which was the religio-historical one conferred on the biblical codes when they were inserted into the pentateuchal narrative.

This analysis, set out here very briefly, is convincing with regard to the cuneiform material.[14] It throws an interesting light on the biblical

---

[10] See in general G. Cardascia, "Droits cunéiformes et droit biblique", *Proceedings of the Sixth World Congress of Jewish Studies—Jerusalem 1973* (Jerusalem, 1977), 63-70. For recent work on parallels between ANE codes and H, see E. Otto, *Rechtsgeschichte der Redaktionen im Kodex Esnunna und im «Bundesbuch». Eine redaktionsgeschichtliche und rechtsvergleichende Studie zu altbabylonischen und altisraelitischen Rechtsüberlieferungen*, OBO 85 (Freiburg & Göttingen, 1989), 48f (Lev 19:20), 103-105 (Lev 25); R. Westbrook, *Studies in Biblical and Cuneiform Law*, Cahiers de la Revue Biblique 26 (Paris, 1988), 82 (Lev 24:17-21).

[11] See Westbrook, "Law Codes". The tendency to align the OT codes with the ANE ones is criticized severely by Schwartz, *Chapters*, 3-10. A very balanced discussion of resemblances and differences between OT and ANE codes is offered by S. M. Paul, *Studies in the Book of the Covenant in Light of Cuneiform and Biblical Law*, SVT 18 (Leiden, 1970), 27-42.

[12] Westbrook, "Law Codes"; Westbrook did not include H (the only biblical law codes he lists are BC and the Deuteronomic code). In his discussion, however, he implicitly shows that H (Lev 24) is structured in the same way as the other codes.

[13] Westbrook, "Law Codes", 254. The arguments for the practical application of the codes are that some of them were found in the gate of a city—the normal location of the court-house in Mesopotamia—and that later collections show signs of updating of the substantive law.

[14] However, it concerns only the final form of the codes, not the older material contained in it. Finkelstein has shown that at the core of the codes lie stipulations that were originally issued in the framework of a *misharum* -act at the beginning of the king's

codes.[15] Yet for a number of reasons, this theory cannot be taken over wholesale by students of biblical law. Unlike the ANE codes, the biblical law-books contain ethical and cultic prescriptions alongside matters of what one might call civil and criminal law.[16] Another difference is that in the OT codes, the laws are accompanied by motivations and admonitions, manifestly aimed at instilling obedience and assent.[17] These characteristics not only distinguish the OT codes from the ANE codes, but also militate against Westbrook's view. The occurrence of provisions for the cult show that the codes were never designed to be reference works for judges. And the presence of paraenesis indicates that they were not destined for scribes or another elite, but for the people at large.[18]

TREATY

A difference between the ANE and biblical codes not yet mentioned is that the entirety of biblical law is derived immediately from the god-

---

reign. These stipulations, concerning the remittance of debts and the fixing of certain prices, did have real force of law. See J. J. Finkelstein, "Ammisaduqa's Edict and the Babylonian "Law Codes"", *JCS* 15 (1961), 91-104. It is by all means possible that a similar distinction should be drawn for biblical law, between older material that was at one point introduced into a reform act and did enjoy force of law, and the final form of the codes.

[15] Nevertheless, the theory would obviously need to be adapted on some points in order to fit the biblical codes. Westbrook seems to extend to the OT codes the supposition that all these codes emanate from the royal court, see Westbrook, "Law Codes", 254, 258. In light of the almost complete absence of questions relating to the royalty from the biblical codes this is not likely (even in Deut 17 the king is rather seen as God's concession to the desire of the people). As to the codes' originating in the circles of the "wise" or the scribes, see M. Weinfeld, *Deuteronomy and the Deuteronomic School* (Oxford, 1972). Weinfeld defends the view that the redaction of Deuteronomy was produced in wisdom circles. With regard to H, we may suppose an origin in priestly circles, though these priests would certainly have shared part of the general education of wise men.

[16] Kaufmann has explained this difference by the fact that the biblical laws are divine laws, whereas the cuneiform laws are essentially royal laws, concerned with matters of state. See Kaufmann, *Toledot*, vol.1, 67. Otto also links the notion of divine law to the blending of different types of prescriptions. However, whereas for Kaufmann this is an original and essential characteristic of biblical law, Otto sees the "theologizing" of law as a late development arising from a breakdown of the traditional authority structures (the clan). See especially E. Otto, *Wandel der Rechtsbegründungen in der Gesellschaftsgeschichte des antiken Israel*, Studia Biblica 3 (Brill, 1988).

[17] See B. Gemser, "The Importance of the Motive Clause in Old Testament Law", in G. W. Anderson et al., eds., *Congress Volume. Copenhagen 1953*, SVT 1 (Leiden, 1953), 50-66; H. Rücker, *Die Begründungen der Weisungen Jahwes im Pentateuch*, Erfurter Theologische Studien 30 (Leipzig, 1973); R. Sonsino, *Motive Clauses in Biblical Law. Biblical Forms and Near Eastern Parallels*, SBLDS 45 (Chico, 1980).

[18] Other differences between OT and ANE law are listed by Paul, *Studies*, 37-41.

head. Though the distinction is not absolute—ANE law too is derived from the gods[19]—the biblical emphasis is unique.[20] These are not simply divinely inspired laws: they have been handed down by this unique god, YHWH, to the people he has chosen to be his own.[21] The Decalogue and the Book of the Covenant, as well as YHWH's *Privilegrecht* in Ex 34:12-26,[22] are presented explicitly as the stipulations of a covenant between YHWH and Israel.[23]

This has prompted a comparison with another ANE type of text, namely the vassal-treaty.[24] The hypothesis has been propounded that the OT law codes transpose into the religious realm the political reality of a vassal treaty:[25] YHWH takes the place of the suzerain, and Israel that of the vassal.[26] An important argument in favour of this view is that some of the OT codes conclude with a collection of blessings and curses, exactly as do the vassal treaties.[27] On the other hand, one necessary criti-

---

[19] In the epilogue of the Codex Hammurabi, the king declares: "I, Hammurabi, am the king of justice to whom Shamash committed law"; translation ANET, 178. See also the prologue to the code of Lipit-Ishtar, ANET, 159.

[20] Cf. Crüsemann, *Tora*, 23-25.

[21] That is, in their present biblical context they are presented in this way. Whether this has always been the character of the law in ancient Israel is a moot point. Gerstenberger has argued that the original *Sitz im Leben* of the apodictic law (in the sense of Alt) is to be found in the family, see E.S. Gerstenberger, *Wesen und Herkunft des apodiktischen Rechts*, WMANT 20 (Neukirchen, 1965). Against Gerstenberger, see H. Graf Reventlow, "Kultisches Recht im Alten Testament", *ZThK* 60 (1963), 267-304. See also the literature quoted above in n.16.

[22] J. Halbe, *Das Privilegrecht Jahwes Ex 34,10-26. Gestalt und Wesen, Herkunft und Wirken in vordeuteronomischen Zeit*, FRLANT 114 (Göttingen, 1975).

[23] For the Decalogue and BC, see Ex 19:5; 24:1-8; for the Decalogue alone, Ex 34:28 (?); Deut 5:2,3; for the *Privilegrecht*, Ex 34:10, 27. Compare also the "Moab Covenant" in Deut 28:69; 29:8,11,13,20; cf. A. Rofé, *Introduction to Deuteronomy* (Jerusalem, 1988), 178-197.

[24] The original observation was made by George Mendenhall, "Covenant Forms in Israelite Tradition", *BA* 17 (1954), 50-76. It is applied to all the different law codes of the OT by de Vaux, see R. de Vaux, *Les institutions de l'Ancien Testament*, vol. I (Paris, 1958), 227. The connection between law and covenant had been observed long before Mendenhall by Mowinckel, *Le décalogue* (Paris, 1927). He was followed by G. von Rad, *Das formgeschichtliche Problem des Hexateuchs*, BWANT 78 (Stuttgart, 1938), 18-23, and by Noth, *Gesetze*, 32-81.

[25] In discussion with those who deemed such transposition unlikely, Reventlow has pointed to the fact that even in its original political application, the treaty had sacral dimensions and notably involved the god of the suzerain. Reventlow, "Kultisches Recht", 276-78.

[26] Usually this view implies the understanding that Israel really did conclude and, in particular, celebrate its "vassal-treaty" with YHWH. The law codes are then taken to have functioned in the framework of this celebration. See, e.g., K. Baltzer, *Das Bundesformular*, WMANT 4 (Neukirchen, 1960), 96f. Others have opted to see in the treaty formulation a mere literary convention. See, e.g., Weinfeld, *Deuteronomy and the Deuteronomic School*, passim.

[27] For other parallels, see de Vaux, *Institutions*, 227.

cism is that the "stipulations" of the biblical covenant are very different from those of the vassal-treaty. These are aimed specifically at assuring the vassal's allegiance,[28] whereas the substance of the biblical codes is law (including ethical and cultic prescriptions).[29]

Though H exhibits some features characteristic of the ANE treaty, notably the blessings-and-curses chapter in Lev 26,[30] it is never explicitly presented as a "book of the covenant", "words of the covenant" or the like.[31] The contents of H are described as the *ḥuqqīm*, *mišpāṭm* and *tōrōt* between YHWH and the people of Israel, given by him through Moses on Mount Sinai (Lev 26:46).[32]

TEACHING OF THE LAW

Whether or not one is to view the covenant as the main framework of the biblical law codes,[33] and the ANE treaties as their literary model, one thing is clear: the laws are addressed by YHWH to the people he considers his own in order to define their mutual relationship. Scholars who

---

[28] Weinfeld, *Deuteronomy and the Deuteronomic School*, 148; Van Houten, *Alien*, 33.

[29] This fact has led Westbrook to his view that the covenant framework is secondary and that the codes were originally law codes comparable to the ANE codes, see above. Weinfeld, *Deuteronomy and the Deuteronomic School*, 250, points to parallels between treaties and law codes and deduces from these that they should not be separated from one another.

[30] Beyerlin has pointed out that the paraenesis of the biblical law codes may also be understood from the vassal treaty, see Beyerlin, "Paränese", 25-28. Compare the paraenesis in H, e.g. Lev 18:3-4: "You shall not do as they do in the land of Egypt, where you dwelt, and you shall not do as they do in the land of Canaan, to which I am bringing you (...). You shall do my ordinances and keep my statutes (...) I am the LORD your God."

[31] Unless I am mistaken, neither is the Deuteronomic law code presented as such (for Deut 5:2,3 and 28:69 see above, n. 23; it seems that Deuteronomy is described as "the book of the covenant" in 2 Ki 23:2,3,21, but this stands in opposition to the way the code presents itself according to the text as it now stands). Perhaps we may see in this circumstance an indication that H and Deuteronomy were not considered to be the most original words of the covenant, a status restricted to BC and the Decalogue, but rather as an interpretation or exposition. Compare G. von Rad, "Deuteronomium-Studien", in idem, *Gesammelte Studien II*, Theologische Bücherei, AT 48 (München, 1973), 109-153, p. 126. See also Lohfink's remarks on Deuteronomy in N. Lohfink, "Kennt das Alte Testament einen Unterschied von »Gebot« und »Gesetz«? Zur bibeltheologischen Einstufung des Dekalogs", *JBTh* 4 (1989), 63-89.

[32] However, H—in contradistinction to P—does know of a covenant at Sinai, see Lev 26:45; 26:25; compare 26:9.

[33] After a first spate of enthusiasm following the original discovery by Mendenhall, some scholars returned to the view that covenant theology is a Deuteronomic innovation, see especially L. Perlitt, *Bundestheologie im Alten Testament*, WMANT 36 (1969). As on so many important points in the study of the OT, the debate is still open.

have given this framework serious consideration have often pointed to the didactic and paraenetic aspects of the law codes.[34] The laws are not simply set down, they are explained, motivated, traced back to their underlying principles.[35]

Already Klostermann had defended the view that the purpose of H was to be publicly recited in the assemblies of the community.[36] Developing the same idea, von Rad traced features typical of the "preaching of the law" (*Gesetzespredigt*) in both Deuteronomy and H.[37] Reventlow went one step further: for him, the totality of H can be understood only against the background of the pre-exilic Israelite covenant celebration (*Bundesfest*).[38] In this framework the law, originally consisting of a number of short apodictic series, was updated, preached, explained and motivated, not least through the appending of a chapter of blessings and curses. Reventlow's theory invokes many unknowns and leaves several questions unanswered;[39] yet in boldly postulating the oral nature of H, he highlights some characteristics of H which are sometimes neglected by its literary critics.[40]

Even if we were to conclude that H is the product of a literary process, we may still ascribe to it the function of teaching the law.[41] And even in a literary creation, links could exist to liturgical traditions of ancient Israel.[42]

---

[34] Beyerlin, "Paränese"; N. Lohfink, *Das Hauptgebot. Eine Untersuchung literarischer Einleitungsfragen zu Dtn 5-11*, AnBib 20 (Rome, 1963), 261-288.

[35] The paraenetic cast of H shows that, if P is to be considered an esoteric writing, H is to be distinguished from it on this point. For the esoteric character of P see C. Cohen, "Was the P Document Secret?", *JANES* 1,2 (1969), 39-44; G. von Rad, *Die Priesterschrift im Hexateuch*, BWANT 65 (Stuttgart, 1934), 187; M. Paran, *Forms of the Priestly Style in the Pentateuch. Patterns, Linguistic Usages, Syntactic Structures* (Jerusalem, 1989), XIV and 243-272.

[36] A. Klostermann, "Ezekiel und das Heiligkeitsgesetz", 374f. Klostermann points to the rhetorical and passionate style of H, to the way single commandments are used to exemplify a whole domain and to the frequent use of formulas of the kind "these are the commandments...".

[37] Von Rad, "Deuteronomium-Studien", 118-126.

[38] Reventlow, *Heiligkeitsgesetz*. Though Reventlow refers to Klostermann, it seems that a subtle difference exists between their views: for Klostermann, H was written in order to be read, whereas Reventlow sees in H the record of originally oral preaching.

[39] See the review of his book by R. de Vaux, *RB* 69 (1962), 297-299.

[40] Compare the discussion of Reventlow's approach in Elliger, *Leviticus*, 15f.

[41] Compare n. 56. See also E. Gerstenberger, "»Apodiktisches« Recht »Todes« Recht?" in P. Mommer et al., Hsg., *Gottes Recht als Lebensraum*, Fs H. J. Boecker (Neukirchen, 1993), 7-20.

[42] Barbiero sees a connection between H and the liturgies of the gate (e.g. Ps 15; Ps 24), cf. Barbiero, *L'asino*, 251, 269. See also K. Koch, "Tempeleinlassliturgien und Dekaloge", in R. Rendtorff und K. Koch, Hsg., *Studien zur Theologie der alttestamentlichen Überlieferungen*, Fs G. von Rad (Neukirchen, 1961), 45-60.

PROGRAMME OF REFORM

We have noted above that the biblical law codes, just like the ANE codes, did not seem to be applied in the practice of law in the courts. However, in one case the historical books do recount how a law-book found a practical application, not however in a law-court setting but as a programme for national reform. In 2 Ki 22-23, it is told that King Josiah completely reformed the cultic organization of his kingdom—a reform, no doubt, with far-reaching political and social ramifications. It is usually submitted that the law code found in Josiah's time was Deuteronomy or a more original form of Deuteronomy.[43] It is also submitted by some scholars that Deuteronomy, or the original core of Deuteronomy, was composed as a programme in order to effect the reform of Josiah.[44] Could not this be the function of the other law codes too,[45] and more specifically of H?

The question has been answered in the affirmative by Knohl.[46] Not only was H designed to be programmatic, it even became operational, at least to a certain extent, under King Hezekiah. The inspiration behind this king's destroying all altars outside Jerusalem was none other than H and the theology which it incorporates.[47]

A similar view of H, though placing it against an entirely different historical background, is held by what is probably a majority of present-day scholars. According to this view, H was composed during the exile as a programme for life in the promised land after the return.[48]

---

[43] However, some scholars thought that H or an earlier form of H was the law-book found in the temple. See G. R. Berry, "The Code Found in the Temple", *JBL* 39 (1920), 44-51; A. Van Hoonacker, "Le rapprochement entre le Deutéronome et Malachie", *EThL* 59 (1983), 86-90; H. Schneider, *Das Buch Leviticus*, Echter Bibel (1958), 4.

[44] See, e.g., S. R. Driver, *Deuteronomy*, ICC (1901³), li-liii. However, this view has been contested on good grounds by Noth, *Gesetze*, 58-67.

[45] Compare J. Hempel, *Die althebräische Literatur* (Wildpark-Potsdam, 1930), 81: BC, Deuteronomy and H are "... Programme, die in historischen Einkleidung für bestimmte Ideen warben...".

[46] Knohl, *Sanctuary*, 220.

[47] 2 Ki 18:4; compare 2 Ki 18:22 and Isa 36:7. According to Knohl, Hezekiah's centralization was focused on the one legitimate *altar* in Jerusalem, as opposed to Josiah's centralization which stressed the one legitimate sanctuary. He sees a parallel between the Rabshakeh's words "this altar" (2 Ki 18:22) and the emphasis in Lev 17:6 on "the altar of YHWH" (compare Jos 22:29). For the archeological record, cf. the debate between N. Na'aman, "The Debated Historicity of Hezekiah's Reform in the Light of Historical and Archaeological Research", *ZAW* 107 (1995), 179-195, and O. Borowski, "Hezekiah's Reforms and the Revolt against Assyria", *BA* 58 (1995), 148-155.

[48] Elliger, *Leviticus*, 16; more explicitly argued in Mathys, *Liebe*, 108; Crüsemann, "Der Exodus als Heiligung. Zur rechtsgeschichtlichen Bedeutung des Heiligkeits-

It is certainly correct that H exhibits programmatic features.[49] One should not, however, jump to the conclusion that it was written with reform in mind. In addition, in the present state of our knowledge (see the preceding chapter) it would be unwise to make the hypothetical historical setting of H a starting point for exegesis.[50]

LITERATURE

As the preceding sections show, most scholars hold that H, or some older form strongly resembling it, once existed as a relatively independent corpus. However, those who see H as an accretion to or an original part of P are led to deny such independent existence.[51] For them, H must be studied in its present literary context.[52]

The most forceful argument in favour of a literary approach has come from Schwartz.[53] In his view, the law corpora of the Pentateuch were never meant to function independently of the narrative framework in which they occur. They were from the outset designed for insertion in the narrative.[54] The various non-legal features occurring in the laws— such as explanatory and motivational clauses, repetitions and omissions, exhortations and admonitions—are functional within the narrative context;[55] they are not indicative of an oral stage in the formation of H.[56] Schwartz therefore pleads for a method of close reading, which gives serious consideration to the law corpora as works of literary art, comparable to prose, poetry or prophecy.

---

gesetzes", in E. Blum, C. Macholz, E. W. Stegemann, Hsg., *Die Hebräische Bibel und ihre zweifache Nachgeschichte. Fs für R. Rendtorff zum 65. Geburtstag* (Neukirchen, 1990), 117-129.

[49] Compare, e.g., the recurring phrase: "When you come into the land..." Lev 19:23; 23:10; 25:2.

[50] Knohl shows himself to be well aware of the risk involved, see Knohl, *Sanctuary*, 199-200.

[51] See Chapter 1, notes 2 and 3.

[52] See Lohfink, "Abänderung" and especially Blum, *Studien*.

[53] Schwartz, *Chapters*, 1-24 and id. "The Prohibition Concerning the 'Eating' of Blood in Leviticus 17" in G. A. Anderson and S. M. Olyan, eds., *Priesthood and Cult in Ancient Israel*, JSOTS 125 (Sheffield, 1991), 34-66.

[54] Schwartz, *Chapters*, 10. Compare also Hempel, *Literatur*, 81. For a fundamentalist approach which comes very close to the one proposed by Schwartz, see J. H. Sailhammer, *The Pentateuch as Narrative. A Biblical-Theological Commentary* (Grand Rapids, 1992), 342-365.

[55] Schwartz, *Chapters*, 17.

[56] However, the narrative and the laws incorporated in it were designed to be read publicly with a didactic aim, see Schwartz, "Prohibition", 35.

The one-sidedness of Schwartz' approach is open to criticism. If the
laws were designed from the start as part of the narrative, why do we
find three law codes, which although largely parallel, all have their own
individual cast? Non-legal features occur in all three codes, but H does
not argue in the same way as the Book of the Covenant, and Deuteronomy is very different from both. This indicates that the non-legal features are not merely a function of the narrative context: they are indicative of the milieu in which the corpus originated. On the other hand, it is
true that the laws as we have them now are integrated into a story, and
this aspect of the texts must be taken into account. As to approaching the
codes as works of literary art, we have already indicated above that this
corresponds to the general trend in biblical studies of taking the text as it
stands more seriously.[57]

Each one of these different models makes a valid contribution to the
study of H. However, one should not view H as an eclectic amalgam or
a hybrid, standing halfway between law code and treaty, though exhibiting some programmatic features. If H and the other pentateuchal law
codes share certain characteristics with extra-biblical material and yet
differ from this material on other points, this should lead us to the understanding that the biblical codes are *sui generis*.[58]

More specifically, we may draw the following methodological conclusions:
a) H certainly presents itself as a piece of literature, integrated—though
loosely so[59]—in a narrative. Our first approach must therefore be a literary, exegetical one. Taking the text as it stands, we should try to discover
what it means and how it expresses what it means.[60]
b) However, H certainly is rooted in a historical context lying outside
the literary context in which we find it today.[61] In order to reconstruct

---

[57] See Chapter 1, n. 20.
[58] A promising new avenue is opened by Gammie, when he points to the fact that
"paraenesis" need not necessarily be opposed to "commandments": "Curiously, scholars of the Hebrew Bible have not sought to exploit the identification among classicists of
paraenesis as a collection of maxims—where the designation would admirably suit
Deuteronomy, the Holiness Code (Leviticus 17-26) and Proverbs as well as Sirach." See
J. G. Gammie, "Paraenetic Literature: Toward the Morphology of a Secondary Genre",
Semeia 50 (1990), 41-77, p. 55
[59] For the relative independence of H, see chapter 1.
[60] Compare Schwartz, *Chapters*, 19-24.
[61] See my criticisms of Schwartz above, and compare M. Noth, "Die Gesetze im
Pentateuch" in idem, *Gesammelte Studien zum Alten Testament*, Thelogische Bücherei,
AT 6 (München, [3]1966), 9-141, p. 21.

this context—a procedure which may be conducive to a better understanding of the text—we must use approaches other than the literary one (historical, sociological, theological etc.). These other methods are ancillary to the literary one and will require to be based on its results.

c) Among these ancillary methods, the juridical approach, including comparison with other ANE law codes and comparable texts, will have pride of place, for neither the narrative framework, nor the paraenesis can obscure the fact that the substance of H is law.[62] This observation remains valid even if it is true—as the juridical approach itself has tended to show—that the law contained in H was never intended to function in a court setting.

---

[62] Christian exegetes have too often tried to minimize the importance of the law, or at least to subordinate it to saving history. See the interesting remarks of J. D. Levenson, "The Theologies of Commandment in Biblical Israel", *HTR* 73 (1980), 17-33; more caustically, Schwartz, *Chapters*, 8.

CHAPTER THREE

THE ADDRESSEES OF THE HOLINESS CODE

A fact of central importance for the exegesis of H is that its audience are the Israelites. Any text, whether spoken or written, will normally be formulated with a specific audience in mind; it will speak on their level, in their language and take into account their cultural milieu. Yet, central though it may be, the notion of the "people of Israel" is also highly problematic. In what sense—ethnic, political, historical, religious—are they to be considered a people? Who are the real addressees: the Israelites in the desert or a later generation, established in the land of Israel or living in exile? A precise analysis of the terms and formulations used in direct address, as well as those referring to persons being indirectly addressed, will afford tentative answers to at least some of these questions.

3.1. THE DIRECTLY ADDRESSED

Israel

Even a cursory reading of Lev 17-26 makes it clear that the law is addressed to "Israel": the name is used 36 times in 10 chapters; 17 of these feature in the various formulas specifying the addressees of the prescriptions. Though the name "Israel" is notoriously polysemic,[1] its meaning here is, at least at first sight, unproblematic. It refers to the people of Israel led out of Egypt by YHWH and now encamped at the foot of Mount Sinai, where in preparation for their entry into the Promised Land they receive YHWH's instruction as related by Moses.[2] Even though in H itself only the tribes of Dan and Levi are mentioned explicitly,[3] we may probably suppose that the concept is that of an Israel with

---

[1] See A. R. Hulst, *Wat betekent de naam Israel in het Oude Testament*, Miniaturen 1, Bijlage bij het maandblad Kerk en Israel 16/9 ('s Gravenhage, 1962); H.-J. Zobel, TWAT III, 986-1012; G. A. Danell, *Studies in the Name Israel in the Old Testament* (Uppsala, 1946).

[2] For this historical setting, see in particular 18:3; 24:10b; 25:1; 26:46.

[3] For Dan see 24:11; for Levi 25:32-34.

13 tribes (counting Manasseh and Ephraim separately), corresponding
to the picture presented in the earlier priestly chapters of Leviticus and
Exodus.[4]

The sons of Israel

In H, as in the priestly tradition in general, the expression $b^e n\bar{e}$ $yi\acute{s}r\bar{a}'\bar{e}l$
is the usual designation whenever the people of Israel is referred to.[5]
Elsewhere in the OT, this expression has to compete with $yi\acute{s}r\bar{a}'\bar{e}l$ used
absolutely,[6] and with the expressions $'\bar{\imath}\check{s}$ $yi\acute{s}r\bar{a}'\bar{e}l$ and $'an\check{s}\bar{e}$ $yi\acute{s}r\bar{a}'\bar{e}l$.[7]
Besters has advanced the theory that the difference between $b^e n\bar{e}$
$yi\acute{s}r\bar{a}'\bar{e}l$ and $yi\acute{s}r\bar{a}'\bar{e}l$ alone can be explained by means of literary criticism: $b^e n\bar{e}$ $yi\acute{s}r\bar{a}'\bar{e}l$ is a mark of later, priestly or Deuteronomistic authors, whereas $yi\acute{s}r\bar{a}'\bar{e}l$ is usual in the older sources.[8] In arguing this
view, however, he is forced to undertake extensive rearrangement of the
delimitation of the different sources.[9] His procedure of arguing the late-
ness of verses because they contain the expression $b^e n\bar{e}$ $yi\acute{s}r\bar{a}'\bar{e}l$ and
then declaring $b^e n\bar{e}$ $yi\acute{s}r\bar{a}'\bar{e}l$ a new criterion for the identification of late
literary strands, is methodologically more than questionable.

A better approach is to look for semantic distinctions between the
different expressions.[10] An investigation of the occurrences of $b^e n\bar{e}$
$yi\acute{s}r\bar{a}'\bar{e}l$ in H leads to the identification of two semantic notions absent
from $yi\acute{s}r\bar{a}'\bar{e}l$ alone. First, it can be shown that in principle the composite expression includes only men. The laws in H are introduced by cer-
tain formulas which, as a rule, specify that the laws are addressed to the

---

[4] For the literary relationship between H and P, see Chapter 1.

[5] The only exceptions in H are the four cases of $b\bar{e}t$ $yi\acute{s}r\bar{a}'\bar{e}l$ reviewed below, and
three cases of $b^e yi\acute{s}r\bar{a}'\bar{e}l$: 20:2; 22:18; 23:42.

[6] Cf. also the expression kol $yi\acute{s}r\bar{a}'\bar{e}l$.

[7] The data are presented exhaustively in A. Besters, "«Israel» et «Fils d'Israel» dans
les livres historiques (Genèse-II Rois)", *RB* 74 (1967), 5-23. In Deuteronomy, the expression $b^e n\bar{e}$ $yi\acute{s}r\bar{a}'\bar{e}l$ is rare; this adds one more example to the list of differences
between H and Deuteronomy that cannot easily be explained by the supposition that one
of the codes is dependent on the other (in the law code of Deut 12-28, the expression is
found only in 23:18 and 24:7).

[8] Besters, "Israel", 6f.

[9] See especially his second article, A. Besters, "L'expression «Fils d'Israel» en Ex.,
I-XIV", *RB* 74 (1967), 321-355.

[10] Cf. the general study of D. I. Block, "'Israel'-'Sons of Israel': A Study in Hebrew
Eponymic Usage", *SR* 13 (1984), 301-326.

$b^e n\bar{e}$ $yi\acute{s}r\bar{a}'\bar{e}l$.[11] Let us consider one example:

18:1f	...ויאמר יהוה אל משה לאמר דבר אל בני ישראל ואמרת אליהם

And the LORD said to Moses, "Say to the sons of Israel..."[12]

The wording of the laws following this formula shows that $b^e n\bar{e}$ $yi\acute{s}r\bar{a}'\bar{e}l$ is to be taken in the sense that the laws are to be addressed specifically to the Israelite menfolk. Thus, Lev 18 contains prohibitions on bestiality both for men and women. However, whereas the commandment concerning men is given in the second person:[13]

18:23a	ובכל בהמה לא תתן שכבתן

And you shall not lie with any beast.

the commandment concerning women is given in the third person:

18:23b	ואשה לא תעמד לפני בהמה לרבעה

Neither shall any woman give herself to a beast to lie with it.

The reason for this variation is that, in the concept of H, the audience of the law are the Israelite men, who are thus made responsible for their own behaviour. Although women are made subject to the law, it is the men that are made responsible for their observance of the laws. The intention behind the use of the phrase $b^e n\bar{e}$ $yi\acute{s}r\bar{a}'\bar{e}l$ is not, therefore, to exclude women—as if they should not hear or keep the laws—but rather to subsume them under the person of the man in whose household they live.[14] The Israelite men are addressed, not so much as individuals, but

---

[11] Moses is commanded to speak to the sons of Israel: 17:2; 18:2; 19:2; 20:2; 22:18; 23:2, 10, 24, 34; 24:2, 15; 25:2; Moses is said to have spoken to the sons of Israel: 21:24; 23:44; 24:23; YHWH is said to have spoken to the sons of Israel: 17:12, 14. On some occasions Moses is commanded to speak only to Aaron or to his sons. It is to be noted, however, that in Lev 21 where Moses is first commanded to speak to the priests, the sons of Aaron (v 1) and then to Aaron himself (v 17), Moses is then said to have spoken to Aaron, to his sons and to all the Israelites (v 24). See for this phenomenon, E. Gerstenberger, ""Er soll dir heilig sein." Priester und Gemeinde nach Lev 21,1-22,9", in F. Crüsemann et al. Hsg., *Was ist der Mensch...? Beiträge zur Anthropologie des Alten Testaments*, Fs H. W. Wolff (München, 1992), 194-210, p. 204.

[12] RSV "say to the people of Israel".

[13] All the laws in c 18 are given from the man's point of view. Cf. also 19:29.

[14] Cf. 22:12f, which stipulates that the daughter of a priest belongs to her father's household until she marries, and may return to it when her marriage comes to an end.

in their quality as head of the family. This principle is especially evident in the following example:

19:29   אל תחלל את בתך להזנותה

Do not profane your daughter by making her a harlot.

Responsibility for the daughter's conduct is placed squarely on the shoulders of the father.[15] The central role of the household in Israel's relationship with YHWH has been the subject of a thorough study by Wright.[16] Reviewing a wide range of evidence, he concludes that the family constituted the basic social fabric through which Israel's relationship with its God was "earthed" and experienced.[17] The same principle is at work in H. The laws are impressed upon every man, in order that they be obeyed by all the Israelites.[18] However, this obedience will not come about by collective pressure of the men on women and children: every man represents his own household. The laws of YHWH are entrusted to the family.[19]

Since the Israelite men, as heads of their families, represent the whole people, it is not surprising to find that the expression $b^e n\bar{e}$ $yi\acute{s}r\bar{a}'\bar{e}l$ may elsewhere designate the entire people of Israel.[20]

Secondly, I would suggest that the expression puts some stress on the

---

[15] It is quite possible that we should give the hiphil in this verse a permissive meaning: do not profane your daughter by permitting her to prostitute herself (or: to be prostituted), see B. K. Waltke, M. O'Connor, An Introduction to Biblical Hebrew Syntax (Winona Lake, 1990), 445.

[16] C. J. H. Wright, God's People in God's Land. Family, Land and Property in the Old Testament (Grand Rapids, 1990), in particlular 1-114.

[17] Wright, God's People, 71. Much of Wright's evidence comes from the Holiness Code. A possible criticism of his work is that he tends to read prescriptive texts as a description of the people of Israel as it historically existed.

[18] Contrast Phillips, who holds that originally only men were included in the covenant with YHWH; women were outside the scope of the law. See A. Phillips, Ancient Israel's Criminal Law. A New Approach to The Decalogue (Oxford, 1970), 14-16. Detailed criticism in Wright, God's People, 90-97.

[19] Nowhere in H is the extent of the family precisely defined. From 22:10-13, it transpires that it comprised slaves and unmarried daughters.

[20] In 23:43 the "sons of Israel" are those involved in the Exodus. See also 22:32. Crüsemann, Tora, 359, has correctly noted that the expression "sons of Israel" refers strictly only to the men, but the further familial and collective aspects of the term seem to have escaped him.

ethnic identity of those it designates.[21] The notion of ethnicity is made explicit in Lev 25:39-46. Here, it is stated that although the Israelites may acquire a slave from the nations that are round about them (25:44), or from the strangers who sojourn with them (25:45), they may not enslave another Israelite:

25:46b ובאחיכם בני ישראל איש באחיו לא תרדה בו בפרך

...but over your brethren, the people of Israel, you shall not rule, one over another, with harshness.

Even if the expression *bᵉnē yiśrā'ēl* were deemed not to express ethnic identity,[22] this passage would show that the underlying conception in H is one of consanguinity. It also illustrates that ethnic identity is not to be interpreted in the sense of racial purity,[23] but of solidarity within the kin group.

Israelite

Ethnic identity is clearly what is expressed by the gentilic adjective *yiśrᵉ'ēlī* (f. *yiśrᵉ'ēlīt*), which is used three times in the account related in 24:10f.[24] A man of mixed descent—his mother an Israelite woman, but his father an Egyptian—came into conflict with a full Israelite (*'īš hayyiśrᵉ'ēlī* [25]). The half-breed blasphemed the Name. The details concerning the ethnicity of the main protagonist are of essential importance in this episode, as will be further explored below in the section on the *gēr* (pp. 63-64).

---

[21] After all, what is expressed by the noun *bēn*—"son"—is the genetic relation. It is true that the noun may be used to designate a member of a guild, order or class (BDB, 121), but this is a derived meaning. Note also that in the historical books, where the expression *bᵉnē yiśrā'ēl* is much rarer than in the Pentateuch, it is used whenever Israel is to be distinguished from other peoples: e.g. 2 Sam 21:2; 1 Ki 9:20. Cf. Block, "'Israel'-'Sons of Israel'"; Crüsemann, *Tora*, 358.

[22] Note also the notion that the sons of Israel are YHWH's slaves (25:55, 42). The underlying conception seems to be that of hereditary bondage (cf. 25:46), see Chapter 4.

[23] The notion of racial purity plays a great part in Ezra and Nehemiah, e.g. Ezra 9:2.

[24] Elsewhere this adjective is attested only in 2 Sam 17:25, where the text appears to be incorrect (see BHS).

[25] For the grammatical construction, see König, *Syntax*, §§ 334n-334q. The Samaritan Pentateuch and the manuscript from Qumran normalize the syntax in different ways.

The house of Israel

The expression *bēt yiśrā'ēl* occurs four times in H, always in the phrase *'īš 'īš mibbēt yiśrā'ēl* (17:3, 8, 10; 22:18).[26] The meaning of *bēt yiśrā'ēl* must be similar to that of *bᵉnē yiśrā'ēl* , for the two expressions interchange in the same formula (cp.*'īš 'īš mibbᵉnē yiśrā'ēl* in 17:13; 20:2), and in the different textual witnesses.[27] Nevertheless, we may suppose that the rarer expression is used to express a certain nuance otherwise absent.[28] A pointer to this nuance is given, I believe, by the progression of cases in Lev 17. The first four laws concern the following subjects: slaughter (vv 3-7), sacrifice (vv 8f), eating of blood (vv 10-12), hunting of animals (vv 13f). In the first three cases we find the expression *bēt yiśrā'ēl*, whereas in the fourth we find *bᵉnē yiśrā'ēl*. This may perhaps be taken as an indication that the first expression includes women, who might occasionally slaughter an animal or bring a sacrifice, and would be concerned by the interdiction against eating blood, but who would not normally go hunting.[29] The phrase *'īš 'īš mibbēt yiśrā'ēl* may be taken to mean any Israelite, man or woman.[30] The other instances of *bēt yiśrā'ēl* in the Pentateuch are in accord with this hypothesis.[31]

The expression certainly does not include the resident alien (*gēr*), as is shown by the fact that he is usually mentioned explicitly alongside the "house of Israel".[32]

---

[26] For study of the expression in the entire OT, see D. I. Block, "Israel's House: Reflections on the Use of *byt yśr'l* in the Old Testament in the Light of its Ancient Near Eastern Environment", *JETS* 28 (1985), 257-275.

[27] See BHS on 17:3 and 20:2.

[28] Note that the use of the term in MT is consistent to the extent that both in c 17 and in c 22 *bēt yiśrā'ēl* is used in the context of sacrifice. We must, however, take account of the possibility that the author of H used *bēt yiśrā'ēl* in 22:18 in order to connect the passage with c 17.

[29] For the entitlement of women to bring sacrifices, see the extensive discussion, with references to earlier literature, in M. I. Gruber, "Women in the Cult According to the Priestly Source", in J. Neusner et al., eds., *Judaic Perspectives on Ancient Israel* (Philadelphia, 1987), 35-48.

[30] Against this interpretation, one might point to the expression *'īš 'ō 'iššāh* (e.g. 20:27), and to 17:5, which mentions only the "sons of Israel". However, both these objections fall when one realizes that sacrifice by a woman was probably the exception.

[31] Ex 16:31; 40:38; Lev 10:6 Nu 20:29. Cassuto's view that the expression includes the Israelites of the desert generation as well as later generations fits Ex 16:31, but not the other occurrences, see U. Cassuto, *A Commentary on the Book of Exodus* (Jerusalem, 1942) [Hebrew], 138. Gispen's comment that the expression may depict the people of Israel as one large family seems to be closer to the mark, see Gispen, *Leviticus*, 166 (comment on 10:6).

[32] For the omission of the *gēr* in 17:3 see below, pp. 65-66.

The native

The term *'ezrāḥ* occurs six times in H and eight times in other priestly texts.[33] It is all but absent elsewhere.[34] Its etymology is usually connected with the verb *zrḥ* "to arise", leading to a meaning "one arising from the soil", "autochthon".[35] Others postulate a second root *zrḥ* related to the Arabic *ṣaruḥa* "to be of pure race".[36] The word is often said to be indicative of late Biblical Hebrew, but this is incorrect; it is no more current in post-exilic than pre-exilic texts. The only thing that can be said is that the word is typical of the priestly tradition.[37]

The term functions as a substitute for "Israelite" in certain contexts, especially in collocation with the term *gēr* "resident alien". In Lev 17, for instance, vv 8, 10 and 13 juxtapose Israel and the *gēr*, but v 15 juxtaposes the *'ezrāḥ* and the *gēr*.[38] The consistent association of *'ezrāḥ* with *gēr*, might be taken as supportive of either etymology given above: autochthon (versus the allochthon *gēr*), or full-Israelite (versus the non-Israelite *gēr*).[39] Only once is the term found in a text where no mention is made of the *gēr* :

23:42 בסכת תשבו שבעת ימים כל האזרח בישראל ישבו בסכת

You shall dwell in booths for seven days; all that are native in Israel shall dwell in booths.

---

[33] In H: 17:15; 18:26; 19:34; 23:42; 24:16, 22; elsewhere in priestly texts: Ex 12:19, 48, 49; Lev 16:29; Nu 9:14; 15:13, 29, 30; cfr Jos 8:33; Ez 47:22.

[34] In Ps 37:35 the word occurs in a different meaning.

[35] BDB, 280. In the OT the verb occurs only in the meaning "to rise, to shine forth" (said of the sun, of YHWH and of leprosy).

[36] HAL I, 270, refers to J. Barth, *Wurzeluntersuchungen* (1902), 15, for this etymology. However, it is found already in W. Robertson Smith, *Lectures on the Religion of the Semites* (Edinburgh, 1889), 75. N. H. Tur-Sinai, EM I, 188, connects the Arabic root with *zrḥ* I "to shine forth" because the notion of purity is underlying in both.

[37] Deller sees the Hebrew word as a very late loan from Assyrian, see K. Deller, "Assyrisch um/unzarhu und hebräisch 'äzrah", ZA 74 (1984), 235-239. His construction is quite hypothetical, however.

[38] Also 18:26; 24:16; 19:34; 24:22 and the instances of the word in other priestly texts.

[39] In any case, the possibility that the term *'ezrāḥ* should designate any class of non-Israelites, as is held by Sulzberger and Albright, is to be excluded. According to Sulzberger the term referred originally to Egyptians who left Egypt together with the Israelites, see M. Sulzberger, "The Status of Labor in Ancient Israel", *JQR* NS 13 (1922-23), 245-302, 397-459, p. 397. Albright connects the term with the adjective *'ezrāḥī* (e.g. 1 Ki 5:11) and has both terms refer to descendants of the original Canaanite population who had become integrated into Israel, see W. F. Albright, *Archaeology and the Religion of Israel* (Baltimore, 1942), 127 and 210, n. 95.

I suggest that here the term *'ezrāḥ* is used in order to restrict the prescription to the Israelites. One could say the non-mention of the *gēr* is emphatic: he is not obliged to dwell in booths.[40] The reason for this restriction is given explicitly in the following verse: "that your generations may know that I made the people of Israel dwell in booths when I brought them out of the land of Egypt." The dwelling in booths makes sense only for the Israelites, whose forefathers took part in the Exodus; the resident alien is not required to participate in the celebration of Israel's past.[41] The wider context of this distinction between *'ezrāḥ* and *gēr* will be explored below, in the section on the resident alien (pp. 63-64).

The assembly and the people of the land

The assembly

The word *'ēdāh* occurs three times in H (Lev 19:2 and 24:14, 16[42]). It is extremely common in priestly texts, where it is used mainly as a designation for the Israelite community; in this sense it is rather rare elsewhere.[43] The related verb is *y'd* "to appoint"; the derivation is regular.[44] The meaning and background of the priestly term are a subject of dispute. On the one side is the position, argued most extensively by Rost, that the term was created by the priestly school during or after the exile.[45] According to this view, its meaning is purely cultic and religious,

---

[40] The association of *'ezrāḥ* and *gēr* is so constant that some commentators suppose that the word *gēr* has been lost from this passage, see e.g. A. Bertholet, *Die Stellung der Israeliten und der Juden zu den Fremden* (Freiburg i. B. & Leipzig, 1896), 171f.

[41] Cf. Elliger, *Leviticus*, 323. A different view has been proposed by C. Bultmann, *Der Fremde im antiken Juda. Eine Untersuchung zum sozialen Typenbegriff >ger< und seinem Bedeutungswandel in der alttestamentlichen Gesetzgebung*, FRLANT 153 (Göttingen, 1992), 205f. Bultmann dates the law to the Persian period. According to Bultmann, the rite of Lev 23:42f was prescribed only for the Israelites who lived in the vicinity of Jerusalem, whereas *gērīm*—converts to the Jewish faith—were found mostly in the Diaspora. In the light of texts like Lev 18:26, where *gēr* and *'ezrāḥ* are emphatically set in the context of the land, his proposal is problematic. Yet another theory is that of M. Cohen, "Le «Ger» biblique et son statut socio-religieux", *RHR* 207 (1990), 131-158, p. 153f n. 50. For Cohen, it was not necessary to command that the *gēr* should dwell in a booth because, as a *persona misera*, he was already doing so.

[42] Also in 22:18 according to the LXX.

[43] Jud 20:1; 21:10, 13, 16; 1 K 8:5; 12:20.

[44] Cf. other derivations of *primae yod* verbs: *'ēṣāh, šēnāh, lēdāh, dē'āh*. Note, however, that all these nouns denote rather an action than a collective.

[45] L. Rost, *Die Vorstufen von Kirche und Synagoge im Alten Testament*, BWANT IV, 24 (1938).

designating the religious community which gathers around the *'ohel mō'ēd*.[46] On the other side are those scholars who argue that in its picture of the *'ēdāh*, P preserves the contours of an institution from the time before the monarchy: the "general assembly" of all male adults which embodies the highest authority of the Israelite tribal league.[47] Although it must be granted that the picture presented in the priestly texts is to a certain extent schematized and anachronistic, it seems to me that the second alternative accounts better for the facts than the first.

Since the noun occurs already in Ugaritic with the precise meaning of "assembly", one may no longer claim that it was invented by priestly writers in the exile.[48] If one wants to defend the view that P "created" the term, one is forced to submit that the priestly writers took an existing word meaning "assembly" and applied it to the community of Israelites in the desert. The view that P created the term in exile may be countered by three arguments. Firstly, the description P gives of the *'ēdāh* is not exactly one of a religious community: though it participates in cultic acts, some of which are expressly said to be performed on its behalf, the *'ēdāh* also goes to war, and functions as a supreme court in case of murder.[49] It is by no means apparent that these elements are meant to be spiritualized. Exilic or post-exilic priests would probably not have included such features in their ideal image of the Israelite religious community, at least not if they were creating it anew. Secondly, the word *'ēdāh* is never used in those parts of the OT known to date from the exilic or post-exilic period.[50] The later biblical books use the word

---

[46] Elliger, *Leviticus*, 70 has argued that the word belongs to a younger literary layer in P (this was argued already by B. Luther, "Kahal und 'edah als Hilfsmittel der Quellenscheidung im Priestercodex und in der Chronik", ZAW 56 [1938], 44-63). However, a text like Num 1:1-3—where the word *'ēdāh* occupies an important place—is generally deemed to be part of the *Grundschrift* of P (even by Elliger himself, see K. Elliger, "Sinn und Ursprung der priesterlichen Geschichtserzählung", ZThK 49 (1952), 121-143, p. 122). In any case, a word may have been in use before its first known attestation; even a later priestly writer may reflect early traditions.

[47] See J. Levy and J. Milgrom, TWAT V, 1079-1093, with literature. Early exponents of this view that are not cited by Milgrom and Levy are B. D. Eerdmans, *Alttestamentliche Studien III. Das Buch Exodus* (Gießen, 1910), 80f; M. Noth, *Das System der zwölf Stämme Israels*, BWANT IV, 1 (Stuttgart, 1930), 102f.

[48] For the Ugaritic examples and their parallel in Ps 82:1, see TWAT V, 1089.

[49] See TWAT V, 1081-1089.

[50] It is attested in Qumran literature, where it was used probably under the influence of the OT, see J. Liver, EM VI, 83-89. It is also attested in the Hebrew text of Ben Sira from Massada, in 41:18; 44:15. It was apparently borrowed into the Aramaic used in the documents from Elephantine, see R. Yaron, "Aramaic Marriage Contracts from Elephantine", *JSS* 3 (1958), 1-39, pp. 14-16.

qāhāl instead of *ʿēdāh*.[51] This indicates that *ʿēdāh* in the sense of "assembly" is an older word that fell from use in the exilic period.[52]

Thirdly, the sporadic occurrences of the word in the historical books accord with the conception of P. This is especially the case for the account of the punitive expedition against Benjamin in Judges 19-21. Here the *ʿēdāh* plays a central part as a sort of inter-tribal court of justice which at the same time executes its own judgments.[53] It is common practice either to date this story to the exilic or post-exilic period,[54] or to excise the clauses containing the word *ʿēdāh* as later, priestly glosses.[55] Both these approaches must be rejected.[56] Whereas the priestly picture can be understood as a development of the notion of *ʿēdāh* as it occurs in Jud 19-21,[57] the concept in Jud 19-21 cannot be explained as an offshoot of P.[58]

We may therefore accept that P's description of the *ʿēdāh* is based on authentic historical tradition or popular recollection of an institution from before the monarchy. This does not mean that P's picture in all its details is a true account of that institution.[59] For the study of H, however, it is P's view of the *ʿēdāh* that is relevant, and it is this view that will be made the basis of the following considerations. In its precise, technical meaning, the *ʿēdāh* includes all male Israelites from the age of 20 upwards, who are able to go to war. The term therefore has the same referent as the expression *bᵉnē yiśrāʾēl*,[60] but whereas *bᵉnē yiśrāʾēl* is the general term, *ʿēdāh* stresses more the group acting concertedly. It has a

---

[51] See TWAT V, 1092.

[52] See A. Hurvitz, *A Linguistic Study of the Relationship between the Priestly Source and the Book of Ezekiel*, Cahiers de la Revue Biblique 20 (Paris, 1982), 65f.

[53] Jud 20:2; 21:10, 13, 16 (cf. the role of the *ʿēdāh* in Josh 22:12, 16, a text from the priestly tradition).

[54] See for extensive discussion, M.-J. Lagrange, *Le livre des Juges* (Paris, 1903), 329-337.

[55] See F. Crüsemann, *Der Widerstand gegen das Königtum*, WMANT 49 (Neukirchen, 1978), 156, n. 2, 158, n. 15.

[56] Noth, *System*, 102f.

[57] This is true also of the use of the term in 1 Ki 12:20.

[58] In Jud 21:16 we find the expression "elders of the assembly" (*ziqnē hāʿēdāh*). Though this expression occurs once in P (Lev 4:15), it is absolutely untypical of P. In the priestly texts the elders play no part whatsoever.

[59] For P's "idealizing" tendency, see J. Milgrom, "Priestly Terminology and the Political and Social Structure of Pre-Monarchic Israel", *JQR* 69 (1978-79), 65-81. For a review of the concrete possibilities and difficulties involved in postulating an "assembly" in the pre-monarchical era, see W. Thiel, *Die soziale Entwicklung Israels in vorstaatlicher Zeit* (Neukirchen-Vluyn, 1980), 137-141 (with literature).

[60] For Num 27:21, where a distinction between the assembly and the sons of Israel seems to be made, see TWAT V, 1085.

communal and a political aspect. The word carries a non-technical meaning when it refers to the whole people, inclusive of wives and children. This general usage is very frequent in priestly texts.[61]

In H the word ʿēdāh is used in the same way as in other priestly texts. Moreover, it seems that in both passages where it occurs it carries its precise, technical meaning. We will now take a closer look at the relevant verses.

19:2   דבר אל כל עדת בני ישראל ואמרת אליהם קדשים תהיו כי קדוש
         אני יהוה אלהיכם

Speak to the entire assembly of the sons of Israel and say to them: You shall be holy, for I the LORD your God am holy.[62]

It is not quite exact, as is sometimes stated, that ʿēdāh here refers to the whole people.[63] It is explicitly stated that the ʿēdāh which Moses is commanded to address is made up of the bᵉnē yiśrāʾēl, the Israelite menfolk (see above)—exactly like the ʿēdāh, in the technical sense of the word, of Num 1. The import of the bᵉnē yiśrāʾēl as addressees of the command to be holy is to be understood in light of the discussion above: holiness is the charge of every single Israelite, but the responsibility for this assignment is entrusted to the families, of which the men are the head.

By the use of the term ʿēdāh, however, another dimension is added to the individual and familial levels expressed by the phrase bᵉnē yiśrāʾēl. To begin with, the term expresses a communal aspect: all the Israelites, the community as a whole, must be holy. Moreover, this community is not a purely religious or cultic association. From the contents of the laws that follow, it transpires that agriculture, the administration of justice and social affairs are also among its concerns. We will not be far wrong, therefore, if we ascribe to the ʿēdāh a social, even a political function. As a result, we may say without exaggeration that Lev 19:2 lays down the blueprint for a nation.

If the exegesis given here is correct, our verse finds a close parallel in Ex 19:5f: "Now therefore, if you will obey my voice and keep my cov-

---

[61] For examples of all these aspects, see TWAT V, 1081-1089.
[62] RSV: "Say to all the congregation of the people of Israel: You shall be holy, for I the LORD your God am holy."
[63] See e.g. Schwartz, Chapters, 110f.

enant, (...) you shall be to me (...) a holy nation (*gōy qādōš*)."[64] The significance of this passage in its context has in my view been well summarized by S. M. Paul:

> First Israel is told what its mission is to be: it was elected for the purpose of becoming a "holy nation" devoted to God. Then the means to achieve and maintain this consecrated status are fully expounded in the Decalogue and legal corpus which together form the constitution of this newly created nation.[65]

Though many of the conceptions underlying Lev 19:2 diverge from those of Ex 19:5f,[66] the thrust of the two passages is the same. Israel must be a holy nation to YHWH; holiness is attained by keeping the commandments.

The second passage mentioning the *ʿēdāh* brings us to a forensic setting. It is again clear that it is used in its limited, technical sense. When a man of mixed descent had blasphemed the Name (Lev 24:11), they—presumably the *bᵉnē yiśrāʾēl* mentioned earlier in the narrative (see 24:10)—brought him to Moses and put him in custody. YHWH then declares that he should be put to death and that the whole *ʿēdāh* must stone him. Subsequently, a new law is formulated:

24:16   ונקב שם יהוה מות יומת רגום ירגמו בו כל העדה

He who blasphemes the name of the LORD shall be put to death, all the assembly shall stone him.[67]

Though the precise nature of the crime, and the reason why it was initially unclear what to do with the blasphemer must be left for consideration below in the section on the resident alien (pp. 68-69), sufficient elements are available to understand the role of the *ʿēdāh* in the present passage. To begin with, it seems that the assembly had an active role in the administration of justice. Admittedly, in the present case the perpetrator of the deed is brought to Moses, while the actual judgment is given by YHWH, through Moses as intermediary. However, this proce-

---

[64] It is more usual to compare Lev 19:2 with Ex 22:30; in the latter, however, we find a more ritualistic understanding of holiness (as opposed to Ex 19:5, which seems, at least in its present context, to exhibit a wider understanding of holiness).

[65] Paul, *Studies*, 31f.

[66] Whereas the Exodus passage uses the concepts of nation (*gōy*) and kingdom (*mamlākāh*), Lev 19:2 speaks of the *ʿēdāh*.

[67] RSV: "all the congregation shall stone him".

dure probably resulted from the complicated nature of the case; had it been more straightforward, the assembly might simply have applied the law and pronounced judgment itself. With regard to Lev 24, this view may seem quite speculative. It is confirmed, however, by the chapter on the cities of refuge, Num 35, where the ʿēdāh functions as supreme judge (Num 35:12, 24f) in cases of homicide.

Whatever its judiciary functions may be, it is clear that the ʿēdāh is responsible for the execution of justice: the entire assembly must stone the blasphemer. The express mention of kol-hāʿēdāh—first in a specific injunction regarding this particular case (v 14) and then again in the more general formulation of a law (v 16)—shows that this is not just a practical matter of having the blasphemer executed. The underlying rationale is that through the blasphemy which occurred "among the Israelites" (v 10), the assembly has incurred guilt which must be eradicated through the execution of the blasphemer.[68] Several arguments may be furnished to illustrate the correctness of this view. First, there is the fact that before the stoning, the ones who heard the blasphemy must lay their hands upon the blasphemer's head (v 14): in this way they transfer on to him the guilt which had been brought upon them through the blasphemy.[69] Secondly, the priestly texts relate a number of occasions where the deeds of one person or one group resulted in the collective guilt of the whole people; the recipient of this guilt is invariably the ʿēdāh. Thus at the death of Nadab and Abihu, Moses commands Aaron and his other sons not to mourn:

Lev 10:6 ראשיכם אל תפרעו ובגדיכם לא תפרמו ולא תמתו ועל כל העדה
יקצֹף

Do not let the hair of your heads hang loose, and do not rend your clothes, lest you die, and lest wrath come upon all the assembly.[70]

Since this command is given in the exact wording of Lev 21:10b, there can be no doubt that Lev 10:6 is akin to H. The doctrine of collective guilt of the ʿēdāh due to the transgression of a few is explicit.[71] On the

---

[68] This point is further underscored by the phrase "he will bear his own guilt" (wᵉnāśāʾ ḥeṭʾō) in v 15: he who curses his own pagan god does not bring guilt upon the collective, but merely upon himself (for the exegesis, see section 3.2.).

[69] For this interpretation, see Wenham, Leviticus, 311.

[70] RSV: "upon all the congregation".

[71] Other passages which exemplify this doctrine: Num 1:53; 16:22; 31:16; Josh 22:17-20.

level of content, the link between Lev 10:6 and 24:14ff lies in the fact that both passages are concerned with a sin against YHWH.

These considerations show why and in what sense the word ʿēdāh is used in Lev 24:14, 16: through a serious transgression against YHWH committed in their midst, the Israelite community incurred guilt; to eradicate that guilt, the collective had to execute the transgressor.[72]

YHWH's command is carried out by the bᵉnē yiśrāʾēl, who, as already shown above, make up the ʿēdāh (v 23).

The role of the ʿēdāh in the present passage raises one more important question. Death by stoning is mentioned also in Lev 20:2, 4, where responsibility for the execution of the judgment is not imposed on the ʿēdāh but on the ʿam hāʾāreṣ.[73] What is the relationship between these two institutions?

The people of the land

The expression ʿam hāʾāreṣ occurs twice in H (Lev 20:2, 4), several times in P (Gen 23:7, 12, 13; Lev 4:27; Num 14:9) and 45 times elsewhere in the OT.[74] It has attracted much scholarly attention, particularly with regard to those occurrences where it denotes a group that actively participated in the history of the kingdom of Judah (2 Ki 11; 21:24; 23:30).[75] The paucity of evidence has led to a bewildering variety of hypotheses, some of which will presumably have convinced only their authors.[76] Yet a relative consensus may be said to exist on the following points. The expression ʿam hāʾāreṣ is often used in a non-technical sense meaning simply: the inhabitants of a given land (e.g. Gen 42:6; Num 14:9; 2 Ki 15:5; 23:3). Furthermore, in a more technical sense it refers to the full citizens of the land: the free, land-owning men, who could in times of crisis constitute a representative assembly (e.g. 2 Ki 23:35; Gen 23 see below).[77] Finally, in the context of the Judean king-

---

[72] Finkelstein has pointed out that the punishment of stoning itself implies a collective aspect, see J. J. Finkelstein, *The Ox That Gored*, Transactions of the American Philosophical Society, Vol. 71, Part 2 (Philadelphia, 1981), 26-29.

[73] Stoning is mentioned also in 20:27, but the executioners are not specified.

[74] See A. R. Hulst, THAT II, 299-301. E. Lipiński, TWAT VI, 190.

[75] See e.g. H. Jagersma, *A History of Israel in the Old Testament Period* (London, 1982), 145.

[76] Recent reviews of the literature in B. Halpern, *The Constitution of the Monarchy in Israel*, HSM 25 (Ann Arbor, 1981), 190-194; and in R. M. Good, *The Sheep of His Pasture. A Study of the Hebrew Noun ʿAm(m) and Its Semitic Cognates*, HSM 29 (Chico, 1983), 109-113.

[77] See Hulst, Lipiński (n. 74 above).

dom, the term is sometimes used to distinguish the population of the provinces from that of Jerusalem (1 Ki 11:20; Jer 2:18).[78]

Since the technical meaning of "the body of full citizens of a given land" is especially relevant to Lev 20:2, 4, we will illustrate it with one very instructive example from P.[79] Gen 23 tells how Abraham went about acquiring a plot of land from the Hittites in Hebron. In this context, the $b^e n\bar{e}$ $\d{h}\bar{e}t$ are called "people of the land":

23:7   ויקם אברהם וישתחו לעם הארץ לבני חת

Abraham rose and bowed to the Hittites, the people of the land.

The "sons of Heth" are further identified in v 10:

23:10   ויען עפרון החתי את אברהם באזני בני חת לכל באי שער עירו

And Ephron the Hittite answered Abraham in the hearing of the Hittites, of all who went in at the gate of his city.[80]

The picture which arises from this passage is that of a fairly loose collective called $^{\zeta}am$ $h\bar{a}^{\jmath}\bar{a}re\d{s}$ (the term also occurs in vv 12f), consisting of the "sons of Heth", who are none other than the male adult citizens, conceived of as a kinship group. This collective could convene in an official manner on important occasions, for instance to witness the sale of a plot of land to one who was not a member of the kinship group.[81]

Turning now to the use of the term $^{\zeta}am$ $h\bar{a}^{\jmath}\bar{a}re\d{s}$ in H, a very similar entity turns out to be meant.

---

[78] Jagersma, *History*, 145 (with literature).

[79] Apart from the term $^{\zeta}am$ $h\bar{a}^{\jmath}\bar{a}re\d{s}$, quite a few other parallels exist between Gen 23 and H: the expressions $g\bar{e}r$ $w^e t\bar{o}\check{s}\bar{a}b$ (Gen 23:4; Lev 25:47); $q\bar{a}m$ l- in the sense of "to be made over" (Gen 23:17; Lev 25:30); the term $^{\jmath a}\d{h}uzz\bar{a}h$ "landholding" (Gen 23:9, 20; Lev 25 *passim*); and the preoccupation with possession of the land. Knohl tentatively assigns the whole chapter to the "Holiness School", see Knohl, *Sanctuary*, 104.

[80] Talmon attempts to draw a distinction between the sons of Heth and "all who went in the gate of his city", see S. Talmon, "Der judäische עם הארץ in historischer Perspektive", in idem, *Gesellschaft und Literatur in der hebräischen Bibel* (Neukirchen-Vluyn, 1988), 80-91, p. 89. However, $l^e kol$ is a well-known priestly expression meaning "namely", see Driver, *Introduction*, 132.

[81] This is the picture as it arises from the story in Gen 23. The historicity of this account is not relevant in the present context.

20:2   איש איש מבני ישראל ומן הגר הגר בישראל אשר יתן מזרעו
                למלך מות יומת עם הארץ ירגמהו באבן

Any man of the people of Israel, or of the strangers that sojourn in
Israel, who gives any of his children to Molech shall be put to death;
the people of the land shall stone him with stones.

All that is said explicitly in this verse is that the people of the land must
execute the man guilty of Molech-worship. It stands to reason, however,
that the ʿam hāʾāreṣ referred to also pronounced the verdict; at least, no
mention is made of any other judiciary authority.[82] If this inference is
correct, the ʿam hāʾāreṣ appears here as a representative assembly with
official status.[83] Thus the ʿam hāʾāreṣ in the present passage exhibits
characteristics of the ʿēdāh of Lev 24:10-23.[84]

The most salient resemblance between the ʿam hāʾāreṣ in Lev 20 and
the ʿēdāh in Lev 24 is their shared role in the execution of justice, as was
stated above. In this connection, two other parallels may be identified.

Though the precise nature of the act proscribed in Lev 20:2 will not
occupy us here,[85] it is clear that it is considered a serious crime against
YHWH (cf. v 3 lᵉmaʿan ṭammēʾ ʾet miqdāšī ulᵉhallēl ʾet šēm qodšī
"defiling my sanctuary and profaning my holy name"). As in Lev 24, a
crime against YHWH is to be punished by stoning at the hands of the
collective.

---

[82] In general, the OT paints the picture of a judiciary system in which every free man
might participate, either as judge or as member of the jury, see L. Köhler, "Die
hebräische Rechtsgemeinde" in id. *Der hebräische Mensch* (Tübingen, 1953), 143-171;
more recent H. Niehr, *Rechtsprechung in Israel. Untersuchungen zur Geschichte der
Gerichtsorganisation im Alten Testament* (Stuttgart 1987). A different view has been
advanced by Crüsemann (*Tora*, 80-104), who argues that the court of elders in the gate
was installed by and represented the king.

[83] De Vaux compares the role of the people of the land in this passage to that of the
elders in several places in Deuteronomy (Deut 19:12; 21:2-6, 19f; 22:15-18; 25:7-9), see
R. de Vaux, "Le sens de l'expression «Peuple du Pays» dans l'Ancien Testament et le
rôle politique du peuple en Israel", *RA* 58 (1964), 167-172, p. 171.

[84] It is therefore incorrect to assert that the ʿam hāʾāreṣ includes the gēr, as is stated
by C. van Houten, *The Alien in Israelite Law*, JSOTS 107 (Sheffield, 1991), 143. Cf. the
expression yōšᵉbē hāʾāreṣ in 25:10, which also seems to include only the Israelites.

[85] The theory of Eissfeldt (still defended by H.-P. Müller in TWAT IV, 957-968),
according to which *molek* is to be understood, in the light of Punic inscriptions, as a type
of sacrifice, is rejected in the most recent studies by Heider and Day, see G. C. Heider,
The Cult of Molek. A Reassessment, JSOTS 43 (Sheffield, 1985); J. Day, *Molech. A God
of Human Sacrifice in the Old Testament*, University of Cambridge Oriental Publications 41 (Cambridge, 1989). For Lev 20:2-5, see Schwartz, *Chapters*, 81-83. Recently,
Smelik has tried to mount a renewed defence of Eissfeldt's theory, see K. A. D. Smelik,
"Moloch, Molekh or Molk-Sacrifice? A Reassessment of the Evidence Concerning the
Hebrew term Molekh", *SJOT* 9 (1995), 133-142.

The second parallel is the notion of collective guilt.

20:4f ואם העלם יעלימו עם הארץ את עיניהם מן האיש ההוא...
ושמתי אני את פני באיש ההוא ובמשפחתו...

When the people of the land do at all hide their eyes from that man...,
then I will set my face against that man and against his family...

If the people of the land do not punish the apostate, YHWH himself will punish. His punishment will fall on the guilty person, and on his *mišpāḥāh*.[86] A further aspect comes into view if we take the context into account. In Lev 20:22f, and more explicitly in 18:24-28, it is stated that if the Israelites engage in such activities—the practices of Egypt and Canaan (18:3), of which the cult of Molech is the most horrendous—they will be defiled, and the land will vomit them out, just as it vomited out its previous inhabitants. On this understanding, the notion of collective guilt in our passage comes into focus: the guilty party must be punished by the people of the land; if they refuse to do their part, the perpetrator will still receive his due; however, by allowing these crimes to happen, the land will be defiled and the entire people will ultimately suffer terrible collective punishment, i.e. exile from their land. In both Lev 24:10-23 and Lev 20:2-5, we find the underlying notion of collective guilt resulting from the crime of one man.[87]

At this point the question arises: if the institutions in Lev 24 and Lev 20 exhibit the same characteristics and are to fulfill the same role in similar contexts, why are they designated by two totally different terms? Many exegetes would be tempted to give an answer from literary criticism: the two passages come from different sources or literary strands.[88] However, a consideration of the respective contexts suggests a less arbitrary explanation. In Lev 24:10ff, we find a narrative relating an event that happened in the desert. In this context the collective body with official authority is the *'ēdāh*, in line with the general priestly picture of Israel in the desert. On the other hand, Lev 20:2-5 is a prescriptive passage on what will require to be done in the land of Israel. This is indi-

---

[86] The extent of the *mišpāḥāh* is difficult to define. According to Greenberg, the biblical text implies a collective penalty imposed on the community that failed to prosecute a notorious idolator, see M. Greenberg, "Biblical Attitudes toward Power: Ideal and Reality in Law and Prophets", in E. B. Firmage et al., eds., *Religion and Law. Biblical-Judaic and Islamic Perspectives* (Winona Lake, 1990), 101-112, p. 108.

[87] Yet another parallel between 20:2-5 and 24:10-13 is the inclusion of the *gēr*.

[88] Older studies usually ascribe Lev 24 to P and Lev 20 to H.

cated by the general framework in Lev 18:3-5 (...the land of Canaan, to
which I am bringing you, v 3), 18:24-30 and 20:22-24 (...the land
where I am bringing you, v 22). More specifically, Molech-worship is
listed as one of the deeds practised in the land of Canaan by its previous
inhabitants (Lev 20:23, cf. 18:24, 27). A case of Molech-worship implies establishment in the land. In that context the function of the ʿēdāh
is ascribed to the ʿam hāʾāreṣ, the corresponding authority under
changed historical circumstances.[89]

The functional equivalence of the "assembly" and the "people of the
land" in different historical contexts must, I believe, be looked at also
from a second, extra-literary perspective. Indeed, even though the notion of the land is explicit in Lev 20, that of the people of the land—
particularly in the sense of an Israelite entity—is somewhat unexpected.
From the point of view of the fiction upheld in H, the Israelites in the
desert, upon hearing the law in Lev 20:2-5, should have reasoned that
they themselves would one day be this "people of the land", once God
had led them there. Such a leap of imagination is inadequately prepared
for by phrases such as: "When you come into the land..." (Lev 19:23).

I suggest, therefore, that in Lev 20:2-5, the author of H lapses into a
mode of speech which is not in tune with the fictional context of H but
instead with his own historical context. He expects his audience to understand what is meant by the term ʿam hāʾāreṣ, not because their imagination has followed the projection of the fictional Israel-in-the-desert
into a setting in the land, but because they are themselves living in the
land and ʿam hāʾāreṣ is for them a notion of everyday life.[90] The fiction
is suspended for a fleeting moment and the audience are directly addressed: you, who are by your own understanding the "people of the
land", must act when this abominable sin is done amongst you. Similar
passages, in which the fiction is for a moment abandoned and the contemporary historical reality of the author breaks in, are found in several
places in H.[91] They would seem to be part of the paraenetic strategy of
the author of H. Just as Nathan told king David: "You are the man" (2

---

[89] In Lev 4 we also find both terms, ʿēdāh in v 13, ʿam hāʾāreṣ in v 27; here it is not
possible, however, to view these terms as reflecting different historical conditions. By
and large, however, it is clear that the assembly is an institution from the desert period
(for the few attestations of the term in a context in the land, see n. 43), whereas the
institution of the "people of the land" belongs in the land.

[90] In the historical and prophetical books, the "people of the land" is an active force
from the 9th century (2 Ki 11) until the early post-exilic period (Hag 2:4; Zech 7:5).

[91] See n. 28 in chapter 1.

Sam 12:7), so the author of H lets his audience know that they are the *bᵉnē yiśrā'ēl* addressed in these chapters.

In other words, it is perhaps no exaggeration to say that the author of H uses a kind of code to address his contemporaries. The symbols of the code are realities of the desert period, the referents are from the period when H was written: the Israelites of the desert are the Israel of his day, the *'ēdāh* is the *'am hā'āreṣ*. Though the fiction of the desert period is held to fairly consistently, from time to time the veil of the fiction is lifted to reveal the contemporary reality of the author.

Singular and plural address

Where direct address is used in H, both second person singular ("thou") and plural ("ye") are found.[92] Such "variation of number" (German: *Numeruswechsel*) has often been used as an index for source-analysis, the underlying ideas being that an author would retain the same grammatical number while addressing an audience, and that a later redactor would preserve the grammatical number used in his sources.[93] However, the literary-critical use of variation of number has been much criticized. It has been pointed out that the mixing of styles is typical of all biblical law codes, and is found also in Ancient Near Eastern texts which are not suspect of being composite.[94] Also, source critical analysis on the basis of the variation of number sometimes leads to results that are at variance with those from source critical analysis using other criteria such as vocabulary and content.[95] Finally, the whole principle of dividing up a given text to correspond to several sources is beginning to be abandoned in favour of approaching the text in its final form.[96]

An extensive study of the variation of number as a stylistic phenom-

---

[92] In the section on variation of number I will quote from the King James Version, since in the English of the RSV the opposition between second person singular and plural is necessarily obscured.

[93] Examples of source-analysis on the basis of the change of number are given in Barbiero, *L'asino*, 206.

[94] See M. Greenberg, "The Design and Themes of Ezekiel's Program of Restoration", *Interpretation* 38 (1984), 181-208, p. 187.

[95] See N. Lohfink, *Das Hauptgebot. Eine Untersuchung literarischer Einleitungsfragen zu Dtn 5-11*, AnBib 20 (Rome, 1963), 239-241.

[96] See in particular on the point of variation of number and with regard to H, E. Cortese, "Levitico 19", in *Evangelizare pauperibus*, Atti della XXIV settimana biblica (Brescia, 1978), 207-217, p. 207; Barbiero, *L'asino*, 206-208; Otto, "Heiligkeitsgesetz", 69, n. 19.

enon has been undertaken N. Lohfink.[97] On the basis of Deut 5-11, he has shown that changing from singular to plural address is a device used in "preaching of the law" which serves to mark intensification at important junctions of the discourse. The variation is entirely functional and may be used for source critical analysis to a very limited extent only. For Deut 5-11, Lohfink establishes that the neutral mode of address (*Normalton*) is the second person singular, addressed to the collective community, whereas the second person plural is more individualizing, more personal.[98]

A most bizarre fact, and one for which I have no explanation to offer, is that in H, though the same phenomenon of variation of number occurs, the relationship between plural and singular is exactly the reverse of that in Deuteronomy.[99] The second person plural is the normal, collective mode of address, the singular being used to address every person individually.[100] Although there are some exceptions, and although it is difficult to prove the precise import of a stylistic usage, a review of some examples will show the phenomenon to be sufficiently salient to oppose it to the Deuteronomic usage observed by Lohfink.

From the above, it is clear that three different types must be distinguished. The common denominator is that of an individual expounding the law to a collective.[101] He may use three modes of address:[102]

a. second person plural addressed to the community; in H this is the neutral mode, being used throughout;[103]

b. second person singular addressing each member of the collective individually; in H this mode is fairly frequent in Lev 18, 19 and 25 and sporadic elsewhere.[104]

c. second person singular addressed to the collective; in H this mode is found in three verses only (25:7-9), which I consider anomalous.

It must be said at the outset that it is impossible to demonstrate the opposition between a. and b. in all cases. In both of the stylistic modes,

---

[97] For earlier discussions cf. C. T. Begg, "The Significance of the *Numeruswechsel* in Deuteronomy. The "Pre-History" of the Question", *ETL* 55 (1979), 116-124

[98] Lohfink, *Hauptgebot*, 248. Cf. also M. Weinfeld, *Deuteronomy 1-11*, Anchor Bible (New York, 1991), 15f.

[99] Cf. Cortese, "Levitico 19", 213; Schwartz, *Chapters*, 119f.

[100] The incongruity between H and Deuteronomy on this point seems to be connected with the one mentioned above, namely the preference for *bᵉnē yiśrā'ēl* in H and for *yiśrā'ēl* alone in Deuteronomy.

[101] In 24:5-7 the second person singular is addressed to an individual.

[102] The three modes are well distinguished by Noth, *Gesetze*, 32, n. 37.

[103] Of course, many laws in H are couched in the third person.

[104] Cortese lists 20:19; 21:8, 17; 22:23; 23:22, see Cortese, "Levitico 19", 213, to which 20:16 must be added.

it is the collective that is addressed, and who is to say whether "thou shalt rise up before the hoary head" (19:32) is more individualizing than "ye shall not steal" (19:11)? It is striking, however, that certain notions are consistently associated with either singular or plural. This may show us a way to understand the effect grammatical number was intended to bring about in the mind of the audience. Let us first consider the words *'ereṣ* "land" and *śādeh* "field". Both of these words refer to the arable land on which the Israelites will live, but whereas the first has a global, "national" connotation, the second refers to the plot belonging to an individual. When second-person suffixes are attached to these words, *'ereṣ* receives a plural suffix,[105] whereas *śādeh* receives a singular suffix.[106] This is most striking where both terms occur in the same verse:

19:9   ובקצרכם את קציר ארצכם לא תכלה פאת שדך לקצר

And when ye reap the harvest of your land, thou shalt not wholly reap the corners of thy field.

The circumstances attending the command are those of the harvest, which concerns the whole collective, as is shown by the noun *'ereṣ*; here the second person plural is used. The command itself, however, is addressed to every Israelite with reference to his *śādeh* ; here we find the second person singular.

Following the pattern of the pair "land"—"field", we may place some other nouns in the collective or individual categories. In the collective "land"-type category, we find notions belonging to the sphere of the people as a whole: *mōšābōt* "dwelling places", *dōrōt* "generations", *'ārīm* "cities", *miqdāšīm* "sanctuaries"; they attract second person plural suffixes and verbforms.[107] In the category of "field" come words describing elements from the sphere of the individual: *kerem* "vineyard", *bǔhēmāh* "cattle", *'ebed* "slave", *rēaᶜ* and *'āmīt* "neighbour", and the members of the family; with these words, second person suffixes and verbs are in the singular.[108]

---

[105]   The occurrences of *'arṣᵉkem* : 19:9, 33; 22:24; 23:22; 25:9, 45; 26:1, 5, 6, 19, 20, 33; *'arṣᵉkā* occurs in 25:7 (see below). In Deuteronomy, *'arṣᵉkem* is found in 11:14 ; *'arṣᵉkā* : 19:2, 3, 10; 28:12; 15:7, 11; 24:14.
[106]   The occurrences of *śādᵉkā* : 19:9, 19; 23:22; 25:3, 4; also Deut 11:15; 24:19.
[107]   See 23:3, 14, 17, 31, 21; 22:3; 23:21, 43; 26:31.
[108]   See 25:3, 4; 19:19; 25:7; 25:6, 44; 19:13, 16, 18; 18:20; 19:15, 17; 25:14, 15 and 18:7-16. The occurrence of *bᵉhemtᵉkem* in 26:22 is rather an exception which confirms the rule.

Some words are used with both singular and plural suffixes. The word 'āḥ "brother" used with a singular suffix carries its literal meaning or refers to individuals close to those addressed:

19:17   לא תשנא את אחיך בלבבך

Thou shalt not hate thine brother in thine heart.

The same word in the plural, with a second person plural suffix refers collectively to the people of Israel:

25:46   ובאחיכם בני ישראל איש באחיו לא תרדה בו בפרך

But over your brethren the children of Israel, ye shall not rule one over another with rigour.[109]

Thus, these two examples confirm the individualizing and collective implications of the second person singular and plural respectively.[110]

Observance of the Sabbath and the feasts is enjoined upon the collective by the use of the second person plural,[111] as is respect for the sanctuary. On the other hand, every man individually is interdicted from sexual abberrations by the use of the second person singular.[112] Finally, the numerous references to the Exodus always employ the plural,[113] as does the final chapter of blessings and curses upon the people.[114]

The cumulative force of these arguments is, I believe, convincing.[115] This means that we may read an individualizing nuance into verses employing the singular even when they give no other indication of it. Respect for the elderly (19:32, quoted above) is indeed commanded to each individual, whereas in the prohibition on stealing (19:11, quoted above) the individualizing nuance is absent.

---

[109] It seems that the variation of number in this verse has to be explained as in 19:9 (see above): the framework is that of the whole people, but the commandment concerns every single Israelite.

[110] Note also the expression betōkᵉkem "among you" 17:12; 18:26; 20:14; 26:11, 12, 25 (contrast bᵉqirbᵉkā in Deut 6:15; 7:21; 13:2, 12, 15; 16:11; 17:2; 19:20; 23:17; 26:11; 28:43).

[111] See Lev 23; contrast Deut 16.

[112] Lev 18; 19:29.

[113] E.g. 19:36; 22:33; 25:38; 26:13; contrast Deut 8:14; 13:11.

[114] Contrast 26:12 wᵉ'attem tihyū lī lᵉ'am with Deut 14:2; 26:17f; 27:9; 29:12.

[115] This conclusion also implies that 2nd person singular and plural are not, in H, free variants which may be exploited in structuring the text, against Otto, "Heiligkeitsgesetz", 69, n. 19: "Der Numeruswechsel ist kompositorisch…"

We must now turn to a few cases of the second person singular which seem to run counter to the hypothesis defended so far. With regard to the first case, I will argue that it is only an apparent exception and that an individual interpretation is in fact demanded by the context.

20:16   ואשה אשר תקרב אל כל בהמה לרבעה אתה והרגת את האשה
ואת הבהמה מות יומתו דמיהם בם

And if a woman approach unto any beast, and lie down thereto, thou shalt kill the woman, and the beast: they shall surely be put to death; their blood shall be upon them.

At first sight, one would surely take the second person addressed in the verb "thou shalt kill" to be the community. This seems to be confirmed by the preceding verse:

20:15   ואיש אשר יתן שכבתו בבהמה מות יומת ואת הבהמה תהרגו

And if a man lie with a beast, he shall surely be put to death; and ye shall slay the beast.

Here the same verb is put in the second person plural, no doubt addressing the community. Yet, the two cases are not treated in the same way. The difference in grammatical person and some other variations seem to me to be significant. Whereas the man who has committed bestiality will receive a proper trial and be condemned to death (*mōt yūmāt*),[116] the woman does not rate such a trial.[117] Instead, she is given the same treatment as the animal, which must also in both cases be killed. The verb *hrg* is not the usual verb expressing capital punishment.[118] It is used, however, to describe the killing of criminals or apostates when, for some reason, no formal trial is held.[119] Now, in v 15 *hrg* is reserved for

---

[116] On *mōt yūmāt*, see J. Milgrom, *Studies in Levitical Terminology, I The Encroacher and the Levite. The Term* 'Aboda (Berkeley, 1970), 5f.

[117] This seems to be what is suggested by the text; whether this procedure would be applied in real life is another question, see Chapter 2.

[118] Fuhs, TWAT II, 483-494, p. 492. The cases listed by Fuhs must be treated with caution: Ex 21:14; Jud 8:21; 9:56; 2 Sam 14:7; 1 Ki 2:32 certainly do not belong in the section on *h r g* as punishment. In Deut 13:10 it may be better to follow the reading reflected by LXX, see BHS. See, however, B. M. Levinson, ""But You Shall Surely Kill Him!" The Text-Critical and Neo-Assyrian Evidence for MT Deuteronomy 13:10", in G. Braulik, *Bundesdokument und Gesetz*, HBS 4 (Freiburg, 1995), 37-63.

[119] See esp. 2 Sam 4:10-12; Num 25:5.

the animal, whereas in v 16 it refers to both the woman and the animal. I think, therefore, that we must take v 16 as prescribing that any man who catches a woman in the act of bestiality must kill her without awaiting formal trial. Only in second instance is death prescribed as a formal legal punishment (*mōt yūmātū*).

In this reading, the second person singular is entirely functional in the same way as in chapter 18.[120]

On the other hand, three verses in Lev 25 exhibit the singular in phrases which can in no way be explained as individualizing. The passage is transcribed in full in order clearly to show the extent of the problem, and to provide a hint as to a possible solution.

25:6-9
והיתה שבת הארץ לכם לאכלה לך ולעבדך ולאמתך ולשכירך
ולתושבך הגרים עמך
ולבהמתך ולחיה אשר בארצך תהיה כל תבואתה לאכל
וספרת לך שבע שבתת שנים שבע שנים שבע פעמים
והיו לך ימי שבע שבתת השנים תשע וארבעים שנה
והעברת שופר תרועה בחדש השביעי בעשור לחדש
ביום הכפרים תעבירו שופר בכל ארצכם

And the sabbath of the land shall be meat for you; for thee and for thy servant, and for thy maid, and for thy hired servant, and for thy stranger that sojourneth with thee, and for thy cattle, and for the beast that are in thy land, shall all the increase thereof be meat. And thou shalt number seven sabbaths of years unto thee, seven times seven years; and the space of the seven sabbaths of years shall be unto thee forty and nine years. Then shalt thou cause the trumpet of the jubilee to sound on the tenth day of the seventh month, in the day of atonement shall ye make the trumpet sound throughout all your land.

The passage begins in the plural, which is entirely expected since the sabbatical year is in H a national occasion. It then slips into the singular, again as expected, because the nouns refer to persons who are seen in relation to the individual ("slave" etc., see above). However, instead of returning to the plural in v 7ff, the text continues in the singular, in prescriptions which are most clearly addressed to the collective. Particularly remarkable are expressions that elsewhere in H appear in the plu-

---

[120] The man is responsible for the sexual conduct of his wife and daughters, see above.

ral, but in these verses in the singular.[121] Then, at the end of v 9, the discourse belatedly returns to the plural, which is the expected form.

To my mind, the singulars in these verses are not sufficient to undermine the theory developed above. They are not indicative of Deuteronomic influence in H, nor of the use of another source. They are a local anomaly and may perhaps be explained as scribal mistakes caused by the singulars in vv 6f.[122] However, these verses together with the numerous variations in number in the different textual witnesses, should make us cautious in the application of the theory when it seems to be contradicted by other facts.

On the whole, the style of H is quite consistent in that the second person plural is used as the normal, collective mode of address, whereas the second person singular addresses each man individually. This stylistic convention stands in stark contrast to the style of the other law codes, especially Deuteronomy.[123] Further study of the phenomenon of variation of number may lead to a better understanding of the difference between H and the other codes on this point.

Several scholars have observed in H, as in Biblical law in general, a certain tension between the individual and the collective.[124] The covenant of God is made with the people as a whole, but it places a demand on every individual belonging thereto. Conversely, although the sin of a man is imputed to him, it also brings guilt on the entire people. Yet another aspect has been pointed out by Greenberg.[125] Biblical law recognizes no central locus of power besides God; therefore, the individual's power, and with it his responsibility, assumes more importance.[126] At the same time, the key position of the individual serves to realize the collective ideal of the "kingdom of priests", of which God is the king.[127]

---

[121] The one case of *'arṣᵉkā* is opposed by 12 cases of *'arṣᵉkem* (see n. 105). Instead of *wᵉsāpartā lᵉkā* in 25:8, we find *usᵉpartem lākem* in 23:15.

[122] The Peshitta has the whole passage (starting in v 6) in the plural. In the LXX the plural begins at v 9a.

[123] The singular is used throughout in the Decalogue; it is also usual in Ex 34:10ff.

[124] See. e.g., J. Hempel, *Das Ethos des Alten Testaments*, BZAW 67 (Berlin, 1938), 32-67; K. Elliger, "Das Gesetz Leviticus 18" *ZAW* 67 (1955), 1-25, p. 21. Elliger ascribes the individual and the collective aspects in Lev 18 to two different layers.

[125] See Greenberg, "Attitude".

[126] Instead of "the individual" it would be better to speak of "the individual family", see above.

[127] It is striking that H knows no other authority than the prophet (i.e. Moses), the assembly and the family. Nowhere do we find any mention of a king, elders or tribal rulers (*nāśî'*).

The tension between the individual and collective aspects finds expression in several ways in H, one of which is the variation of number. This stylistic device allows the author to combine those elements which are specifically within the scope of the individual (or the individual family) and those which are a matter for the people as a whole, without blurring the distinction between them.

3.2. THE INDIRECTLY ADDRESSED

The Holiness Code directly addresses the people of Israel, as has been documented in section 3.1. In some cases, however, consequences are drawn for certain categories of persons who do not belong to the people of Israel. Since these persons are therefore in a sense part of the audience of H—albeit as it were potential bystanders—it is necessary to include them in the discussion. In addition, the characterization of these categories further delimits and defines the entity which is "Israel".

The resident alien

The term *gēr* occurs 21 times in H. The word does not always refer to a person distinct from the Israelites,[128] and where it does, the *gēr* is not always required to obey the law.[129] However, the nine cases (accounting for 13 occurrences) where a law is indeed binding on the *gēr* illustrate that we are justified to include this category of persons in the present section on the indirect addressees of H.

The term *gēr* is also found in priestly passages outside H,[130] in most of the other biblical law codes, in narrative texts and in some prophetical books (Jeremiah, Ezekiel, Zechariah, Malachi). Grammatically, it is a verbal noun of the form *qaṭil* (in BH *qāṭēl* with strong roots, as e.g. *kābēd*), which usually expresses a stative characteristic, derived from the root *gwr*.[131] As the meaning of the verb is "to stay somewhere as a *gēr* ", it is not helpful for determining the sense of the noun. The word

---

[128] The exceptions are 19:34; 25:23; 25:35.
[129] In 19:10, 33; 23:22 the *gēr* is recommended to the goodwill of the Israelites.
[130] Gen 23:4; Ex 12:19, 48, 49; Lev 16:29; Num 9:14; 15:14, 15, 16, 26, 29, 30; 19:10; 35:15.
[131] F. E. König, Historisch-kritisches Lehrgebäude der hebräischen Sprache, Bd II (Leipzig 1895), 82f.

finds a cognate in Arabic *jār*, which however has the slightly different meaning of "guest, protégé".[132] Other derivations and cognates are more far-fetched.[133]

The historical books sketch out a fairly homogeneous picture. The *gēr* is the sojourner, who for some reason has left his country to settle elsewhere.[134] Being in principle landless, he is more or less dependent on the local inhabitants;[135] his social status is fragile. A comparison with the words meaning "stranger, alien" (*nokrī, ben nēkār, zār*), "exile" (*gōleh*), "hireling" (*śākīr*), "task-worker(s)" (*mas*), "slave" (*'ebed*), shows that within its semantic field, the word *gēr* has a very specific meaning. It is practically a technical term: the *gēr* is a person (possibly a family or group) conceded a certain juridical status because of the fact that he has settled among a foreign tribe or people.[136]

In spite of the reasonably clear picture in the historical books, the meaning of the term where it occurs in the law codes is disputed, particularly with regard to the priestly laws. In the wake of the Graf-Kuenen-Wellhausen view of P, the thesis that the term *gēr* in the priestly writings refers to a person seeking integration in the religious community of Israel has become influential.[137] "Indeed, in P the term is already on the

---

[132] Robertson Smith defends the essential identity of the Hebrew and Arabic words, deriving them both from a primitive Semitic institution of guest-friendship, see W. Robertson Smith, *Lectures on the Religion of the Semites* (Edinburgh, 1889), 75-77.

[133] See D. Kellerman, TWAT I, 980; M. Görg, "Der »Fremde« (*ger*): ein Fremdwort im Alten Testament?", *BN* 25 (1984), 10-13; B. Greger, "Beobachtungen zum Begriff גֵּר (ger)", *BN* 63 (1992), 30-34.

[134] Examples include the patriarchs in Canaan (Gen 20:1; 21:23,34; 26:3; also 23:4 P), Moses in Midian (Ex 2:22), Israel in Egypt (Gen 15:13; 47:4; Deut 26:5), an Amalekite in Israel (2 Sam 1:13), the Beerothites in Gittaim (2 Sam 4:3). The only real exception is Josh 8:33, 35 where the *gēr* is present among the people of Israel before the conquest of the land.

[135] He might serve an indigenous inhabitant as a "hireling" (*śākīr*): so Jacob, who is said in Gen 32:5 to *gwr* with Laban, and in 29:15 discusses his *maśkoret* "hireling's wages" with him. Cf. also Deut 24:14. Whether he might receive landed property, then called *gērūt*, from an Israelite overlord, as was argued by A. Alt on the basis of 2 Sam 19:38-41 and Jer 41:17, is debated; see D. Kellerman, TWAT I, 958.

[136] Thus the connotation of the word is sociological and juridical, and not primarily ethnic. An Israelite might under circumstances become a *gēr* in Israel. Conversely, when David wants to stress the fact that Ittai is not "one of them," he uses the word *nokrī*, 2 Sam 15:19, though Ittai is probably to be considered a *gēr* (cf. 2 Sam 1:13).

[137] See A. Bertholet, *Die Stellung der Israeliten und der Juden zu den Fremden* (Freiburg i. B. & Leipzig, 1896), 152-178, in part. pp. 155, 174f; Baentsch, *Heiligkeits-Gesetz*, 137 "Er ist nicht mehr nur ein Gegenstand des Mitleids und der Duldung, sondern ein mit Rechten und Pflichten ausgestaltetes Glied des Gottesstaates. Hier ist der Punkt, wo der religiöse Gesichtspunkt die nationale Schranke zu durchbrechen beginnt"; Elliger, *Leviticus*, 227 (but see also 224); D. Kellermann, TWAT I, 987f; more cautiously, R. Martin-Achard, THAT I, 409-412; M. Smith, *Palestinian Parties and*

way to assume the later technical sense of προσήλυτος, the foreigner
who, being circumcised and observing the law generally, is in full religious communion with Israel."[138] The most recent exponent of this view
is C. Bultmann, who argues that wherever in the priestly laws the *gēr* is
juxtaposed with the Israelite (*beʾnē yiśrāʾēl, bēt yiśrāʾēl, ʾezrāḥ*), a person is referred to who is ethnically not an Israelite but who has been
integrated in the Israelite religious community.[139]

Another view has been mooted by Cazelles: the laws juxtaposing *gēr*
and *ʾezrāḥ* are editorial additions which must be understood in the light
of Ezra's mission.[140] Here, according to Cazelles, the term *gēr* does not
mean "sojourner" or "alien" as in earlier texts, nor "proselyte" as in
post-Biblical Hebrew; it carries an entirely different meaning. The *gēr*
is the Israelite living in or just returning from exile, who is viewed as a
stranger, a sojourner in Palestine. On the other hand, the *ʾezrāḥ* is the
"Samaritan", the Israelite who is native to the land.[141] The mission of
Ezra aimed at surmounting the tensions which existed between the two
communities during the time of Nehemiah by demanding that "one law
should be binding for both groups".[142] Cazelles' theory was received
favorably by Grelot.[143] It has been rejected by most others who have
studied the question.[144]

Vink also adopts the main lines of the theory, but modifies it by in-
verting the terms: the *gēr* is the Samaritan, the *ʾezrāḥ* the Jew who returns from exile.[145] The thesis has recently been revived by Van Houten

---

Politics that Shaped the Old Testament (New York & London, 1971), 178-182. The view
that the *gēr* is a proselyte was anticipated by the ancient versions and rabbinic exegesis,
see K. G. Kuhn, TWNT VI, 727-745, esp. 730-742; more recently I. Cardellini,
"Stranieri ed «emigrati-residenti» in una sintesi di teologia storico-biblica", *RivBib* 40
(1992), 129-181, pp. 154-164.

[138] S. R. Driver, *Deuteronomy*, ICC (Edinburgh, 1895), 165.

[139] C. Bultmann, *Der Fremde im antiken Juda. Eine Untersuchung zum sozialen
Typenbegriff >ger< und seinem Bedeutungswandel in der alttestamentlichen Gesetzgebung*, FRLANT 153 (Göttingen, 1992). Bultmann also recognizes two other meanings of the term in priestly texts ("resident alien", in Lev 19:9f, 33; "foreigner" in
25:47ff). All his considerations are heavily influenced by his view that H and P reflect
the realities of the post-exilic period. It is to be regretted that Bultmann has not entered
into a discussion with any of the literature cited in n. 152.

[140] H. Cazelles, "La mission d'Esdras", *VT* 4 (1954), 113-140.

[141] Cazelles, "La mission", 126ff.

[142] Cazelles places Ezra after Nehemiah, following a theory of Van Hoonacker. See
for this question Jagersma, *History*, 201-202, with literature.

[143] P. Grelot, "La dernière étape de la rédaction sacerdotale", *VT* 6 (1956), 174-189, p.
177. He also extends the theory to include Ez 47:22 and Josh 8:33.

[144] Kilian, *Untersuchung*, 171; Mathys, *Liebe*, 42f; Bultmann, *Fremde*, 204.

[145] J. G. Vink, "The Date and Origin of the Priestly Code in the Old Testament", *OTS*
15 (1969), 1-144, pp 47ff. Vink also modifies the theory in that he does not limit it to a

in the form given to it by Vink:[146] in the priestly laws requiring equal treatment of the *gēr* and the Israelite, the term *gēr* referred originally to those who had remained in the land and after the exile joined the cultic community created by those who returned to Judah.[147]

Yet another theory regarding the meaning of the term *gēr* in P has been advanced by Cohen.[148] According to this, the generic term *gēr* is univocal and denotes the nationals of Northern Israel subjected to Judean control, especially after the downfall of Samaria.[149] In fact, the hypothesis that many Israelites from the North came to stay in Juda as *gērīm* after the exile of the Northern Kingdom in 722 BC, and that it is to them that certain laws in the Pentateuch refer, had already been floated in the 19th century,[150] though it had never been applied specifically to the priestly texts.

Notwithstanding the many competing hypotheses on offer,[151] several scholars have held to the view that in P, as in the other law codes, the term *gēr* carries the same meaning as in the historical books.[152] The

---

number of late additions in P, but extends it to the totality of the priestly material in the Pentateuch. It is because of this that he has to invert the terms: taken as a whole, it is clear that P privileges the *'ezrāḥ* over the *gēr*; the first term could, therefore, scarcely refer to the "Samaritans", who seem to have been the weaker group in the religious confrontation at the time of Ezra and Nehemiah.

[146] C. van Houten, *The Alien in Israelite Law*, JSOTS 107 (Sheffield, 1991). It is nowhere clearly stated by Van Houten that she is adopting the theory of Vink.

[147] Van Houten, *Alien*, 155. In her view, this was the original meaning of the term; at a later stage it took the more general meaning of convert to the Jewish faith (proselyte).

[148] M. Cohen, "Le «Ger» biblique et son statut socio-religieux", RHR 207 (1990), 131-158. Though Cohen's theory extends to all cases of *gērīm* in Israel, his discussion is focused mainly on P.

[149] Cohen, "Ger", 131.

[150] See A. Geiger, *Urschrift und Uebersetzungen der Bibel in ihren Abhängigkeit von der innern Entwickelung des Judenthums* (Breslau, 1857), 351ff; see also De Vaux, *Institutions* I, 118; I. Cardellini, "Stranieri", 149f (Cardellini does not yet know of Cohen's article).

[151] Some modern scholars hold that in a number of texts *gēr* should be used to designate the original Canaanite inhabitant of the land, who lost his full citizenship under Israelite rule. This theory is found already in Geiger, *Urschrift*, 351. See also de Vaux, *Institutions* I, 116, Noth, "Gesetze", 77. Sulzberger ("The Status of Labor in Ancient Israel", JQR NS 13 (1922-23), 245-302, 397-459) claimed that this was the principal meaning of the word in the law-texts: the Israelites had conquered the land, but not being able to work it they retained the original inhabitants as dependent laborers, i.e. *gērīm*. For criticism of this view, see S. Japhet, *The Ideology of the Book of Chronicles and its Place in Biblical Thought* (Jerusalem, 1977), 286ff.; S. E. Loewenstamm, "Law" in B. Mazar, ed., *The World History of the Jewish People, Vol. 3. Judges* (Tel Aviv, 1971), 231-267, p. 336, n. 50.

[152] Y. Kaufmann, *The Religion of Israel. From its Beginnings to the Babylonian Exile*, translated and abridged by M. Greenberg (London, 1961), 206: "The ger of P is a free man, a foreigner who has settled in the land of Israel and has been assimilated culturally

peculiar status accorded to the *gēr* in priestly legislation derives from the priestly theology and world-view, not from changed historical conditions or from a different meaning of the term *gēr*. A discussion of all the passages in H that mention the *gēr* will show that it is this latter view that is most in accord with the texts.[153]

The Israelites as resident aliens

Two paraenetic verses in H speak of the Israelites as *gērīm*. Although these examples do not concern persons indirectly addressed by the law, they are included here because they help clarify the meaning of the word in H.

25:23 והארץ לא תמכר לצמתת כי לי הארץ כי גרים ותושבים אתם
עמדי

The land shall not be sold in perpetuity, for the land is mine; for you are strangers and sojourners with me.

The verses Lev 25:23f have a pivotal function in Lev 25. They form the transition from the laws concerning the jubilee proper (25:8-22) to the laws concerning real estate (25:25-34) connected with it. They set out the rationale for the regulations regarding redemption and restoration of landed property.[154]

The idea that Israel, or the Israelite, is a *gēr* with YHWH is also found in the Psalms (39:13; 119:19; cf. 1 Chron 29:15). In our text, however, this metaphor is interpreted very realistically: YHWH is the owner of the land, with the Israelites each of whom has occupied his own property (*ʾaḥuzzāh*) his "tenants". The notion that the land of Israel belongs to YHWH is found in various places in the OT (e.g. Ex 15:17; Isa 14:2, 25; Jer 2:7; Ez 36:5; 38:16; Hos 9:3; Ps 10:16; 85:2). Its roots

---

and hence religiously." See also M. Weinfeld, *Deuteronomy and the Deuteronomic School* (Oxford, 1972), 228ff; J. Milgrom, "Religious Conversion and the Revolt Model for the Formation of Israel", *JBL* 101 (1982), 169-76; F. Crüsemann, "Fremdenliebe und Identitätssicherung. Zum Verständnis der »Fremden«-Texte im Alten Testament", *Wort und Dienst* 19 (1987), 11-24, pp. 22f.

[153] A general consideration which supports this view is that one should not postulate a semantic development in a word unless there are clear indications of such development. Contrast Bultmann (above, n. 139), who distinguishes three meanings of the term in the priestly texts alone.

[154] See Wright, *God's People*, 55-58.

are very old.[155] However, what was originally a cultic element receives in these verses a practical, social application: the land may not be sold in perpetuity.[156]

Although these two verses, which are quite typical of the general ideology of H, do not furnish any precise indication concerning their date, it is clear that they address a period when the Israelites actually own the land on which they are settled.[157] They sound a critical note on land ownership and the buying and selling of real estate, which would not make sense to people who are not landowners. The meaning of the term *gēr* poses no problem. What is intended is the meaning usual in the historical books. The Israelites are viewed as people coming from elsewhere and finding refuge in the land of YHWH, who in turn accords to them the right to settle on and live off his land.[158]

The second example reminds the Israelites that they themselves have been *gērīm* in Egypt:

19:34   (כאזרח מכם יהיה לכם הגר הגר אתכם ואהבת לו כמוך)
כי גרים הייתם בארץ מצרים

(The stranger who sojourns with you shall be to you as the native among you, and you shall love him as yourself;) for you were strangers in the land of Egypt.

The author of H seems to have taken the entire clause from the Israelite legal tradition, for it is also found in exactly the same form in the earlier Book of the Covenant, Ex 22:20; 23:9, and in Deut 10:19 in the context of the commandment to love the *gēr*.[159] Moreover, if it were not for the

---

[155] Wright, *God's People*, 10-11, 58-65 (with literature).

[156] The idea that the land of one's inheritance may not be sold is not to be found in BC or Deuteronomy. It is subjacent in the complaint of the daughters of Zelophehad (Num 27:1-11; 36) and the story of Naboth (1 Ki 21); cf. also the book of Ruth and Jer 32:1-15.

[157] This does not directly tell us anything about the date of these verses. Wright, *God's People*, 58f (citing earlier literature), stresses that laws and institutions of great antiquity may occur in a late literary composition.

[158] We may compare Gen 23:4 where Abraham is termed a *gēr* because he has no land of his own.

[159] The notion that the Israelites were *gērīm* in Egypt is not altogether unproblematic. It is found only in Gen 15:13, 47:4; Deut 26:5; in the law-texts listed above and in Deut 23:8. Elsewhere it is made clear that for most of their stay in Egypt, the Israelites were not *gērīm* but slaves, *ʿabādīm*. Heaton has defended the view that the OT conflates two different traditions about Israel's stay in Egypt, one of which has them as *gērīm* (cf. the Joseph story) and the other as slaves, see E. W. Heaton, "Sojourners in Egypt", *Expository Times* 58 (1946), 80-82. Some other views are collected by J. Wijngaards, *Deuteronomium*, BOT, 256 (comment on Deut 23:8).

weight of this tradition, the author might have employed his own conception of Israel's being *gērīm* with YHWH (25:23 v.s.), particularly since the condition of Israel in Egypt is described elsewhere in H as slavery, not sojourning (Lev 26:13; cf. 25:42, 55).[160]

There is no reason to suspect that the term *ger* carries any different meaning here from that in the Book of the Covenant. It refers to the status of the Israelites in Egypt, which was apparently conceived not as that of slaves, but of sojourners to whom the right to live in a foreign land was granted.

The resident alien as a disadvantaged member of society

Three passages in H speak of the *gēr* as one who is in need of assistance. This recalls the position of the *gēr* in the Book of the Covenant and, particularly, Deuteronomy.

19:9f   ובקצרכם את קציר ארצכם לא תכלה פאת שׂדך לקצר ולקט
            קצירך לא תלקט וכרמך לא תעולל ופרט כרמך לא תלקט
            לעני ולגר תעזב אתם

When you reap the harvest of your land, you shall not reap your field to its very border, neither shall you gather the gleanings after your harvest. And you shall not strip your vineyard bare, neither shall you gather the fallen grapes of your vineyard; you shall leave them for the poor and for the sojourner.

With minor variations the same prescriptions are given in 23:22.[161] They find a close parallel in Deut 24:19-22 (compare also Ruth 2). However, the many differences in formulation in the treatment of the exact same subject matter make it most unlikely that there is a direct relationship between H and Deuteronomy in this case.[162] The rationale of these prescriptions is given by the definition of the *gēr* which

---

[160] These facts militate against Cazelles' suggestion that the clause is original in Lev 19:34 whence it was taken over by priestly redactors of the Book of the Covenant, see H. Cazelles, "Histoire et Institutions dans la Place et la Composition d'Ex 20,22-23,19", in R. Liwak, S. Wagner, Hsg., *Prophetie und geschichtliche Wirklichkeit im Alten Israel*, Fs S. Herrmann (Stuttgart, 1991), 52-64, pp. 58f.

[161] For the insertion in 23:22, see Wenham, *Leviticus*, 304f.

[162] Cholewinski (*Heiligkeitsgesetz*, 270f) sees in these differences an argument for the dependence of H on Deuteronomy: H has consciously rewritten the law of Deuteronomy in order to cover certain eventualities which Deuteronomy had overlooked.

emerges from the historical books. Being landless—a displaced person—he is generally dependent for his well-being on the goodwill of the inhabitants of the land. Lev 19:9f and parallels aim to induce practical application of this goodwill.

As it is formulated, the passage addresses the Israelites in their capacity as land-owners. The meaning of the term *gēr* cannot be open to doubt. It refers to the foreigner who has settled in Israel and who has been granted the right to stay in the land.

19:33f   וכי יגור אתך גר בארצכם לא תונו אתו כאזרח מכם יהיה
            לכם הגר אתכם ואהבת לו כמוך

When a stranger sojourns with you in your land, you shall not do him wrong. The stranger who sojourns with you shall be to you as the native among you, and you shall love him as yourself.

The substance of this passage, namely the injunction not to oppress the *gēr*, is found in the Book of the Covenant (Ex 22:20 *wᵉgēr lōʾ tōneh wᵉlōʾ tilḥāṣennū*; 23:9 *wᵉgēr lōʾ tilḥāṣ*),[163] with the same motive clause.[164] The present passage has sometimes been interpreted as establishing equal legal status for the *gēr* and the *ʾezrāḥ*.[165] It is to be noted, however, that the law is not addressed to the *gēr*, but only to the Israelite. Furthermore, the phrase *hyh l-* x *k-* y means: "x treated him as y",[166] not "for x he became equal to y." It seems, therefore, that the meaning of the present injunctions is equivalent to that of the parallel texts in the Book of the Covenant (and Deuteronomy), even though the formulation is different. The *gēr* remains a *gēr*, but rather than taking advantage of his weak position, the Israelites should treat him as a native. Indeed: "You should love him as yourself" (in the same way as you should love your fellow-Israelites, 19:18).

In view of these considerations, it is fairly certain that *gēr* must be taken here in its usual sense of sojourner. This is also indicated by the

---

[163] For the difference between the verbs *lḥṣ* and *ynh* (hiphil), see N. Lohfink, "Gibt es eine deuteronomistische Bearbeitung im Bundesbuch?", in C. Brekelmans and J. Lust, eds., *Pentateuchal and Deuteronomistic Studies*, BEThL 94 (Leuven, 1990), 91-113, pp. 105-107.

[164] There is no exact parallel in Deuteronomy (but cf. Deut 24:17 and 10:19).

[165] Jagersma, *Leviticus 19*, 115, 129. Cazelles, "La mission".

[166] See, e.g., Jud 17:11 *wayᵉhī lō kᵉʾaḥad mibbānāw* "and he treated him as one of his sons" and cf. Jud 17:12 *wayᵉhī lō lᵉkōhēn* "and he became his priest" (see also 2 Sam 12:3 *watᵉhī lō kᵉbat* and contrast Ex 2:10 *wayᵉhī lāh lᵉbēn*).

accompanying motive clause, which has been discussed above. It is not
likely that the same term would carry different meanings in the law-text
and in the motive clause.[167]

The resident alien as a prosperous member of society

The *gēr* is typically a person in need, but not necessarily so.[168] The inversion of the relationship between native and *gēr*, whereby the latter
unexpectedly achieves higher social status than the former, is mentioned
in the Deuteronomic chapter of curses (Deut 28:43f; no parallel in Lev
26). In H, some practical implications are spelled out:[169]

25:47f   וכי תשיג יד גר ותושב עמך ומך אחיך עמו ונמכר לגר תושב
                עמך או לעקר משפחת גר אחרי נמכר גאלה תהיה לו אחד מאחיו
                יגאלנו

If a stranger or sojourner with you becomes rich, and your brother
besides him becomes poor and sells himself to the stranger or
sojourner with you, or to a member of the stranger's family, then after
he is sold he may be redeemed; one of his brothers may redeem him.

This is the concluding law of redemption in the chapter on the jubilee.
After considering the possibility of an Israelite selling himself to a com-
patriot, the bitter eventuality of an Israelite selling himself to a non-
Israelite is left until last.[170]

The stringent rules by which H regulates this kind of transaction ad-

---

[167] Against Bultmann, who distinguishes three stages and two meanings of the term
gēr within the two verses 19:33f, see Bultmann, *Fremde*, 177f. His principal criterion is
the variation of number, for which I refer to the end of section 3.1. above.

[168] In Gen 23, Abraham—the *gēr*—is depicted acquiring a plot of land.

[169] Because in this passage the *gēr* is depicted as a man of means, Bultmann takes the
word to have another meaning than in 19:9f: in 25:47ff the word refers to a member of
one of the neighbouring peoples (referred to as "the nations that are round about you" in
25:44), see Bultmann, *Fremde*, 179-190, in particular p. 187. However, the text explicitly indicates that in order to attain his economically strong position, the *gēr* had to rise
from the ranks and that the whole situation is exceptional (v 47a).

[170] The expressions *gēr wᵉtōšāb*, *gēr tōšāb* and *ʿēqer mišpaḥat haggēr* are for all
practical purposes synonymous: what is important in this context is that the person in
question is not an ethnic Israelite. For the term *tōšāb* see below.

dress an historical situation in which Israel is politically independent.[171] The meaning of the term *gēr* is the same as in the examples above: he is a sojourner with a well-defined juridical status, which is clearly differentiated from that of the native Israelite.[172]

Sacral laws which must be observed by the gēr

A series of prescriptions occurring in H contain the provision that the law is binding on the *gēr* as well as on the native. One passage explicitly states "You will have one law for the *gēr* and the native" (24:22). These texts have often been regarded as typifying a tendency toward equalizing the legal status of the *gēr* and the Israelite.[173] Since these laws concern matters which may be considered sacral, scholars have concluded that they imply incorporation of the *gēr* in the religious system of Israel. These texts are then taken as evidence for the meaning "proselyte".[174]

Against this view, however, it should be noted that the existence of laws stipulating compliance by native and *gēr* alike does not entail general legal equivalence of the two. In fact, equivalence is contradicted by the form of these commands themselves. Where they are formulated in the second person, they address the Israelites alone and refer to the *gēr* in the third person, showing that he does not have full legal status. It must also be stated that a certain degree of incorporation does not mean general equivalence. The inclusion of the *gēr* in the Decalogue, Book of the Covenant and Deuteronomy also implies incorporation of the *gēr* into the socio-religious system of Israel, but that does not make him a "proselyte", let alone an Israelite.

Furthermore, in several places in H, the *gēr* is in fact treated differently from the Israelite: in 23:42 the prescription on dwelling in booths

---

[171] Such a reality existed only before the exile. Bultmann attempts to derive the whole practice prescribed in Lev 25 from the initiative of Nehemiah related in Neh 5:1-13. In the Book of Nehemiah, however, it is explicitly stated that the Jews had no authority over the nations (Neh 5:8). The historical reality is that described by Weinberg and incorporated into his theory of a "citizen-temple community", see J. P. Weinberg, *The Citizen-Temple Community*, transl. by D. L. Smith-Christopher, JSOTS 151 (Sheffield, 1992).

[172] Note that the law refers to the *gēr* in the third person; the addressees are the Israelites.

[173] See, e.g., Kilian, *Untersuchung*, 17. See also the exegesis of 19:33f above.

[174] Mathys, *Liebe*, 40-45, has a much more nuanced view of the status of the *gēr* in H than most scholars. However, he continues to maintain that the word means "proselyte" in such texts as 17:8, 22:18, 19:34.

during the feast is limited to the native Israelite;[175] according to 25:44ff,
Israelite slaves must go free at the jubilee, but the sons of sojourners
(hattōšābīm haggārīm) may be enslaved for life.[176] The laws of Lev 17
also differentiate between Israelite and gēr, as will be shown below.
These facts make it difficult to claim that H displays a tendency toward
equalizing the legal status of native and gēr.[177]

An alternative theory to explain the extension of certain prescriptions
to embrace the gēr has been advanced by Weinfeld and elaborated by
Milgrom.[178] The suggestion is that the gēr is not obliged to comply with
all the positive requirements of Israel's religious law (such as celebrat-
ing the different feasts, cf. 23:42), but only with the apodictic prohibitions. Transgression of apodictic prohibitions, even at the hand of non-
Israelite residents, profanes the land and the people among whom
YHWH resides, and this must be avoided.[179] Thus a gēr is not required
to celebrate Pesach, but if he wishes to celebrate it he must first be circumcised (Ex 12:48).[180] He is not obliged to fast on the tenth day of the
seventh month, but must on that day abstain from work (Lev 16:29).

This view implies that the gēr in all these texts is nothing other than
as has been seen in the examples discussed hitherto: a resident alien to
whom certain rights have been conceded, and who in turn must observe
certain duties. He may seek integration into the Israelite religion but
does not automatically do so. This view will now be tested in the case of
the texts from H.

---

[175] See above, pp. 35-36. This probably does not mean that the gēr is excluded from
this celebration (see Deut 16:14), only that he is not obliged to participate in it.
[176] Cf. also the fact that in 25:39-43 the possibility of redemption is not mentioned,
whereas in 25:47-54 it is the central notion.
[177] Pace Knohl, Sanctuary, 182; Crüsemann, Tora, 347, 359.
[178] Weinfeld, Deuteronomy, 230f. Milgrom, "Religious Conversion". This hypothesis
covers all of P (including H). See also M. Smith, Parties, 179 (on the gēr in H).
[179] Cf. the comment of Ibn Ezra on Lev 18:26; Weinfeld, Deuteronomy, 228f. The
same idea is expressed by Mathys, Liebe, 44, without reference to his predecessors. It
must be added that the crucial notion is not that of the land per se, but the sanctuary and
the presence of YHWH. Therefore, even in the desert period, the gēr must observe the
law (Lev 17; 24). See J. Milgrom, "Israel's Sanctuary: The Priestly «Picture of Dorian
Gray»", RB 83 (1976), 390-399.
[180] M. Cohen, "Ger", 153-56, takes Ex 12:48 and Num 9:14 to mean that the gēr must
be circumcised and that his participation at Pesach is compulsory. However, his arguments for this exegesis are very weak; the main reason why he defends it seems to be
that it accords with his theory regarding the gēr in the OT (see above). For a correct
understanding of Ex 12:48, see Japhet, Ideology, 294: "...the right to eat the Pesach
offering and to be circumcised in view of it is a result of the social status and not vice
versa. Therefore also, this status does not change because of circumcision."

The opening chapter of H gives us a good starting point. In five paragraphs (vv 3-7, 8-9, 10-12, 13-14, 15-16), Lev 17 deals comprehensively with the slaughtering of animals for meat, which in the OT usually has a sacrificial aspect,[181] and with the closely related matter of the disposal of blood.

17:3   ...איש איש מבית ישראל אשר ישחט

If any man of the house of Israel slaughters...[182]

17:8   ...איש איש מבית ישראל ומן הגר אשר יגור בתוכם אשר יעלה

Any man of the house of Israel, or of the strangers that sojourn among them, who offers...

17:10   ...איש איש מבית ישראל ומן הגר הגר בתוכם אשר יאכל כל-דם

If any man of the house of Israel, or of the strangers that sojourn among them, eats any blood...[183]

17:13   איש איש מבני ישראל ומן הגר הגר בתוכם אשר יצוד ציד חיה

Any man of the people of Israel, or of the strangers that sojourn among them, who takes in hunting any beast...

17:15   ...וכל נפש אשר תאכל נבלה וטרפה באזרח ובגר

And every person that eats what dies of itself or what is torn by beasts, whether he is a native or a sojourner...

What is striking with regard to our subject is that whereas in the latter four paragraphs the *gēr* is explicitly mentioned (v 8, v10, v 13, v 15), he is absent from the first (v 3). This has often been explained as an accidental omission. I will argue, however, that the MT makes perfect sense if one takes it seriously. The MT rules that, to the Israelites, all slaughter of domestic animals is forbidden except as *zebaḥ šelāmīm* at the tent of meeting (17:3, 4). However, this rule does not apply to the resident al-

---

[181] The authorization of profane slaughter in Deut 12:13-28 is clearly a novelty which needs much explanation and hedging.

[182] RSV: "If any man of the house of Israel kills..."

[183] The *gēr* is also mentioned in the reiteration of the command in 17:12.

iens, which implies that to them profane slaughter is permitted (though it is not encouraged).[184] Such a reading of the first paragraph is further supported by the formulation of the motive clause in v 5: "This is to the end that *the people of Israel* may bring their sacrifices..."[185]

Sacrifices, on the other hand, may only be brought to YHWH and only at the tent of meeting, be it by Israelites or by resident aliens (17:8).[186] A sacrifice to a foreign deity, even at the hand of a foreigner, is an abomination to YHWH. The other prescriptions too, the prohibition to eat blood and the law concerning $n^e b\bar{e}l\bar{a}h$ and $t^e r\bar{e}p\bar{a}h$, belong to the apodictic rules, to which the *gēr* as well as the Israelite must submit.

If the exegesis proposed here is accepted, it is impossible for the term *gēr* to designate "proselyte". Were this the case, he would certainly have been included in the first paragraph concerning the slaughtering of animals fit for sacrifice.[187] On the other hand, on viewing the *gēr* as a resident alien, the meaning of the present passage falls into place. The *gēr* is in an exceptional situation: not an Israelite, yet entitled to live as a free man among the people. Taking account of this, the sacral law does not oblige him to behave like an Israelite: he is not required to bring sacrifices to YHWH. Yet he must observe certain prohibitions, such as those prohibiting sacrifices to other gods or the eating of blood.[188] A transgression against those prohibitions would bring guilt on the whole people; it must not be tolerated.[189]

---

[184] See Baentsch, *Heiligkeits-Gesetz*, 137; Wenham, *Leviticus*, 244; Schwartz, *Chapters*, 205f, n.17; J. Milgrom, "Ethics and Ritual: The Foundations of Biblical Dietary Laws", in E. B. Firmage et al., eds., *Religion and Law. Biblical-Judaic and Islamic Perspectives* (Winona Lake, 1990), 159-191, p. 169; Eerdmans, *Studien IV*, 87, takes note of this possibility but rejects it. Bultmann explains the omission of the *gēr* in 17:3 in the same way as for 23:42 (see above, n. 41), see Bultmann, *Fremde*, 194.

[185] It is possible that 17:5-7 is a later addition; note that a different verb meaning "to slaughter" is used. However, even a later addition may bring out the correct meaning of a text.

[186] This understanding solves the problem of the relationship between vv 3-7 and vv 8f. If both were addressed to exactly the same group of people they would be tautological: if slaughter is forbidden, then certainly sacrifice, which involves slaughter, is too.

[187] The LXX version of v 3 does include the *gēr*. This may be more than a simple harmonization with vv 8. 10; 13: if in the understanding of the LXX the *gēr* is a proselyte, it is logical that he should be included in the first paragraph as well.

[188] The impurity resulting from eating $n^e b\bar{e}l\bar{a}h$ or $t^e r\bar{e}p\bar{a}h$ is included for sake of completeness. The subject of the whole chapter is the attitude to be taken towards slaughter and the eating of meat; but what if the animal is already dead? This question is answered in vv 15f. If the main subject were sacrifice, then the question of animals with a blemish ought to have been addressed (cp. Deut 15:21; Lev 22:20-25).

[189] Note that Zimmerli, from a comparison of Lev 17 with Ez 14, has concluded that the legal form represented by Lev 17—with its inclusion of the *gēr*—is pre-exilic, see W. Zimmerli, *Ezekiel*, BKAT (1969), 303.

Although the use of the word *gēr* in Lev 17 accords with the theory of Weinfeld, the principles of collective guilt and of the contaminating force of crimes against the apodictic prohibitions are not made explicit. Both of these notions are, however, found in Lev 20:2f.

20:2f   איש איש מבני ישראל ומן הגר הגר בישראל אשר יתן מזרעו
למלך מות יומת עם הארץ ירגמהו באבן ואני אתן את פני באיש ההוא
והכרתי אתו מקרב עמו כי מזרעו נתן למלך למען טמא את מקדשי...

Any man of the people of Israel, or of the strangers that sojourn in Israel, who gives any of his children to Molech shall be put to death; the people of the land shall stone him with stones. I myself will set my face against that man, and will cut him off from among his people, because he has given one of his children to Molech, defiling my sanctuary...

For the notion of collective guilt, I refer the reader to the discussion on *'am hā'āreṣ* above in 3.1. (pp. 45). This notion is brought into even clearer focus by the final clause of the quotation: *lᵉma'an ṭammē' 'et miqdāšī*—Molech-worship, be it at the hand of Israelites or of resident aliens, pollutes the sanctuary.[190] The problem with sins against YHWH is not first and foremost that they contaminate others in some way. The matter is much more serious: those sins defile the earthly dwelling of God, and thus raise the possibility that God will leave his earthly dwelling and, therefore, his people.

18:26   ושמרתם אתם את חקתי ואת משפטי ולא תעשו מכל התועבת
האלה האזרח והגר הגר בתוככם

But you shall keep my statutes and my ordinances and do none of these abominations, either the native or the stranger who sojourns among you.

The paraenetic framework of the laws on sexual relations in 18:6-23 stresses that it was the practice of the former inhabitants of Canaan to do "these things", and that it is because of this that they were—or rather,

---

[190] For Molech-worship, see n. 85. Bultmann, following Eissfeldt and Müller, connects the practice with the Punic *molk*-sacrifice, and uses it to date Lev 20:2-5 in the 5th century. He does not attempt to explain the expression "playing the harlot after Molech" in 20:5, which cannot easily be explained on the supposition that *molek* is a type of sacrifice.

will be—cast out of the land (18:3, 24f, 28).[191] By transgressing the prescriptions contained in the chapter, the Israelites would defile the land, just as the former inhabitants defiled it before them.[192] At this point, the * gēr* is included in the discussion: he too should observe these laws. Thus the context indicates that it was relevant to mention the *gēr* precisely because he inhabits the land. Although the meaning "proselyte" would not, on first sight, be impossible, close attention to the context actually leads to the conclusion that *gēr* carries here the same meaning as in the examples discussed above. As a sojourner among the Israelites he must submit to certain prescriptions for fear of desecrating the land.

22:18   ...איש איש מבית ישראל ומן הגר בישראל אשר יקריב קרבנו

When any one of the house of Israel, or of the sojourners in Israel presents his offering...

Here, as in 17:8, the *gēr* is seen to bring sacrifices, which could lead one to think of a proselyte. However, the priestly laws nowhere limit the bringing of sacrifices exclusively to the Israelites.[193] Note also that the present law does not require that the *gēr* offer sacrifices to YHWH, but merely regulates for that eventuality. The picture which emerges is of an alien residing among the Israelites in their land to whom the possibility of sacrificing at the Israelite shrine is open. Should he wish to bring sacrifice, however, then his offering must meet all the usual requirements.

24:16   ונקב שם יהוה מות יומת רגום ירגמו-בו בל-העדה כגר כאזרח
                   בנקבו שם יומת

He who blasphemes the name of the LORD shall be put to death, all the assembly shall stone him; the sojourner as well as the native, when he blasphemes the Name, shall be put to death.

---

[191] Verses 25 and 28 regard the casting-out of the Canaanites from their land as already completed, see Chapter 1, n. 28.
[192] The land and the temple are analogous notions both expressing the idea of YHWH's earthly dwelling, see R. E. Clements, *God and Temple* (Oxford, 1965), 52-54.
[193] Cf. the sacrifice brought by the foreigner in 22:25 (see below, p. 76), and Num 15:14 where both *gērīm* and "whoever else living among you" are permitted to bring sacrifices.

The verb *nqb* in the sense of "to curse", as well as the notion of cursing the name of YHWH, are limited to the present verse.[194] It seems that the point of Lev 24:10ff is to determine which attitude should be taken toward aliens who curse the name of Israel's God.[195] In the narrative part of the passage, the perpetrator of the deed is said to be the son of a foreigner—though his mother is an Israelite[196]—who lives among the Israelites: in other words, a *gēr*. The verdict is unambiguous: he must be stoned. However, the legal casuistics stated in v 15-16 are carefully nuanced: if someone—presumably a non-Israelite—curses his (own) god(s), he will merely "bear his sin",[197] but if anybody, resident alien or Israelite, curses the name of YHWH, he will be put to death.[198]

If this is a correct reading of the passage, then it is clear that the term *gēr* cannot possibly mean anything akin to "proselyte". Rather, he is seen as a resident alien, and provision is made for the possibility that he continues to revere his own god(s). Whereas the inclusion of the *gēr* in 24:16 is paralleled in 20:2, the implications of 24:15 are reminiscent of 17:3f: the privilege of the *gēr* to practice profane slaughter.

24:22   משפט אחד יהיה לכם כגר כאזרח יהיה

You shall have one law for the sojourner and for the native.

This general statement serves as a conclusion to the legislative part of the passage, after which the narrative closes (v 23). It is clear that the term *gēr* is used here in the same sense as in the preceding prescriptions.

The requirement that there shall be one law for native and *gēr* alike is found in four other places in P. In Ex 12:49 and Num 9:14, it comes at the conclusion of prescriptions concerning Passover; in Num 15:15f, it concerns the bringing of sacrifice; and in Num 15:29, the atonement for inadvertent sins.

---

[194] In light of the problems this passage poses, Gabel's and Wheeler's conclusions as to its late date seem to be precipitate, see J. B. Gabel and C. B. Wheeler, "The Redactor's Hand in the Blasphemy Pericope of Leviticus XXIV", *VT* 50 (1980), 227-229.

[195] See the discussion in M. Fishbane, *Biblical Interpretation in Ancient Israel* (Oxford, 1985), 100-102.

[196] Perhaps his mixed descent is stated expressly in order that he might serve as an example for both *gērīm* and Israelites.

[197] I.e., presumably, his god will punish him himself (cf. Jud 6:31).

[198] For this exegesis of the passage, see Dillmann, *Exodus und Leviticus*; 657; Fishbane, *Interpretation*, 101.

Ex 12:49 תורה אחת יהיה לאזרח ולגר הגר בתוככם

There shall be one law for the native and for the stranger who sojourns amongst you.

Num 9:14 חקה אחת יהיה לכם ולגר ולאזרח הארץ

You shall have one statute, both for the sojourner and for the native.

Num 15:15,16 הקהל חקה אחת לכם ולגר הגר
חקת עולם לדרתיכם ככם כגר יהיה לפני יהוה
תורה אחת ומשפט אחד יהיה לכם ולגר הגר אתכם

For the assembly, there shall be one statute for you and for the
stranger who sojourns with you, a perpetual statute throughout your
generations; as you are, so shall the sojourner be before the LORD.
One law and one ordinance shall be for you and for the stranger who
sojourns with you.

Num 15:29 האזרח בבני ישראל ולגר הגר בתוכם תורה אחת יהיה
לכם לעשה בשגגה

You shall have one law for him who does anything unwittingly, for
him who is native among the people of Israel, and for the stranger
who sojourns among them.

It seems that in all these passages, the requirement is limited to the cultic
prescriptions concerned. The statement has more general force only in
Lev 24:22, where the law on cursing the name of YHWH is followed by
three other prescriptions (24:17-21).[199] Yet, even Lev 24:22 is unlikely
to constitute a requirement for complete legal equivalence of gēr and
Israelite. Rather, it seems to extend the gēr's subjection to Israel's (civil
and criminal) law to certain sacral matters.[200]

---

[199] Note that the other prescriptions represent three different types of law: apodictic,
casuistic, talion. If we could be sure that the Israelites distinguished between these categories in the same way we do, we might suppose that 24:17-21 is a sort of summary of
the Book of the Covenant, indicating that the gēr is beholden to follow the whole body
of Israelite law.

[200] Deut 1:16 states that the Israelite judges must judge between a man and his brother
and between a man and his gēr : This also implies that the existing law was valid for the
gēr.

Problematic case

In one final example, the context is not sufficiently clear to allow any firm conclusions to be drawn:

25:35   וכי ימוך אחיך ומטה ידו עמך והחזקת בו גר ותושב וחי עמך

And if your brother becomes poor, and cannot maintain himself with you, you shall maintain him;[201] as a stranger and a sojourner he shall live with you.

The fact that the syntactical function of the words *gēr w^etōšāb* is not clear has led many commentators to regard these words as a gloss.[202] If we want to take the text as it stands,[203] we must analyse these words as a circumstantial phrase referring to the suffix in *bō* : "you shall support him as a *gēr* …".[204] Even so, it is not certain whether the verse states that the impoverished brother is to be treated as one should treat a *gēr*,[205] or whether under these circumstances he really becomes a *gēr*.[206] In view of the fact that *gēr* is a juridical term defining social status—it does not stress ethnic difference but rather the social position of one who has left his own social matrix—I opt for the second alternative.[207] The Israelite who sells his own heritage and leaves it in order to settle elsewhere in the land becomes a *gēr* in relation to his "brother".[208]

---

[201] Ehrlich and Speiser take the expression *w^eheh^oezaqtā bō* in the sense "you will seize him"—as a stand-in for his debt, see Ehrlich, *Randglossen II*, 94f; E. A. Speiser, "Leviticus and the Critics", in J. J. Finkelstein , M. Greenberg, eds., *Oriental and Biblical Studies. Collected Writings of E. A. Speiser*, (Philadelphia, 1967), 123-142, p. 134. In light of the progression of cases in 25:35-54, I would translate it rather: "you shall give him hospitality" (cf. 2 Ki 4:8; Jud 19:4).

[202] Baentsch, Noth, Elliger. The problem with this view is that the words do not really clarify anything, which is, after all, the *raison d'être* of a gloss.

[203] Disregarding, however, the Masoretic accents which mark a separation between *bō* and *gēr* . The Masoretic division is reflected in the interpretation of the verse found in Rashi's commentary: "even if he is a *gēr* or a *tōšāb* ". Cf. Geiger, *Urschrift*, 357. This interpretation does not fit the context: throughout the laws contained in Lev 25, the focus is on the empoverished Israelite (the "brother").

[204] König, *Syntax*, §§ 412h-i.

[205] This interpretation is found in the Septuagint and the Vulgate, see also Wenham, *Leviticus*, 321. Wenham gives a psychological interpretation: rather than turning him away in shame, you must treat him as you would treat a resident stranger.

[206] Cf. the comment in König, *Syntax*, 601: "nimm dich seiner an als eines etc. oder indem er wird ein etc."

[207] In spite of Wenham's remark (n. 205 above), I think it unlikely that H would hold the *gēr* up as a model for what should be done to an Israelite, albeit an impoverished one.

[208] This could apply to Northern Israelites settling in Judah after 721 (see the theory of M. Cohen, above). It is, however, neither an obvious nor a necessary interpretation of these verses.

Against Wellhausen, who considers this a clear instance of *gēr* meaning "proselyte",[209] none of the possible interpretations requires such a meaning. If the word is a gloss, we do not know what its author meant by it. If it is part of the original text, the most obvious meaning is that which the word has been shown to have in all other texts in H.

Conclusions

Our case-studies have shown both who the *gēr* is and why he is included in H. The *gēr* envisaged by the author of H, though ethnically not an Israelite (except in 25:35), resides among the people of Israel, in the Promised Land.

As a resident alien, he is a free agent and nobody's charge. The law therefore seeks to protect him from oppression and recommends him to the goodwill of the Israelites. His freedom is real: the *gēr* may retain his foreign culture and religion with its practices,[210] though he would be welcome to participate in the Israelite religion with its practices.[211] In any case, however, he should observe the apodictic prohibitions for fear of defiling the land and the sanctuary, the earthly dwelling of YHWH among the people.[212]

Extensive comparison of the treatment of the *gēr* in H with that in the other law codes is not within the scope of this study.[213] A clear difference is that in H the *gēr* is taken far more seriously than in the other codes. Many of its rules mention the *gēr*, and he is never referred to as an afterthought. In some longer passages such as Lev 17 and 24:10-23, the whole legal casuistry revolves around his borderline status. We observe a conscious effort to come to grips with this "borderline category": how, and to what extent is this resident alien, who is at the same

---

[209] Wellhausen, *Composition*, 154; Wellhausen's reading of the verse was probably based on the (incorrect) traditional Jewish interpretation discussed in n. 203.

[210] See the exegesis of 24:15, 17:3, 23:42. Cf. Wenham, *Leviticus*, 244.

[211] See the exegesis of 17:8; 22:18. Cf. also Ex 12:48, Num 9:15, which may belong to the same school as H (Knohl's "Holiness School", see Chapter 1).

[212] See 17:8-13; 18:26; 20:2. Contrast Deut 14:21, where it appears that according to Deuteronomy, the resident alien is not subordinate to the purity laws.

[213] Weinfeld has sought to reduce the difference in treatment of the *gēr* in P and in Deuteronomy to the divergence between the dominant idea of holiness of the land in P and holiness of the people in Deuteronomy, see Weinfeld, *Deuteronomy*, 228f. It is to be noted, however, that a) the land is not seen as holy *per se* in H (nor in P), the decisive factor being the presence of YHWH in his earthly dwelling; b) in H as in Deuteronomy the people of Israel has a special status different from that of non-Israelites who dwell in the land (see in particular the exegesis of 17:3).

time a guest and a stranger, to be integrated into the cultural/religious system of Israel? He is respected in his own individuality as a person with a different history and socio-cultural background.[214] He is not to be excluded from the day-to-day privileges of Israelite life: economic solidarity, the entitlement to bring sacrifices, justice. Equity demands that the same law should be valid for *gēr* and Israelite alike. But at the same time it is necessary to protect the Israelite from potential oppression at the hand of the *gēr*, who might not feel obliged to behave in the "Israelite" way toward an impoverished Israelite. In 25:45-55 we may detect an element of national pride, which goes so far as to allow a certain inequality between Israelites and resident aliens in that only the latter may be acquired as slaves "forever".

The sojourner

The word *tōšāb* occurs eight times in H and three more times in other priestly texts;[215] it is very rare elsewhere.[216] The form of the noun, with a *t*-prefix and designating a person, is exceptional;[217] it is related to the verb *yšb* "to dwell". The meaning of the term cannot be very different from that of *gēr*, as is shown by the frequent collocation of the two terms, either joined by the copula (Gen 23:4; Lev 25:35, 47; Num 35:15; compare Lev 25:23; Ps 39:13; 1 Chr 19:15), or in apposition (Lev 25:47).[218] Note also the fact that the subject of the verb *gwr* is the *tōšāb* in 25:6, 45. Yet it seems that *gēr* and *tōšāb* are not exact synonyms. In one text outside H, they are clearly distinguished. Ex 12:43-49, gives some indications as to who may and may not participate in the Pesach meal. Although as a general rule, "no foreigner (*ben nēkār*) shall eat of it" (v 43), slaves must be circumcised and do so (v 44). "No sojourner (*tōšāb*) or hired servant (*śākīr*) may eat of it" (v 45). If a *gēr* wishes to keep the passover, he must first be circumcised with all his males.[219]

---

[214] The motive clause "for you were strangers in the land of Egypt" invites the Israelites to put themselves in the shoes of the *gēr*.

[215] Gen 23:4; Ex 12:45; Num 35:15.

[216] Ps 39:13; 1 Chr 29:15; for 1 Ki 17:1 see BHS.

[217] Cf. *tōlāl* Ps 137:3; *talmīd*.

[218] The constant association of *gēr* and *tōšāb* casts doubt on the theory that when the word *gēr* took on the meaning "proselyte", a new word was introduced meaning "resident alien", as held by Bertholet, *Stellung*, 159; Smith, *Parties*, 182.

[219] The structure of the passage, proceeding from a general rule to exceptions to the rule and then to exceptions to the exceptions, is paralleled in Lev 22:10-13.

The meaning of the word *tōšāb*, almost synonymous with the word *gēr* and yet distinct from it, can best be approached, I believe, by supposing that the words belong to different spheres. The term *gēr*, as we have defined it above, is a juridical term, defining the rights of a free man who has left his original environment in order to settle elsewhere. The term *tōšāb* does not define rights, but objectively describes a social condition: a "sojourner", one who immigrated from another locality and who must typically attach himself to a free citizen in order to assure his livelihood.[220] The words can, therefore, refer to the same person: socially he is a *tōšāb*, juridically a *gēr*.[221] In his capacitiy as a *tōšāb*, a stranger living among the Israelites, he may not automatically partake in the Pesach meal; but in his capacity as a *gēr*, to whom certain rights have been conceded, he may be circumcised and then partake.[222]

This understanding of the word throws some light on Lev 25:44-46, where it is stated that the Israelites may take slaves from among the sojourners (*mibbᵉnē hattōšābīm*) who sojourn with them, whereas they may not take them from among the Israelites. It is remarkable that the term *gēr* is not used here for persons who must certainly be considered *gērīm*, unless our definition of the term is wrong. That the author of H did not desire to lay stress on the juridical status of this category of individuals is understandable. A *gēr*, it is well known, may not be oppressed (19:33f). However, in their position as non-Israelites with a weak social status who might thus reach a point where the only viable solution is to sell themselves as slaves—i.e. in their position as *tōšābīm*—they may be bought as slaves.

The other instances where the word is used in H also fit this proposed definition.[223]

---

[220] The word is found in the construct state with a genitive referring to the person with whom he is staying, see 22:10 (*tōšab kōhēn*); 25:6 (*tōšabkā*). Note that in H and P the noun *gēr* never occurs with a genitive as it does in the decalogue or in Deuteronomy (Ex 20:10; Deut 1:16). In H and P the *gēr* is said to be "with" (*'et, 'im*) someone.

[221] Cf. Elliger, *Leviticus*, 293: "תושב bezeichnet doch wohl unter wirtschaftlichem Gesichtspunkt denselben Mann, der nach seinem rechtlichen Status גר heißt." However, the corresponding economic term is *śākīr* "hireling" (cf. Deut 24:14), so that it is better to speak of the social aspect with regard to the term *tōšāb*. See also Cardellini, "Stranieri", 151 (with other literature).

[222] Note that it is implied that the *gēr* will celebrate Pesach in his own house: the decisive criterion is not that he lives with the Israelites, but that he takes an active part in their religion.

[223] See 25:6; 22:10; 25:40.

The foreigner

The term *ben nēkār* occurs once in H and three times in other priestly texts, but nowhere else in the Pentateuch.[224] In the rest of the Pentateuch, the synonym *nokrī* is used (see esp. Deut 14:21; 15:3; 17:15). In all its occurrences in priestly texts, *ben nēkār* means "one who is ethnically not a member of the people of Israel" (cf. *ʾašer lōʾ mizzarʿakā hūʾ* "who is not of your offspring" Gen 17:12). Though the meaning of the term is clear, the verse in which it occurs in H is problematic. Lev 22:17-25 stipulates certain rules with regard to the unblemished state of animals fit for sacrifice; these rules are valid both for the house of Israel and for the resident alien in Israel (v 18). The general rule is that the animal must be male and without blemish (v 19). Certain types of blemish are then detailed: natural or accidental blemishes that render the animal unfit for any type of sacrifice (v 22); natural blemishes that may be tolerated in a freewill offering but not in a votive offering (v 23); finally, different types of castration: these do not only render the animal unfit, they must not be practised in the land at all (*ubeʾarṣekem lōʾ taʿaśū* "you must not do this in your own land [NIV]" v 24). There then follows the problematic verse:

22:25   ומיד בן נכר לא תקריבו את לחם אלהיכם מכל אלה

And from the hand of a stranger you shall not offer the food of your God from any of these (author's translation).

Many modern commentators take this verse to mean that the Israelites may not acquire blemished animals from foreigners to offer them to YHWH.[225] A contextual justification of this reading may be found in v 24, where it is said that the Israelites may not do this, i.e. practise castration, in their land.[226] Verse 25 would then aim to close a loophole: even if the animal was not castrated in your own land, but imported by a foreigner, you may not offer it to YHWH.

However, a possible criticism of this exegesis is that the subject of the whole paragraph is the state of animals fit for sacrifice, not castration. The prohibition of castration in v 24b is added almost as an after-

---

[224] Gen 17:12, 27; Ex 12:43.
[225] Noth, Elliger, Wenham.
[226] Some exegetes deny that v 24 prohibits castration, see Gispen, *Leviticus*, 317f.

thought. It is likely, therefore, that v 25 returns to the main subject, rather than prolonging the excursus on castration. Close attention to the wording of the verse confirms this view. The expression *miyyad* "from the hand of" is usual in sacrificial contexts;[227] in the present verse, it calls up the picture of the priest who offers the sacrifice brought by the worshipper.[228] Also, the phrase *mikkol ʾēlleh* "from any of these" should not be limited to the four types of castration: it refers to all the types of blemish enumerated in the preceding verses.

It thus transpires from this verse that, according to H, the foreigner may bring sacrifices at the Israelite sanctuary.[229] As far as this aspect is concerned, he is put on the same footing as the *gēr*.[230] And as in the case of the *gēr*, his offering must meet all the usual requirements. Should the priest be tempted to think: "He doesn't know any better" or "What can you expect, from a foreigner?"—the law recalls the essence of sacrifice: it is the food of God; the quality of the gift should not be determined in relation to the donor but to the recipient.

The human being

The treatment of resident aliens and foreigners in H shows that although the laws are directly addressed solely to the Israelites, the outlook is not narrowly ethnocentric. This point is further confirmed by two references to *ʾādām* "human being".[231] The word is fairly frequent in P, where in certain passages it holds a central theological position (Gen 1:27; 9:6); in other priestly texts, however, it is used without any special theological weight.[232]

The first time we encounter the word in H is in the paraenetic introduction in Lev 18. It is stated, in the second person plural, that the Israelites must not act according to the deeds of the land of Egypt, nor ac-

---

[227] See Num 5:25; and in non-priestly texts: Deut 26:4; Jud 13:23; Mal 1:10, 13.

[228] Cf. Num 5:25; Deut 26:4; for the synergy between the worshipper and the priest see, e.g., Lev 1:1-9. In this exegesis, the second person plural in 22:25a is addressed to the priests, in 22:25b to the Israelites. However, this multiplicity of addressees is in keeping with the introductory formula in 22:18.

[229] This is in agreement with Num 15:14, see n. 193.

[230] From the ethnic point of view, the resident alien is a *ben nēkār* ; yet in view of the fact that the resident alien is already mentioned in 22:18, it seems that *ben nēkār* here refers to foreigners not resident among the Israelites.

[231] A third use of the word *ʾādām* (22:5) where it means "human" as opposed to "animal" (*šereṣ*) will not be discussed here, cf. n. 232.

[232] See, e.g., Lev 5:3; Num 19:11; cf. Lev 22:5.

cording to the deeds of the land of Canaan (v 3); on the contrary, they must keep the ordinances and statutes of YHWH (v 4). This injunction is then reiterated and provided with a motive clause:

18:5   ושמרתם את חקתי ואת משפטי אשר יעשה אתם האדם וחי בהם

You shall therefore keep my statutes and my ordinances, by doing which a man shall live.

The precise meaning of this verse, the paramount importance of which is underscored by the fact that it is quoted in Ez 20:11, 13, 21 and in Neh 9:29,[233] cannot be discussed here.[234] What is relevant in the present section is that when the ultimate goal or scope of the commandments is explicitly stated,[235] the party concerned is defined as *ha'ādām* and not as Israel.[236] The laws are handed down to the Israelites, and it is to them that the paraenesis is addressed so that they may keep the laws; the human being who will live by them will therefore usually be an Israelite. However, the force of YHWH's commandments is not limited to Israel. To begin with, the resident alien is also subject to the laws (see above). Moreover, according to Lev 18:24-28 even the previous inhabitants of the land were in a sense subject to these laws: it is because they did not observe them that they were vomited out by the land. If non-Israelites are liable to punishment for transgressing the law, it is logical that they should also be included with regard to the recompense for keeping them; even if this inclusion be largely theoretical.

I venture to submit, therefore, that Lev 18:5 intimates the universal tenor of the OT message, which is expressed in Gen 1:27 and in different terms in Gen 12:3, etc.

The second passage where *'ādām* is used in a significant fashion is in the summary of the law in Lev 24:15-21. After the laws on blasphemy (vv 15f) follow some other rules, the first of which concerns homicide:

---

[233] Hurvitz has demonstrated on linguistic grounds that the verse is original in H and a quotation in Ezekiel, see A. Hurvitz, *A Linguistic Study of the Relationship between the Priestly Source and the Book of Ezekiel*, Cahiers de la Revue Biblique 20 (Paris, 1982), 46-48.

[234] See Schwartz, *Chapters*, 66f.

[235] Schwartz (*Chapters*, 66) affirms that 18:5 refers only to the commandments in Lev 18; however, the meaning of the expression "my commandments" (18:4) should not be restricted in this way (cf. the interpretation in Ezekiel and Nehemiah).

[236] For Talmudic discussion on this point, see Schwartz, *Chapters*, 239, n. 33.

24:17   ואיש כי יכה כל נפש אדם מות יומת

He who kills a man shall be put to death.

Since the following verse speaks of slaying animals, one might claim
that 'ādām in this verse does not have a universal connotation.[237] However, it cannot be overlooked that the content of the verse is very close to
that of Gen 9:6: human life ("blood" in Gen 9:6) is sacred, because the
human being is made in the image of God. This parallel, from a context
where the people of Israel is not yet spoken of, indicates that in our
passage the term 'ādām does have a wider meaning: not just the Israelite, but any human being. Another argument in favour of this view is that
intertextually Lev 24:17 may be contrasted with its parallel in the Book
of the Covenant:

Ex 21:12   מכה איש ומת מות יומת

Whoever strikes a man so that he dies shall be put to death.

Here 'īš may have the restricted meaning "free citizen",[238] as is shown
by the fact that slaves are excluded from this rule in cases of unpremedi-
tated manslaughter.[239] It is likely that the author of H consciously substituted the more universal term 'ādām for the at least potentially more
restrictive term 'īš as found in the Book of the Covenant. All human life,
whether Israelite or not, is sacred and therefore protected by the law.[240]

A comparable idea lies at the basis of the law on bodily harm in Lev
24:19f. Initially it is stated that when a man causes a disfigurement in
his neighbour ('ªmītō), the ius talionis will apply (v 19). When the law is
recapitulated, however, the general term 'ādām is used instead of the
specific 'āmīt :

24:20   כאשר יתן מום באדם כן ינתן בו

As he has disfigured a man, he shall be disfigured.

---

[237] Cf. 22:5 above, n. 232.
[238] See T. J. Meek, "The Origin of Hebrew Law", in idem, *Hebrew Origins* (Revised
edition, New York, 1950), 49-81, p. 59. Meek compares the 'īš of the Book of the Covenant with the *awêlum* of the Codex Hammurabi.
[239] Ex 21:21; cf. 21:32.
[240] See M. Greenberg, "Some Postulates of Biblical Criminal Law", in M. Haran, ed.,
Yehezkel Kaufmann Jubilee Volume (Jerusalem, 1960), 5-28.

What is true for life, is true for corporal integrity: it is sacred not just in Israel, but throughout all humanity.

3.3 THE PEOPLE OF ISRAEL

The group to which H is addressed, whose composition, internal organization and capacity to integrate outsiders have been described above on the basis of data from H, is referred to as a "people" (*'am*). Before presenting some general conclusions concerning the people of Israel, it is first necessary to pay some attention to the way the word *'am* is used in H.

The use of the noun 'am

The noun occurs 23 times in H in its different grammatical forms. It refers both to the people of Israel and to other peoples,[241] but is also used in its older meaning of "kinsman".[242] Two important expressions will not be reviewed in the present section: "people of the land" (20:2, 4), dealt with above, and "you shall be my people" (26:12) which will be discussed in the next chapter.

The punishment of "cutting off"

On thirteen occasions in H, in different formulations, we find a punishment described by the verb *krt* (niphal or hiphil)—"to cut off".[243] In all but three of the instances, it is specified that the cutting-off will be from among the *'am* (sg or pl) of the culprit.[244] Similar expressions occur in other priestly texts and in Ezekiel.[245] The meaning of "cutting off" as a

---

[241] Other peoples 20:24, 26; Israel 26:12; cf. also 20:2, 4.

[242] For the etymology, see HAL, 792.

[243] 17:4, 9, 10, 14; 18:29; 19:8; 20:3, 5, 6, 17, 18; 22:3; 23:29; cf. 23:30 with the verb *'bd* (hiphil).

[244] The exceptions are 17:14 (no specification), 20:17 (*le'ēnē benē 'ammām*); 22:3 (*millepānāy*).

[245] For extensive discussion, see W. Zimmerli, "Die Eigenart der prophetischen Rede des Ezekiel. Ein Beitrag zum Problem an Hand von Ez. 14 1-11", ZAW 66 (1954), 1-26, pp. 13-20; H. Schüngel-Straumann, *Tod und Leben in der Gesetzesliteratur des Pentateuch unter besonderer Berücksichtigung der Terminologie von "töten"*, (Bonn, 1969), 146-177; D. J. Wold, "The *Kareth* Penalty in P: Rationale and Cases", *SBL 1979 Seminar Papers*, Vol. 1 (Missoula, 1979), 1-45.

punishment for certain transgressions has been much debated.[246] Schematically, the main interpretations are a) death penalty imposed by human agency,[247] b) excommunication,[248] and c) some type of divine punishment.[249] Most recent studies opt for the third interpretation. With regard to H, the instances where YHWH himself declares in the first person that he will "cut off" (hiphil) the transgressor, show that the third interpretation is to be preferred.[250] Example:

17:10   ונתתי פני בנפש האכלת את הדם והכרתי אתה מקרב עמה

> I will set my face against that person who eats blood, and will cut him off from among his people.

This example leaves no doubt that the punishment involved in the expression "cutting off" will be executed by YHWH himself, without human assistance.[251] The general meaning of the verb *krt* in other passages indicates that a death penalty is meant.[252] We should not hesitate to use the present formulation, in the first person of the hiphil, to interpret the other instances which are formulated passively with the niphal.[253] It is not likely that in 17:4, 9, 14, where we find the passive expression, a different punishment is meant from that in 17:10. The difference between the active and the passive is merely one of degree of intensity: the

---

[246] See G. F. Hasel, TWAT IV, 362-364; Schwartz, *Chapters*, 28f.

[247] See, e.g., R. M. Good, *The Sheep of His Pasture. A Study of the Hebrew Noun 'Am(m) and Its Semitic Cognates*, HSM 29 (Chico, 1983), 87.

[248] See, e.g., E. Lipiński, TWAT VI, 186f; van Houten, *Alien*, 135f.

[249] Wenham, *Leviticus*, 285f. Schwartz, *Chapters*, 28f (with exhaustive literature); Milgrom, *Leviticus 1-16*, 457-460; Wold, "*Kareth* ". Elliger (*Leviticus*, 101) agrees that in P the connotation is that of death by divine agency, though he holds that the original meaning of the formula was death by human agency or expulsion from the family.

[250] 17:10; 20:3, 5, 6; cf. 23:30.

[251] In 20:2-4 (and in Ex 31:14) "cutting off" is juxtaposed with a call for the death penalty imposed by human agency; for these cases see Schwartz, *Chapters*, 29, and Milgrom, *Leviticus 1-16*, 460.

[252] See, e.g., Jud 4:24; 1 Sam 24:22; 1 Ki 11:16; 18:4. Schwartz has argued convincingly that the formula implies premature natural death (as opposed to miraculous death such as that of Nadab and Abihu in Lev 10). Milgrom, Wold and Wenham see death of the offender as just one of the possible interpretations.

[253] Knohl has pointed out that the older priestly texts (his "Priestly Torah) are extremely wary of attributing concrete actions (other than speaking) to God, at least in the Mosaic period; usually some type of impersonal circumlocution is used (see, e.g., Lev 10:2). See Knohl, *Sanctuary*, 88, 107; and idem, "The Priestly Torah Versus the Holiness School: Sabbath and the Festivals", *HUCA* 58 (1987), 65-117, pp. 71 and 73. In texts of the Holiness School, actions are more frequently ascribed immediately to God; in these texts it is also more usual for God to speak in the first person.

active wording is more direct, and therefore more terrifying, than the passive.

Our central question, however, is not what is implied by the *krt* formula, but the meaning of the word '*am* contained in it. This meaning is uncontroversial where the noun occurs in the plural. Example:

23:29   וכל הנפש אשר לא תענה בעצם היום הזה ונכרתה מעמיה

For whoever is not afflicted on this same day shall be cut off from his people.[254]

The plural of '*am* is usually taken to mean the circle of kinsmen.[255] Some scholars hold that although "kinsmen" is the original meaning of the term, the priestly writers reinterpreted it in the sense of a cultic community; *weᵉnikrᵉtāh mēᶜammehā* would then mean "he will be cut off from his fellow Israelites".[256] However, this is unlikely in light of the fact that both P and H use the plural in other expressions where the meaning "kinsmen" is unequivocal.[257] The priestly formula *neᵉᵉsap ʾel ᶜammāw* ("was gathered to his people", Gen 25:8 and eight more times in P) is particularly relevant in this connection. In this expression, the plural '*ammīm* certainly refers to kinsmen—in fact, dead kinsmen—and not to the people, or to a cultic community.[258]

However, if the plural means "kinsmen", how are we to read the cases where the singular is used, as in 17:10 quoted above?[259] Zimmerli—who accepts for the plural the meaning "Verwandten"— postulates that the singular "[...] denkt dagegen deutlich an das Volk Israel, das Bundesvolk Jahwes."[260] This interpretation is supported by the places where *yiśrāʾēl* is substituted for '*am* in the *krt* formula (Ex 12:15; Num 19:13; see also Ex 12:19; Num 19:20; Ez 14:8f). It should

---

[254] The plural is found also in 17:9; 19:8. For the cases of the plural in other priestly texts, see Zimmerli, "Eigenart", 17.

[255] See HAL, 792.

[256] See, e.g., Good, *Sheep*, 87.

[257] For the examples from H, see below on the relatives of the priest.

[258] This formula also raises the possibility that the punishment of "cutting off" not only implies death but concerns the after-life as well. See particularly the argument in Milgrom, *Leviticus 1-16*, 457-460. An example from the historical books seems to be provided in the story of the death of Hophni and Phinehas in 1 Sam 2-3, see M. Tsevat, "Studies in the Book of Samuel", *HUCA* 32 (1961), 191-216, in part. pp. 195-209. In that passage, the death of the offenders results in extirpation of the line.

[259] The other examples with the singular: 17:4; 20:3, 5, 6, 18; 18:29; 23:30.

[260] Zimmerli, "Eigenart", 17, 25.

be noted, however, that all these cases occur outside H.[261] As for the examples in H, the meaning "people of the covenant" does not always accord well with the context. In 17:10; 18:29; 20:3, 5, the formula with singular ʿam is used where the law applies to both the Israelites and the resident alien. Now, whereas for Israelites it would make sense to say that they are cut off from "their people" in the sense of the people of the covenant, the mention of the resident alien ill suits that context. For instance, in the example of 17:10 referred to above, if the person who ate blood were a resident alien, then "his people"—i.e. from whom he would be cut off—could not well be Israel. I am, therefore, of the opinion that it is better to ascribe the same meaning to the singular as to the plural; in both cases the word refers to the circle of kinsmen, i.e. the community of day-to-day life. We may say, therefore, that there is a development in the wording of the formula regarding the sphere from which one is cut off: the older instances envisage the kinsmen, the later instances envisage the people of Israel; the examples in H, however, stand in the older tradition.

The relatives of the priest

Lev 21 lays down a number of rules for the priest and the high priest, which are all aimed at safeguarding their holiness. In this context the plural ʿammāw is used four times. Unfortunately, two of the verses in which the expression occurs are obscure. Verse 4 lōʾ yiṭṭammāʾ baʿal beʿammāw is a noted crux interpretum, and v 15 welōʾ yeḥallēl zarʿō beʿammāw is almost equally difficult. The other two instances, however, are clear: the priest may not defile himself for a dead person among his kinsfolk—except for a near relative (v 1); the high priest must marry a virgin from among his kinsfolk (v 14). Both these examples reveal that the extent of the group designated as one's ʿammīm was wider than the family; the first instance also shows that it was more restricted than the whole people. In both cases the term seems to refer to the group of people constituting a person's social matrix, the community of day-to-day life.[262]

---

[261] Zimmerli, "Eigenart", 19, finds an argument in 22:3, where millepānāy is substituted for mēʿammāw or the like; he states: "Israel, die Gemeinde, ist der Raum, der vor dem Angesichte Jahwes ist". Since, however, this expression occurs in a prescription of purity for priests, it is better to interpret it contextually as referring to the temple—the working area of the priest.

[262] Cf. 19:16 lōʾ tēlēk rākīl beʿammekā "you shall not go up and down as a slanderer among your people".

The sons of your/their people

The expression $b^e n\bar{e}$ 'am + suffix occurs twice in H. For the first passage, Westbrook has advanced a very original interpretation:

19:18   לא תקם ולא תטר את בני עמך

You shall not take vengeance or bear any grudge against the sons of your own people.

On the basis essentially of comparative Ancient Near Eastern material, Westbrook attempts to find in this passage an interdiction of vicarious retaliation: you shall not take vengeance on the children of the guilty.[263] This exegesis is extremely speculative. It is also contradicted by the second occurrence of the expression, in a *krt* formula:

20:17   ...ונכרתו לעיני בני עמם

...they shall be cut off in the sight of the children of their people.

Here the expression clearly does not refer to the children. Rather, it seems that in both passages, the expression $b^e n\bar{e}$ 'am + suffix refers to the members of the community among which an Israelite would live from day to day; i.e. it is roughly synonymous with 'am as defined above.

The co-citizen (?)

The word 'amīt occurs nine times in H, twice in P and once in Zech 13:7. Its etymology and precise meaning are debated. It is not impossible that it is related to the noun 'am and means "a member of the same people".[264] This meaning could be made to fit the cases in H and P (but not Zech 13:7).

---

[263] See R. Westbrook, *Studies in Biblical and Cuneiform Law*, Cahiers de la Revue Biblique 26 (Paris, 1988), 97-99.
[264] See HAL, 799; see also the critical remarks in Hurvitz, *Study*, 74-78.

General conclusions

One conclusion which emerges from our study of the word 'am in H is somewhat unexpected: the word has no particular theological weight. That Israel should be a people is considered a matter of course. The notion is nowhere elaborated theologically. That the term is free of theological implications is shown by the fact that in the majority of occurrences it does not refer to Israel, but to the extended family.[265] Moreover, even where it refers to the people of Israel, the notion of peoplehood is subservient to other, theologically significant ideas. The expression "people of the land" probably does refer to Israel, but the passage where it occurs (20:2-5) is concerned with collective responsibility and purity of the sanctuary (see section 3.1.). The phrase "you shall be my people" (26:12) is not intended to demonstrate that Israel is a people, that it is in danger of no longer being a people, or that it should become one—that Israel should be a people is as self-evident as that YHWH should be a god. The significance of the statement is that they belong to each other (see Chapter 4).

This does not, of course, mean that peoplehood and the notions attached to it are not fundamental for H. What was said at the beginning of this chapter still stands: since it is thought of as the audience, the idea of the people of Israel is determinative of the form and content of H. We will now attempt to draw some general conclusions.

The composition of the people

The picture of the people of Israel presented by H, as it arises from our study, is that of a concrete historical entity constituted along ethnic lines. The sons of Israel are related to each other as brothers who all together, with their wives and children, may be considered one large family, the "house of Israel". Quite a number of the laws in H operate on the principle of kinship. An Israelite is distinguished from a non-Israelite by birth. Non-Israelites may live among the people, they may participate in the social, economic and religious life of the people; but even

---

[265] This phenomenon would be unimaginable in Deuteronomy, where the Israelites are constantly reminded that they are one people of brothers, see G. von Rad, *Das Gottesvolk im Deuteronomium*, BWANT 47 (Stuttgart 1929); L. Perlitt, "»Ein einzig Volk von Brüdern.« Zur deuteronomischen Herkunft der biblischen Bezeichnung »Bruder«", in D. Lührmann und G. Strecker, Hsg., *Kirche*, Fs G. Bornkamm (Tübingen, 1980), 27-52.

where they do, they remain quite distinct from the Israelites, even after several generations.[266]

The conclusions which are presented here run counter to the conception that in P and H "the people of Israel" is not so much an ethnic as a religious community.[267] The background to this view is the theory, dominant in present-day biblical scholarship, that the priestly laws date from a period when the group referring to itself as "Israel" had lost any semblance of statehood and had reconstituted itself as a cultic community (the image of which was then projected back into the stories of the Exodus and of the giving of the law).[268] According to this view, the picture of the people in H should be that of a religious community constituted on the basis of common worship of the same god. Our review of the evidence shows, at the very least, that this is not the way the people are explicitly presented in H.

Ethnic identity is the exclusive criterion for the notion of peoplehood which underlies H. For the author of H, this criterion is self-evident; in his view, a people is made up of individuals who descend from the same forefather. On the other hand, we find in H no fanaticism on this point. The appearance on the scene of a half-breed does not elicit any judgment (24:10-23); true, this particular half-breed turned to be bad, but it is nowhere stated that his genealogy was to be blamed for this. Nowhere in H do we find the prohibition to marry non-Israelite women; in view of the great emphasis on this point in other law codes, and in view of the extensive marriage-laws in H, this is a significant omission.[269] The provision regarding the high priest that he should take "a virgin from among his people" (21:14) is surely the exception that proves the rule: if it is expressly forbidden to the high priest to take a wife from outside his people, does this not mean that it was allowed to other Israelites? Moreover, if our analysis is correct that the term 'ammāw does not refer to the entire people of Israel, then this verse proves indeed to be far removed from the passages in other law codes prohibiting marriage to

---

[266] See in particular the expression 'ēqer mišpaḥat gēr "a descendant of the family of a gēr" (Lev 25:47).

[267] See, e.g., Jagersma, Leviticus 19, 129.

[268] Even in the post-exilic period, it is highly questionable whether Israel was constituted purely as a cultic community. The books of Ezra and Nehemiah evince an interest in genealogy bordering on the fanatical (see, e.g. Ezra 2:59; 9:1f). A more realistic view of the post-exilic community is that proposed by Weinberg, Citizen-Temple Community.

[269] Crüsemann's attempt to explain this omission by saying that the priestly composition, of which H was a part, had already dealt with that subject in Gen 27:46-28:9 is strained. Cf. Crüsemann, Tora, 326; 328, n. 31; 344-345.

non-Israelites. The absence of fanaticism can also be observed in the laws concerning the resident alien. The distinction drawn between the Israelite and the *gēr* is razor-sharp; no procedure is provided for to turn a foreigner into an Israelite. Yet we find a remarkable openness toward resident aliens: they are free to participate in all the aspects of Israelite life. The resident alien, though not an Israelite, must be treated as one, and the Israelites are to love him as they are to love their fellow-Israelites.[270]

The national perspective

The demands put upon the Israelites in the laws of H do not only concern each individual Israelite, or each individual family; they are first and foremost addressed to the people as a whole. In other words: the Israelites are called upon to become a nation, to act concertedly, to realize as a group the ideals that are set before them. This national perspective, which informs most parts of H (see the section on the variation in grammatical number, pp. 47-54), becomes more concrete when Israel is seen in the context of the land. The Sabbath and the feasts will be celebrated "in all your dwellings" (Lev 23). The sabbatical year and the jubilee are national institutions; the jubilee is proclaimed by a trumpet which is "sent abroad throughout all your land" (Lev 25). The catastrophes that will come upon the people if they do not keep the commandments of YHWH are of national dimensions (18:24-28; Lev 26).

The conception which most strongly expresses the national perspective is that of collective guilt. Transgression of the commandments by any individual brings guilt upon the people, it defiles the land, it profanes the sanctuary. This conception creates a certain tension between the freedom of the individual and his responsibility towards the collective. On the one hand, an appeal is made to every man's conscience in order that he should keep the commandments; on the other, it is made clear from the outset that failure to do so will put a blight on the nation and will eventually result in dire consequences for the entire people. It is

---

[270] Some scholars view the openness towards non-Israelites in the light of prophetical statements to the effect of the inclusion of the nations in God's plan (e.g. Isa 66:18-21; Zech 2:15), see e.g. Jagersma, *Leviticus 19*, 116. However, in 3.2. above we have seen that the inclusion of the *gēr* in the laws of H entirely proceeds from the fact that he is already present among the Israelites, in the land. This is a far cry from the prophetical promise that non-Israelites will come to the land (or to Zion) in order to seek the presence of the God of Israel.

true that the collective is authorized to right the wrongs, and certain procedures are set up to eradicate the guilt; however, the peculiar power structure described in H (see below) apparently leaves the enforcement of these procedures to the individuals who make up the people. Thus the national perspective of H, which is an essential part of its ideology, generates a certain tension between the sphere of the individual and the sphere of the collective.

The internal organization of the people

The power structure underlying the description in H is quite simple. At the head stands Moses, who represents YHWH and transmits his word. This word is authoritative and without appeal, though its authority is— paradoxically—enhanced by appeals to the numinous presence of YHWH and by references to salvation history. Yet one could say that Moses, in his capacity as mediator, stands with one foot outside the people, at the side of God.

The internal organizational structure of the people is limited to two levels: the family and the assembly. Every male adult Israelite is made responsible for what happens in his house and family. Parents are to be respected (19:3). The family is the basic unit of which the people is constituted, and it is in the family that most of the laws will be put into practice. Thus, the importance of the family exceeds the merely social dimension: it is also fundamental in education, the economy and religion. The hierarchical level above the family is occupied by the assembly, which is constituted by all the male adult Israelites.[271] This body is empowered to oversee the families and to punish wrong-doers. All matters touching the whole nation are of its resort: religion and worship, law and order, social affairs and the regulation of agriculture. Next to the absolute authority of the divine law it is the only locus of power, which implies that it bears the highest responsibility.

It does not lie within the scope of H to give an exhaustive description of the power structure of the people of Israel. Even so, the lack of any mention of other executive bodies or institutions within this structure is remarkable. From H we learn nothing about the existence—even the future existence—of a king (contrast Deut 17), nor of an institution of elders (as elsewhere in Deuteronomy), nor of a tribal ruler, *nāśî'* (as in

---

[271] On the distribution of the expressions *'ēdāh* and *'am hā'āreṣ* see above in section 3.1.

Ex 22:28 and in P). It is sometimes supposed that in H as in P, the priests, and especially the high priest, hold the power which in other sources is ascribed to the king; these texts are then said to point to the hierocratic Jewish society of the Persian period.[272] This view, already highly problematic with regard to P, can in no way be supported by the data from H. In H an important place is given to the priests and the high priest (c 21; 22:1-16). The responsibility of the priests is great, and the demands imposed upon them are stricter than those on the other Israelites. They must be revered by every Israelite (21:8). Yet all these provisions result from the greater holiness of the priest, not from his greater political power. Because he works in the sanctuary and approaches YHWH, he must be consecrated for fear of bringing guilt upon the Israelites (22:16). H has nothing to say of the political power of the priests, nor are the priests ever mentioned in juridical contexts.[273]

The real addressees of H

A question which still needs to be tackled is that of the historical reality lying behind the image of the people in H. The priestly concept of a 13-tribe Israel in the desert, encamped around a central movable shrine, is widely recognized to be fictitious, and this aspect of the problem need not occupy our attention any further. However, the fictional "Israel in the desert" is probably meant to correspond to a reality from the time when H was composed; for the main objective of H is not to give an account of what YHWH said to the desert generation, but to teach the law to its own generation (see Chapter 2). In light of this we must now ask: what group is ultimately addressed through the picture of the people in H?

Von Rad has formulated a similar question with regard to Deuteronomy, only to reject it on the grounds that Deuteronomy itself does not intend to be interrogated on that point. The image of the people in Deuteronomy is wholly ideal and theoretical, that of "the people of the promise".[274] The same may be said of H: the text does not intend to give information on the real addressees. The picture of the people of Israel contained in it is a fiction, a model and an example (see, e.g., 24:23),

---

[272] For criticism of this position, see Y. (J.) Kaufmann, "Probleme der israelitisch-jüdischen Religionsgeschichte", ZAW 48 (1930), 23-43.
[273] Priests do appear in juridical contexts in Deuteronomy (Deut 17:9, 12; 19:17; 21:5). See also Ez 44:24.
[274] G. von Rad, Das Gottesvolk im Deuteronomium, BWANT 47 (Stuttgart 1929), 22.

destined for the generation of the authors of H. It is not an image of that later generation, to be decoded by present-day scholars. All this does not mean, however, that the question as to the historical identity of the real addressees of H may not be raised—although this question does imply moving from the literary to the historical domain. Since the aim of the present study is exegetical rather than historical, no more can be done here than to evaluate certain approaches that have been essayed and to indicate an avenue for future study.[275]

A view enjoying great currency, is that the real addressees of H are the members of the Jewish religious community (*Gemeinde, Kultgemeinde*) during, or after, the exile.[276] One of the results of the present chapter which might be interpreted as an argument in favour of this position is the absence in H of legislation concerning a king and other political institutions (except for the assembly). This lacuna may indicate that for the authors and the audience of H, kingship was not an important institution. Does this not mean that H is to be set in a historical situation where there was no king in Israel? Such an historical situation existed after the fall of Jerusalem: in exile, Israel had no king nor any other well-defined political institutions;[277] after the exile, an elaborate political organization may be supposed to have existed, part of which can be reconstructed, but it had no room for a king. The argument is not entirely convincing, however. The omission of legislation concerning the king may at least partly be understood within the narrative framework: in the desert period there was no king in Israel; one should not, therefore, expect that legislation given in such a setting would contain rules concerning kingship. On the other hand, even in the monarchical period, circles may have existed in Israel which considered the king relatively unimportant (see below).

A number of results of the present chapter definitely militate against a setting in the exilic or post-exilic period. The functions attributed to the collective addressed in H largely exceed those of a cultic or religious community. The fact that they encompass such matters as the adminis-

---

[275] It will not be useful in the present section to review the whole debate on the dating of H, for which the reader is referred to Chapter 1.

[276] This view is taken for granted in the works of Elliger, Jagersma, Mathys, Barbiero, to name but a few. A recent explicit statement can be found in E. Gerstenberger, "»Apodiktisches« Recht »Todes« Recht?", in P. Mommer et al., *Gottes Recht als Lebensraum*, Fs H. J. Boecker (Neukirchen, 1993), 7-20, pp. 16-19.

[277] Note, however, the frequent mention of the elders in Ezekiel (7:26; 8:1, 11, 12; 14:1; 20:1, 3). The elders are never mentioned in H.

tration of justice and the organization of economic life does not accord
well with the conditions of Israel in the Babylonian and Persian periods,
when large parts of public life were directed by a foreign power.[278] The
rules concerning the treatment of the resident alien show with particular
clarity that the Israelite people, as presented by H, are free to impose
laws on non-Israelites living among them.[279] One may be tempted to
spiritualize some of the functions attributed to the Israelite people,[280] or
to treat them as utopian,[281] but there is no peremptory reason why we
should do so. Rather, we are led to the conclusion that the historical
conditions addressed by H are those of the pre-exilic period. It seems
likely that the real audience of H should have lived under these same
conditions, i.e. before the exile.[282]

In an elaborate answer to the question of the identity of the real addressees of the main law codes, Noth has argued for a setting in the pre-
exilic period.[283] On the basis of a number of characteristics of these
codes—the Book of the Covenant, the Deuteronomic code, H—he derives all of them from a setting in the sacral confederation of the Israelite
tribes, the "amphictyony".[284] During the monarchical period, this institution persisted as a sacral, religious body relatively independent of the
State (be it Judah or Israel). Its center was the Temple at Jerusalem—or
rather the ark of the covenant placed there by David—where the confederation continued to assemble and hear the covenant-statutes of YHWH.
The community of addressees (*die angesprochene Gemeinschaft*) of the

---

[278] However great the autonomy granted to it within the Persian Empire, the Jewish
community in Judah was not an independent political entity (see, e.g., Ezra 9:9; Neh
9:36-37).
[279] The treatment of the resident alien is so pervasive a theme in H that it cannot easily
be ascribed to older sources; it is clearly a preoccupation of the authors of the text as it
lies before us.
[280] As does Gerstenberger on the death penalty in Lev 20 and 24, see Gerstenberger,
"Recht", 17f.
[281] As does Bultmann on the inclusion of non-Israelites in the jubilee legislation, see
Bultmann, *Fremde*, 188.
[282] A supplementary argument against seeing the audience of H as a religious community is, I believe, afforded by the numerous warnings in H against worshipping other
gods (see 17:7; 18:21; 19:4; 20:2-5; 26:1, 30). This topic is so important in H that it
cannot be disparaged as empty rhetoric, nor can it be viewed as an element deriving
exclusively from the framework of the fiction. However, if the real addressees of H must
be warned against idolatry, this means that common worship of the same god is not what
binds them together.
[283] Noth, *Gesetze*, 32-53.
[284] The characteristics he lists are: the laws address a group of people who are bound
by their common worship of YHWH; this group is distinguished from the original inhabitants of the land, the Canaanites; the laws presuppose the Exodus and the taking of
the land; the audience is called "Israel". See Noth, *Gesetze*, 43.

laws is therefore that of the amphictyony: the assembled followers of YHWH who regard themselves as descendants of the Israel of the Exodus. Although these "Israelites" are at the same time citizens of the kingdom of Judah or Israel, it is not in that capacity that the law is addressed to them; neither are all the citizens of these states, which include many non-Israelite groups, members of the amphictyonic assembly.

Noth's hypothesis has the great merit of taking the biblical law codes on their own terms. Nevertheless, when he hypostatizes the Israel depicted in the laws and postulates that it really existed, as a sacral confederacy of 12 tribes settled around a central sanctuary and bound to the one God, YHWH, and that it continued to exist until late in the time of the monarchy, he departs from the path of sober historical research. His hypothesis of a pre-monarchical amphictyony has not survived the criticism levelled at it, let alone his thesis that this institution remained in existence in the monarchical period.[285] It is therefore impossible to accept his grand design.

Nevertheless, on one point Noth's observations are very acute. H certainly is not a state law addressed to the citizens of the State of Judah. Yet if the historical setting of H is to be sought in the pre-exilic period, this almost certainly implies an origin in Judah in the monarchic period.[286] What, then, is the collective addressed by H? I will present two clues, one from H and one from the historical books, which will, it is hoped, show that it is at least possible that an audience such as seems to be supposed in H could have existed in this period. The first clue, which has been discussed in section 3.1., is the substitution of the term "people of the land" for the term "assembly" in the context of establishment in the land. If the conclusions of our discussion there are accepted, then it would seem that the intended audience of H could be referred to as "the people of the land". In view of the considerations mentioned above, a connection might be established between this entity and the "people of the land" occasionally described as an active force in the history of the Judean kingdom.[287] These "people of the land" are not to be viewed as a

---

[285] See C. H. J. de Geus, *The Tribes of Israel. An Investigation into Some of the Presuppositions of Marthin Noth's Amphictyony Hypothesis*, Studia Semitic Neerlandica 18 (Assen, 1976).

[286] This would seem to be implied by the relationship between H and P: P has close ties to the temple in Jerusalem, and H depends on P (see above in Chapter 1).

[287] In Chapter 5 it will be shown that the outlook of H is definitely provincial; this ties in with the fact that the term *'am hā'āreṣ* is sometimes used to distinguish the population of the provinces from the inhabitants of Jerusalem, see above in section 3.1.

well-defined political party. Nevertheless, they were able to convene in an official manner, as transpires both from H and from the Book of Kings (see above, pp. 42, 44). An audience in this circle would seem to fit several of the characteristics of H (see further in 5.3. below, pp. 154-163).

The second clue also involves the noun ʿam. 2 Ki 4:13 relates how a Shunammite lady, in response to Elisha's offer to speak to the king or the commander of the army on her behalf, says: "I dwell among my people" (beṭōk ʿammī ʾānōkī yōšābet). The noun ʿam is here used in its more restricted sense of "kinship group", also attested in H. What is more important, however, is the implication of the Shunammite's words: she has no need for a king or a commander, since her kinship group is sufficient to provide for all her needs. What emerges here is a picture of Israelites living in a social environment in which the political organization of the state is irrelevant.[288] Although the Elisha stories derive from a different time and place, the social reality described in 2 Ki 4 demonstrates that it is not totally implausible to posit an audience in the monarchical period to which the simple power structure of H would be relevant.[289]

These two clues could perhaps be combined in order to argue that the ʿam hāʾāreṣ of the Judean countryside functioned more or less like the ʿam of the Shunammite, and that the intended audience of H is to be found in such a social environment.

---

[288] Elements of a sociological analysis of the Elisha stories can be found in T. Hoover Rentería, "The Elijah/Elijah (sic) Stories: a Sociocultural Analysis of Prophets and People in Ninth Century B.C.E. Israel", in R. B. Coote, ed., *Elijah and Elisha in Socioliterary Perspective* (Atlanta, 1992), 75-126; for 2 Ki 4, see in particular pp. 91, 104-108.

[289] Compare also 1 Sam 20:28f, which seems to attest that the family (mišpāḥāh) and the king might at times become competing spheres of authority. Of course, these verses refer again to a different period.

CHAPTER FOUR

THE STATUS OF THE PEOPLE

The people of Israel are not only the specific audience to whom the discourse of H is addressed—they also constitute as it were the domain where its objectives are to be realized. In all its different parts H contains a vision for the people, which decisively colours the notion of peoplehood. This vision is anchored in what YHWH has done for the Israelites in the past when he led them out of Egypt; it is realized in a durable relationship between YHWH and the people; and it entails consequences for the Israelites' conduct in all spheres of life. In the present chapter we will review these three main aspects.

4.1 THE EXODUS

On eight occasions in the discourse of H, YHWH recalls that he brought the Israelites out of the land of Egypt: 19:36; 22:33; 23:43; 25:38, 42, 55; 26:13, 45. The statements on the Exodus exhibit stereotyped diction, with certain elements recurring in every instance: the verb used is invariably *yṣ'* (hiphil),[1] the grammatical subject is YHWH and the direct object the sons of Israel, even where they are not expressly mentioned,[2] the domain out of which the Israelites are brought is called "the land of Egypt" (*'ereṣ miṣrayim*). These formulas seem to sum up a whole narrative complex, stretching from the account of slavery (26:13 "...out of the land of Egypt, that you should not be their slaves") to that of the desert period (23:43 "...I made the people of Israel dwell in booths when I brought them out of the land of Egypt"). Two other passages are merely reminders that the Israelites dwelt in the land of Egypt: 18:3; 19:34.

---

[1] For the different formulations of the Exodus, see E. Zenger, "Le thème de la «sortie d'Egypte» et la naissance du Pentateuque", in A. de Pury, éd., *Le Pentateuque en question* (Genève, 1989), 301-331, pp. 302-305 (with literature).

[2] The direct object is: the sons of Israel 25:55; 23:43; the second person masculine plural suffix 19:36; 22:33; 25:38; 26:13; the third person masculine plural suffix 25:42; "the ancestors" (*ri'šōnīm*) 26:45.

Formulaic statements summing up the Exodus occur throughout the entire OT; they play an important part in Deuteronomy,[3] but less so in the priestly laws.[4]

All but one of the places in H where the Exodus is referred to contains the formula *'ani yhwh ('oelōhēkem)*,[5] which recalls the celebrated statement in Hos 12:10: "I am the LORD your God *('oelōhekā)* from the land of Egypt." The possibility needs to be considered that the formula *'ani yhwh ('oelōhēkem)* itself, which is used abundantly throughout H, harks back to the great events surrounding the Exodus. Indeed, this formula occurs again and again in the priestly version of the Exodus,[6] accentuating that it is by liberating the Israelites from the power of Pharaoh that YHWH proved himself to be their God (Ex 6:7; compare Lev 26:45). However this may be, the theme of the Exodus is quite pervasive. The question arises, therefore, as to the significance of this theme in the context of the laws in H.

In a recent article, Crüsemann has argued that the main implication of the Exodus in H is that of "sanctification" or "consecration" *(Heiligung)*: when YHWH led the Israelites out of Egypt he consecrated them to himself.[7] Crüsemann's exegetical starting point is Lev 22:31-33: "So you shall keep my commandments and do them: I am the LORD. And you shall not profane my holy name, but I will be hallowed among the people of Israel;" and then:

---

[3] Deut 13:6, 11; 15:15; 16:1, 3, 6; 20:1; 23:5; 24:9, 18, 22; 25:17

[4] Reference is made to the Exodus in Ex 29:46; Lev 11:45 and Num 15:41. It is not sure that any of these passages belongs to the priestly *Grundschrift*; on stylistic grounds they are ascribed to the "Holiness School" by Knohl. See Knohl, *Sanctuary*, 65, 69, 90.

[5] In 19:36; 25:38 and 26:13 before the statement concerning the Exodus; in 23:43; 25:55 and 26:45 after the Exodus statement; in 22:33 before and after the statement. The exception is 25:42. For general discussion, and the essential identity of the long and short formulas, see W. Zimmerli, "Ich bin Jahwe", in idem, *Gottes Offenbarung. Gesammelte Aufsätze*, Theologische Bücherei, AT 19 (München ,1963), 11-40; K. Elliger, "Ich bin der Herr—euer Gott", in idem, *Kleine Schriften zum Alten Testament*, Theologische Bücherei, AT 32 (München 1966), 211-231

[6] The longer formula occurs in the highly significant verse Ex 6:7 (and later in 16:12; 29:46); the shorter formula in Ex 6:2, 8, 29; 7:5, 17; 8:18; 10:2; 12:12; 14:4, 18 (perhaps not all of these verses belong to P).

[7] F. Crüsemann, "Der Exodus als Heiligung. Zur rechtsgeschichtlichen Bedeutung des Heiligkeitsgesetzes", in E. Blum, C. Macholz, E. W. Stegemann, Hsg., *Die Hebräische Bibel und ihre zweifache Nachgeschichte*, Fs für R. Rendtorff zum 65. Geburtstag (Neukirchen, 1990), 117-129. See already, W. Zimmerli, "Heiligkeit nach dem sogenannten Heiligkeitsgesetz", *VT* 30 (1980), 493-512, p. 503.

22:32b, 33

אני יהוה מקדשכם
המוציא אתכם מארץ מצרים להיות לכם לאלהים אני יהוה

I am the LORD who sanctify you, who brought you out of the land of
Egypt to be your God: I am the LORD.

According to Crüsemann, the two participle phrases *meqaddiškem* and
hammōṣî' 'etkem are in parallel to one another and refer to the same
event: the Exodus. YHWH, by leading the Israelites out of Egypt, sanctified them—i.e. he separated them from all the other peoples in order
that they be his own (cf. Lev 20:24-26; 18:3). Crüsemann then proceeds
to oppose this putative priestly understanding of the Exodus to the
Deuteronomic interpretation of the Exodus as liberation which, in his
view, stands in relation to the fact that Deuteronomy is addressed to the
free, land-owning men.[8] He further connects the notion of Exodus-as-
sanctification with the loss of freedom and landed property which came
about through the exile: holiness—unlike liberation—is an idea which
may be presented as the basis of God's laws even to a people that has
lost its independence and its land. Confirmation of the (post-)exilic
background of this complex of ideas is found in the books Ezra and
Nehemiah (Ezra 9:2 "the holy seed"; Neh 9:2 the Israelites separating
themselves from all foreigners).

Crüsemann's theory is well constructed and accords with other recent approaches to the Holiness Code.[9] Nevertheless, it is open to criticism.[10] To begin with, his analysis of Lev 22:31-33 is unsound. The
assertion that the participle phrases *meqaddiškem* and *hammōṣî' 'etkem*
must refer to the same time frame is contradicted by the fact that they
are differently constructed: the first participle has a suffix pronoun attached to it, whereas the second participle is determined by the article
and followed by the particle *'et*. Although it is difficult to ascribe different syntactic functions to these constructions as such,[11] the fact that they

---

[8] "Der Exodus nicht als primär sozial und rechtlich zu beschreibende Tat Gottes, die
die Existenz der freien und grundbesitzenden Israeliten prägt oder die politische Situation des Volkes als Ganzes, sondern der Exodus als Aussonderung aus den Völkern und
Trennung von ihren Sitten und damit die Zuordnung zu Gott wird zur entscheidenden
Begründung…" p. 124.

[9] Particularly that of E. Blum, see above in Chapter 1.

[10] The post-exilic date of H is accepted without argument by Crüsemann. His view
that the society addressed by H is more egalitarian than that envisaged in Deuteronomy
(p. 121) is problematic: the addressees of H, too, may on occasion acquire slaves from
among their own people (Lev 25).

[11] The phrase *haqqōneh 'ōtō* in Lev 25:28 seems to be substantially identical with
qōnēhū in 25:50.

occur here within one and the same verse opens up the possibility that
they were intended to refer to different time frames ("who sanctifies
you" vs. "who has led you out"). Secondly, the expression *ᵃnī yhwh
mᵉqaddiškem* occurs in two other places in H (20:8; 21:8; see also Ex
31:13), and twice with a third person suffix referring to the priests
(21:15; 22:9). A review of these cases shows that the implication of the
expression is that YHWH sanctifies the priests through his holy presence in the sanctuary, and the Israelites through his commandments (cf.
20:8 "Keep my statutes, and do them; I am the LORD who sanctify
you").[12] This interpretation fits 22:32b perfectly. It appears, then, that
the first participle phrase refers to an ongoing process, while the second
one expresses a past event; the claim that they express different aspects
of the same divine act is therefore untenable.

More generally we must take note of the fact that holiness is never
described in H as something the Israelites already possess, be it even by
the grace of God. Israel is never called a "holy people" (*ᶜam qādōš*) as
in Deuteronomy (Deut 7:6; 14:2, 21). Holiness is the calling of the Israelites, the aim to which they must devote their entire lives. Even where it
is explicitly stated that YHWH has separated the Israelites from the
other peoples—an expression which may well allude to the Exodus—
this separation is not said to result in the holiness of the people; holiness
remains their calling (20:26 "You shall be holy to me; for I the LORD
am holy, and have separated you from the peoples").[13] This call to holiness will be further explored below. For our present purpose, it is sufficient to have shown that there is no direct link between the Exodus and
holiness according to H. Neither the exegesis of 22:31-33, nor the general idea of holiness obtaining in H warrants the view that the Exodus
was interpreted in H as sanctification or consecration.

Fortunately, however, some very explicit indications may be found
which open up a different view of the place of the Exodus in the conceptual universe of H. In the provisions concerning the impoverished Israelite (25:25-55), the three latter paragraphs are motivated with an appeal
to the Exodus. In the third paragraph (25:39-46), on the Israelite who
has sold himself to a fellow-Israelite, the prohibition to treat him as a
slave (*lō' taᶜᵃbōd bō ᶜᵃbōdat ᶜābed*) is motivated as follows:

---

[12] Cf. Knohl, *Sanctuary*, 182-183. See also below in 4.3.
[13] As opposed to W. Zimmerli, "Heiligkeit nach dem sogenannten
Heiligkeitsgesetz", *VT* 30 (1980), 493-512, p. 503. See below, section 4.3.

25:42   כי עבדי הם אשר הוצאתי אתם מארץ מצרים

לא ימכרו ממכרת עבד

For they are my servants, whom I brought forth out of the land of
Egypt; they shall not be sold as slaves

A very similar statement closes the fourth paragraph, on the Israelite
who sells himself to a resident alien (25:55). The tenor of these
motivations is, of course, that since one should not dispose of someone
else's slaves, no man may dispose of an Israelite for he already belongs
to YHWH. Whereas in reality an Israelite might be forced to sell himself
in debt-slavery, in theory he always remains the slave of God. Once
every fifty years, reality is to be adjusted to the theory, all Israelite debt-
slaves will go free.[14]

But how did the Israelites come to be YHWH's slaves? In a booklet
which has unfortunately been widely neglected by theologians,[15] the
jurist David Daube has shown that in certain passages in the OT, the
Exodus was interpreted in the light of contemporary law and custom.[16]
YHWH was pictured as the mighty redeemer who freed his kinsmen
from captivity in the hands of foreigners. The Exodus meant a change of
master, from the rule of Pharaoh and the Egyptians to the rule of
YHWH. In this juridical interpretation, "The kind of salvation portrayed
in the exodus was not, by its nature, an isolated occurrence, giving rise
to nebulous hopes for similar good luck in the future: it had its roots in,
and set the seal on, a permanent institution—hence it was something on
which absolute reliance might be placed."[17] Whether or not it is true, as
Daube claims, that this understanding underlies the account of the Exodus in all the different sources and literary layers contained in the OT,
what is important for our purpose is that such a reading is explicitly
attested in the verses quoted above. Through the Exodus, the Israelites
were subjected to a change of master: no longer would they be slaves of

---

[14] Crüsemann turns the message topsy-turvy when he extracts from Lev 25 that
YHWH will remain the God of the Israelites even if they are enslaved. See Crüsemann,
"Exodus", 124f. The object of the law is not to comfort enslaved Israelites, but to guarantee them their freedom; even if an Israelite is enslaved, one day he, or at least his
children, will again be free.

[15] S. Herrmann, in his article "Exodusmotiv. I Altes Testament", *TRE* 10, 732-737,
mentions neither Daube's work, nor the juridical aspect ascribed to the Exodus in the
OT. Superior in this respect is the review of Zenger, "Sortie d'Egypte", 303-308 (though
Zenger does not quote Daube either).

[16] D. Daube, *The Exodus Pattern in the Bible*, All Souls Studies 2 (London, 1963).

[17] Daube, *Exodus*, 14.

the Egyptians (cf. 26:13 "I am the LORD your God, who brought you forth out of the land of Egypt, that you should not be their slaves"), but slaves of YHWH. Thus, the relationship between YHWH and the Israelites was defined in legal terms. In the context, it is possible to go even further and to draw two other inferences: (a) in the precise legal understanding it is the "sons of Israel", i.e. the male adults, that are slaves, whereas their women and children find themselves in this position merely because they are dependent on the *pater familias* ; (b) since children of slaves were regarded as the master's property, the Israelites will be slaves of YHWH down the generations.[18] Of course, the point of the whole motif is not the utter and irredeemable wretchedness of the Israelites, but their supreme and perennial dignity.

The "realistic" view of the Israelites as slaves of YHWH is fully functional in the context of Lev 25, since it serves to motivate certain limits on human slavery.[19] We must not, however, loose sight of the fact that the concept is essentially metaphorical: the slaves of a god are his worshippers, his faithful. Although it rarely receives so realistic an interpretation as in Lev 25, the metaphorical use of the word "slave" to designate the worshipper of a god is extremely common in the OT. Now, if the metaphor of the Israelites' servitude implies, on the human side, a guarantee of freedom from bondage, on the divine side the implication is that YHWH will be "served" by the Israelites, that he will be worshipped by them. Or in other terms: that he will be their God. It is stated explicitly in three places in H that the aim of bringing the Israelites out of Egypt was for YHWH "to be their God", see 22:33 (quoted above); 25:38 (quoted below) and 26:45.[20]

Thus we observe that the juridical aspect of the Exodus expressed by the master-slave analogy is not naive. What YHWH did to the Israelites when he led them out of Egypt may be described in legal terms on the analogy of a mighty kinsman who redeems slaves or prisoners from a foreign power. The relevance of this analogy, however, is limited to contexts where the subject matter is the social status of the Israelites. In

---

[18] See also below pp. 120-122.

[19] Cf. the "realistic" view of Israel as *gērīm* in 25:23, discussed above in 3.2.

[20] It has been argued by Clements that YHWH's promise "to be the God of Israel" implies very concretely that he will dwell in a sanctuary in their midst, see Clements, *God and Temple*, 112. This fits in very well with further implications of the Exodus as they will be developed below.

other contexts, it is stated in uncoded form that by delivering the Israelites from Egypt, YHWH became not their master but their God.[21]

Yet another element linked to the Exodus is that of the giving of the
land:

25:38   אני יהוה אלהיכם אשר הוצאתי אתכם מארץ מצרים
               לתת לכם את ארץ כנען להיות לכם לאלהים

I am the LORD your God, who brought you forth out of the land of
Egypt to give you the land of Canaan, and to be your God.[22]

Although it is here called by its historical name "land of Canaan", in H
the land is viewed first and foremost as YHWH's possession. When the
Israelites are settled in the land they are said to be YHWH's tenants
(25:23, cf. above, pp. 58-59 and below, pp. 181-184); all inhabitants of
the land must respect YHWH's rules for fear of polluting it. Not observing these principles will lead to expulsion from the land (see the conclusions to 3.2. above, pp. 181-184). The ideas attached to the notion of the
land of YHWH remain to be fully investigated in 6.1. (pp. 169-180).
What can be said, however, in the present context is that the relationship
instituted between YHWH and Israel at the Exodus had a territorial implication.

Some light is thrown on this territorial aspect by some extra-biblical
parallels. Weinfeld has identified a pattern in Mesopotamian, Hittite and
Greek texts of cities or regions being liberated from the hand of worldly
kings—meaning concretely that they did not have to pay taxes—and
made over to the godhead so that he might be served in his sanctuary.[23]
In these cases, the population are viewed as slaves of the god who are
settled around the sanctuary on land belonging to the god.[24] The underlying idea of H seems to be much the same: if YHWH took the Israelites
for his slaves so that they might serve him, he must also provide them

---

[21] As against Kalluveettil, who holds that the word "slave" in 25:42, 55 depicts the
Israelites as YHWH's vassals. See, P. Kalluveettil, *Declaration and Covenant. A Com-
prehensive Review of Covenant Formulae from the Old Testament and the Ancient Near
East*, AnBib 88 (Rome, 1982), 191.

[22] Note that the expansions of the Exodus formula depend on the context: vv 42, 55,
which state that the Israelites became YHWH's slaves, occur in sections on slavery; v
38, where the gift of the land is alluded to, comes in the section on the Israelite who has
lost his landholding.

[23] M. Weinfeld, *Justice and Righteousness in Israel and the Nations. Equality and
Freedom in Ancient Israel in Light of Social Justice in the Ancient Near East* (Jerusalem,
1985) [Hebrew], 133-139.

[24] Cf. Weinberg, *Citizen-Temple Community*, 103.

with a dwelling-place; he therefore settles them on his land around his sanctuary.

A last notion attaching to the Exodus is a simple corollary of all that has been said so far. Becoming YHWH's slaves brings important advantages to the Israelites; it also comports one key requirement: the Israelites are to keep his commandments:

19:36f   אני יהוה אלהיכם אשר הוצאתי אתכם מארץ מצרים

ושמרתם את כל חקתי ואת כל משפטי ועשיתם אתם אני יהוה

I am the LORD your God, who brought you out of the land of Egypt. And you shall observe all my statutes and all my ordinances, and do them: I am the LORD.

This same notion is also explicitly expressed in the verses preceding the mention of the Exodus in 22:33 (quoted above); it is implicit in all the other occurrences of the Exodus formula.

Thus the import of the Exodus in H comes into focus. When he liberated the Israelites, YHWH became their God and they became his "slaves", in which capacity they were granted the right to live in his land (the land of Canaan).[25] This state of affairs guarantees the Israelites freedom from bondage and a share of inalienable property, at least theoretically.[26] It also implies that they will observe all YHWH's commandments.[27] We may suppose that this pattern of thought is typically priestly, for it derives the essence of the people and the land from their relationship to God and his sanctuary; all the parallels cited by Weinfeld come from the sacral sphere (sanctuary cities, etc.).   .

If this is a tolerably exact description of the understanding of the Exodus found in H, it is easy to see why the theme is so pervasive; in fact, the theme of the Exodus underpins the entire discourse of H. The obedience to the commandments, the relationship between YHWH and the people, the dignity of the Israelites, the special status of the land, the

---

[25] The Exodus is explicitly interpreted in these terms in Ex 6:6-8.

[26] Contrast Crüsemann, "Exodus", 124-127.

[27] The whole conception has been well appreciated by Levenson in a remark on Lev 25, cf. J. D. Levenson, *The Hebrew Bible, the Old Testament, and Historical Criticism. Jews and Christians in Biblical Studies* (Louisville, 1993), p. 144: "The image that Leviticus 25 evokes is that of Israel as a huge temple estate, worked by people who are in the simultaneously exalted and humble role of slaves consecrated to their God, humble because they are only slaves, exalted because they have been chosen for service to the God of the universe."

punishment in the event of disobedience and YHWH's continuing faithfulness in spite of it—there is not one single subject treated in H which is not directly connected in some way with that momentous event from the past.

4.2 THE RELATIONSHIP BETWEEN YHWH AND ISRAEL

If the Exodus is the basis of the discourse in H, the relationship between YHWH and the Israelites is its centre. Already, the preceding section has demonstrated that this relationship was thought of in very precise terms, analogous to inter-human law and custom. However, the slave/master metaphor is not the only conception of the bond between God and his people; several other elements come into play on this point. Each of these will be reviewed in the present section.

The covenant formula

YHWH's stated purpose to be the Israelites' God (*lihyōt lākem lēʾlōhīm* 22:33; cf. 25:38; 26:45) is entirely comprehensible in the conceptual framework described above in 4.1. In scholarly literature, however, it is usually included in a discussion of the so-called covenant formula, of which it is said to be the first member. The complete formula is found once in H:

26:12   והייתי לכם לאלהים ואתם תהיו לי לעם

And I will be your God, and you shall be my people.

With slight variations, this formula is attested 19 times in the OT, to which are usually added nine cases where only the first member is found (YHWH will be Israel's God), and nine instances of the second member (Israel will be YHWH's people).[28]

---

[28] See N. Lohfink, "Dt 26,17-19 und die "Bundesformel"", in idem, *Studien zum Deuteronomium und zur deuteronomistischen Literatur I*, SBAB 8 (Stuttgart, 1990), 211-261, p. 211. For the different variations of the formula, see R. M. Good, *The Sheep of His Pasture. A Study of the Hebrew Noun ʿAm(m) and Its Semitic Cognates*, HSM 29 (Chico, 1983), 65f.

Because of its abundant attestations and its obvious theological weight, the formula has become easy prey for traditio-historical treatment. Scholars have expended considerable effort to determine which of the two parts of the statement is the earlier, whether the two-member proposition is early or late, what its original *Sitz im Leben* may have been—if it was not just a literary creation—and how it was transmitted in different milieux from the moment it was first coined.[29] In spite of abundant data, however, the theories that have been proposed remain extremely speculative. Moreover, it must be said that in most of these studies the priestly attestations of the formula have received a very perfunctory treatment.[30] What can, in my opinion, reasonably be concluded with regard to the tradition history of the formula is, firstly, that it is indeed traditional; the numerous occurrences in the books of Ezekiel and Jeremiah, in particular, point in this direction. Secondly, the fact that where only one member is quoted, priestly writings invariably render the first clause whereas the Deuteronomic and Deuteronomistic literature always have the second clause, shows that neither school borrowed the formula from the other.[31] Thirdly, the systematic variation of the formula in Deuteronomy, whereby a further specification is attached to the noun "people", is a clear sign that in Deuteronomic circles the formula was adapted to the dominant election-theology.[32] In light of these conclusions, it would seem that the priestly attestations merit close attention in their own right.

More certainty obtains with regard to the meaning of the clause. It has been correctly observed that it exhibits a certain similarity with formulas of adoption and marriage. A full parallel is found in the divine declaration of adoption of the Davidide:

2 Sam 7:14   אני אהיה לו לאב והוא יהיה לי לבן

I will be his father, and he shall be my son.[33]

---

[29] See R. Smend, "Die Bundesformel", in idem, *Die Mitte des Alten Testaments. Gesammelte Studien Band 1* (München, 1986), 11-39; Lohfink, Good (see the preceding note). Criticisms in L. Perlitt, *Bundestheologie im Alten Testament*, WMANT 36 (Neukirchen, 1969), 102-115.

[30] The most extensive treatment of the priestly attestations is that of Smend, "Bundesformel", 35f.

[31] Compare, e.g., Lev 11:45 with Deut 4:20, see Smend, "Bundesformel", 13.

[32] See A. Rofé, *Introduction*, 182f.

[33] Other examples: 1 Chron 17:13; 22:10; 28:6; Jer 31:9; Ex 2:10.

For the analogy with the words spoken at a wedding, Hos 2:4 is usually referred to ("she is not my wife, and I am not her husband"),[34] but other parallels may be found that are grammatically closer, e.g.

Gen 24:67   ויבאה יצחק האהלה שרה אמו ויקח את רבקה
                     ותהי לו לאשה

Then Isaac brought her into the tent, and took Rebekah, and she be-came his wife.

Though this is a narrative and not a declaration, we find here the same construction *hyh l-* x *l-* y as in the covenant formula.[35]

Usually, these are the only analogies cited,[36] and the inference is drawn that by the use of the formula, the founding of the relationship between YHWH and his people is pictured as an adoption or a wed-ding.[37] However, what is characteristic of the formula of adoption is the word-pair "father—son", and of that of marriage the word-pair "man—wife"; when these words are absent there is no reason whatsoever to see in the naked grammatical structure of the formula an allusion to adop-tion or marriage.[38] This point is further underscored by some other par-allels, which have not yet been brought to bear on our subject. In Jud 17 the story is told of a wandering Levite who is engaged as a priest by a certain Micah:

Jud 17:10   ויאמר לו מיכה שבה עמדי והיה לי לאב ולכהן
                     ואנכי אתן לך עשרת כסף לימים וערך בגדים ומחיתך

And Micah said to him, "Stay with me, and be to me a father and a priest, and I will give you ten pieces of silver a year, and a suit of apparel, and your living."

Clearly what is here expressed by the construction *hyh l-* x *l-* y is the drawing-up of a type of contract. Admittedly, the second member of the

---

[34] Marriage contracts from Elephantine are also viewed as a parallel, see Lohfink, "Dt 26, 17-19", 214.

[35] Other examples: Gen 20:12; Num 36:11.

[36] Good has proposed the analogy of a tribe adopting a client, see Good, *Sheep*, 82-85. The parallel in Ruth 1:16f is remote, however. Moreover, it is not clear to me how YHWH could be compared to a client (in spite of Jer 14:8).

[37] See in particular Lohfink, "Dt 26, 17-19", 213f. Criticisms in Good, *Sheep*, 81f.

[38] Moreover, it is unlikely that the covenant formula would allude to both adoption and marriage all at once, since these institutions are quite different from one another.

contract is absent; or rather, it is represented by the commitment of
Micah to pay a fixed salary. Nevertheless, in my opinion, this example is
on a par with the adoption formula quoted above. In both cases, a precisely defined relationship is instituted.[39]

We now turn to our last example. Jacob, on his way to Mesopotamia,
has seen God in a dream and having woken up he makes the vow that if
God will keep him on his journey there and back, then he will serve him:

Gen 28:21   ...וְהָיָה יְהוָה לִי לֵאלֹהִים

...then the LORD shall be my God.[40]

This clause is, of course, very similar to the first member of the covenant formula—and to my mind it must be included in any discussion of
the topic.[41] However, confining ourselves to the meaning of the clause
in its immediate context, what we may definitely say is that it is Jacob's
solemn declaration of his intention to enter into a precise type of relationship with YHWH. What these examples show is that the construction *hyh l*- x *l*- y is a very general expression which is used to establish
a type of contract between two individuals, or between an individual
and a god. Or between a god and a people. Since "covenant" may indeed
be understood in the sense of such contract, the term "covenant formula" proves to be quite adequate, at least with regard to its occurrence
in H.

One might object that, among the parallels, it is only the adoption
formula that expresses the reciprocal relationship by using two balanced
clauses. The dual structure is not, however, an essential characteristic of
the covenant formula; either one of the two clauses may be used to define the whole god/people relationship. Nor is the twofold structure essential to express adoption; as with the covenant formula, either the first
clause (Jer 31:9) or the second (Ex 2:10) is sufficient to express the
contract. The balancing of two complementary—almost tautological—
statements merely serves to add solemnity to the declaration. The adoption formula is illuminating as an analogy, but it is not necessary to sup-

---

[39] Yet another parallel is 1 Sam 27:12 *wᵉhāyāh lī lᵉˤebed ˤōlām* "he shall be my
servant always"—i.e. my vassal, see Kalluveettil, *Declaration*, 165.

[40] Rofé regards Gen 28:21 as an instance of the covenant formula, see Rofé, *Introduction*, 182.

[41] It is included only by Rofé (see the preceding note) and Good, *Sheep*, 65, n. 1.

pose that the covenant formula was modelled upon it, or alludes to it in any way.[42]

The god/people relationship defined by the covenant formula in Lev 26:12 may be further specified. Several facts indicate that it is identical with the relationship instituted by the act of the Exodus (see section 4.1.). The first part of the formula "I will be your God" should not be divorced from the infinitive phrase "to be your God" which is joined several times to references to the Exodus (22:33; 25:38; cf. 26:45 "to be their God"), particularly since this infinitive phrase also employs the construction *hyh l- x l- y*. What had been YHWH's objective when he led the Israelites out of Egypt is recapitulated in extended form in the covenant formula. Confirmation of this view is afforded by the reference to the Exodus in 26:13, immediately following the covenant formula in 26:12.[43] We may conclude that the use of the covenant formula in H links up with the thought-complex attached to the Exodus event. The god YHWH acquired a group of worshippers by liberating the Israelites from slavery in Egypt, whom he intended to settle on his land so that they might serve him in his sanctuary and in their daily lives.

What is new in the covenant formula is that the group of worshippers is called a "people" (*'am*). Good has suggested that in the priestly attestations of the covenant formula, the noun should be taken in the sense of "congregation".[44] He opposes the priestly examples to Deut 14:2 "the LORD has chosen you to be a people for his own possession (*lihyōt lō lᵉ'am sᵉgullāh*), out of all the peoples that are on the face of the earth", where the opposition with the other peoples shows that the entire people of Israel is meant. In view of what was said in 4.1. above, the rendering "congregation" would seem to be defensible. Nevertheless, the conclusions to Chapter 3 illustrate that this congregation was thought of as a people, i.e. an ethnically defined entity. This is confirmed by what looks like an amputated instance of the second member of the covenant formula:

20:26   והייתם לי קדשים כי קדוש אני יהוה ואבדיל אתכם מן העמים
להיות לי

---

[42] Rofé has deduced from the marriage and adoption analogies that the idea underlying the covenant formula is that of monolatry as opposed to monotheism, see Rofé, *Introduction*, 182. However, if the formula is not necessarily to be seen in the light of these institutions, Rofé's inference is not compelling.

[43] Cf. Ex 6:6f.

[44] Good, *Sheep*, 68.

You shall be holy to me; for I the LORD am holy, and have separated
you from the peoples, that you should be mine.

Here we find the same opposition to the other peoples as in Deut 14:2,[45]
which shows that the group YHWH separated for himself is thought of
as a people. Israel's peoplehood precedes, logically, its association with
YHWH. However, the absolute "that you should be mine" (lihyōt lī) is
indeed remarkable; one would expect "that you should be my people"
(lihyōt lī le'am). Maybe this remarkable wording was used to avoid any
suggestion of kinship between YHWH and Israel.[46] In the two-member
formula there was no risk of such an ambiguity, since the first member
clearly defined the type of relationship.

A possible objection to the view developed here, that the covenant
formula refers to the relationship instituted at the Exodus, is that 26:12
is formulated in the future tense. In fact, it is the apodosis to the condition set in 26:3 "If you walk in my statutes and observe my commandments and do them..."; if the Exodus and the relationship it inaugurated
are elsewhere looked upon as events of the past, how can it now be said
"I *will be* your God, and you *shall be* my people"?[47] Does not the use of
the future tense indicate that a different relationship is being thought of,
one that has not yet been established, but will be if the Israelites obey the
commandments? I do not think that such an interpretation is feasible.
Rather, the discrepancy between the past and future tenses must be
taken to mean that if the Israelites obey the commandments, the relationship between them and YHWH will blossom: If you obey me, I will
indeed be your God, and you my people. From what follows in Lev 26,
it transpires that if Israel will not obey, YHWH will nevertheless remain

---

[45] On the basis of the idea of election and the use of the root *bdl* (hiphil) as in 1 Ki
8:53, Thiel holds that Lev 20:24, 26 indicates influence of the Deuteronomistic tradition; see Thiel, *Erwägungen*, 72. Note, however, that the typically Deuteronomic root
bhr is absent from H and that whereas *bdl* is frequent in priestly texts, it is unattested in
Deuteronomic literature except 1 Ki 8:53. A priestly author, such as the author of H, is
therefore more likely than a Deuteronomistic one to have inaugurated this use of the root
bdl.

[46] Note that the expressions "people of YHWH", "my/your/his people" are absent
from the laws in P and H, see N. Lohfink, "Beobachtungen zur Geschichte des
Ausdrucks יהוה עם", in H. W. Wolff, Hsg., *Probleme biblischer Theologie*, Fs G. von Rad
(München, 1971), 275-305, p. 279. These expressions could easily be interpreted in the
sense of kinship between YHWH and the people, see A. Hulst, THAT II, 303.

[47] Lohfink,"Beobachtungen", 297, has argued that *hyh l-* must be translated "to become". See against this, Hulst, THAT II, 305.

their God: he will punish them severely and then again take pity on them (26:44f).[48]

The covenant

The term $b^e r\bar{\imath}t$ occurs nine times in H.[49] The etymology of the noun is obscure, and its sense controversial.[50] The occurrences of the term which refer to a relationship between YHWH and a human party, a "covenant", set apart the priestly literature, which knows only the covenants of Abraham and Noah,[51] from the rest of the Pentateuch,[52] where the term refers almost exclusively to the covenant of Horeb-Sinai.[53] Interestingly, most of the occurrences in H seem to side with non-priestly texts in situating the $b^e r\bar{\imath}t$ after the Exodus.

The covenant in non-priestly texts

The word $b^e r\bar{\imath}t$, and more particularly the origins and background of the concept of a "covenant" between YHWH and Israel, have been the subject of much controversy. Schematically, one may distinguish two pronounced views (though many scholars have adopted a mediating position). On the one hand, there are those scholars who hold that the OT notion of a "covenant" with God was a literary invention of Israelite theologians attempting to parry the criticisms of the prophets, while incorporating the essential points of the prophetical message.[54] On the other hand are those who connect OT "covenant theology" with the birth of the Israelite nation and explain most of its features in the light of Ancient Near Eastern parallels like the vassal treaty and the covenant of

---

[48] Cf. v 11 "and I will make my abode among you"—stated as already having happened in Ex 40:34ff. For v 9, see below, pp. 115-117.

[49] Lev 24:8; 26:9, 15, 25, 42, 42, 42, 44, 45.

[50] For the etymology, see E. Kutsch, THAT I, 339-352; M. Weinfeld, TWAT I, 781-808. For the semantic opacity of the word, J. Barr, "Some Semantic Notes on the Covenant", in H. Donner et al., Hsg., *Beiträge zur alttestamentlichen Theologie*, Fs W. Zimmerli (Göttingen, 1977), 23-38.

[51] A priestly text mentioning the covenant of Sinai is Ex 31:16. It seems likely that this text was influenced by H (Knohl attributes it to his Holiness School).

[52] The most important texts are Ex 20-24; Ex 34; Deuteronomy. Cf. also Jos 24.

[53] An exception is Gen 15.

[54] An influential exponent of this view is L. Perlitt; his ideas were conveyed to the English-speaking world by E. W. Nicholson. For bibliography, see TWAT.

grant.[55] Though the first position is not entirely devoid of justification, it seems to me that the second view is to be preferred on methodological grounds.

Whatever the precise meaning of the word $b^e r\bar{\imath}t$, its use in referring to a fairly well defined political concept should not be in doubt. The importance of this concept can be proven without reference to extra-biblical material: suffice it to point to the passages in the OT where the $b^e r\bar{\imath}t$ is confined to the human sphere. A $b^e r\bar{\imath}t$ is concluded between a clan of semi-nomads and a city-state (Gen 26:26-31);[56] between the Israelites and a Canaanite clan (Josh 9); between two kings (1 Ki 5:26); between a monarch and his subjects (2 Sam 5:3).[57] In all these examples the word refers to a bond or a treaty instituted between the two parties in question. As might be expected with regard to a political reality which expressly, though not exclusively, concerns international relations, the practice of treaty-making evinced by the OT, in all its variety, with its customs, terminology and ideology, enjoys numerous parallels in Mesopotamian, Hittite and Ugaritic texts.[58] Thorough study of this whole complex has led to a fairly definite idea of what a "covenant" implied in Israel's historical environment. Briefly, the following characteristics of the concept may be mentioned: (a) it would usually involve two parties of different standing, with the more powerful of the two dictating its terms; (b) in most cases, both parties would take on certain obligations, though in some cases only the weaker party's obligations are spelled out; (c) two complementary notions—expressed by different terms, but inherent in every treaty established—constitute the base of the relationship, namely, obligation or commitment on the one hand, and loyalty and love on the other.[59] This type of relationship is covered by the English word covenant.

---

[55] This view is argued by D. J. McCarthy, M. Weinfeld and many others. For bibliography, see TWAT.

[56] A striking Ancient Near Eastern parallel to the making of the pact in Gen 26:26-31 is signalled by J. D. Safren, "Ahuzzath and the Pact of Beer-Sheba", ZAW 101 (1989), 184-198.

[57] Note also the pacts between Jacob and Laban (Gen 31:44) and between David and Jonathan (1 Sam 18:3), which contain a strong political element. In Prov 2:17 and Mal 2:14, however, the term designates the marriage relationship. See for these latter texts G. P. Hugenberger, *Marriage as Covenant. A study of Biblical Law and Ethics Governing Marriage Developed from the Perspective of Malachi*, SVT 52 (Leiden, 1994).

[58] See M. Weinfeld, TWAT I, 781-808; Kalluveettil, *Declaration*.

[59] Kutsch has argued in many publications that $b^e r\bar{\imath}t$ means not "covenant" but "stipulation" or "obligation"—i.e. it refers to the obligation taken on by a stronger party with regard to a weaker party, or imposed on the weaker party by the stronger one. His methodology has been much criticized, see, e.g., Barr, "Semantic Notes", 37. Weinfeld has correctly pointed out that the obligations taken on or imposed in a $b^e r\bar{\imath}t$ presuppose a strong and dependable relationship.

It would be a grave mistake to divorce the OT picture of inter-human treaty-making from its Ancient Near Eastern background. It is equally indefensible, however, to separate the human $b^e r\bar{\imath} t$ from the $b^e r\bar{\imath} t$ between God and his people. To all appearances, the OT "covenant theology" was born when the political concept of a human covenant was projected into the spriritual realm and applied to the relationship between YHWH and Israel. To a large extent, the terminology and concepts which are used to describe the covenant between YHWH and Israel are identical with the terms and customs occurring in secular contexts. If, therefore, covenant theology in the OT requires to be seen in the light of the non-theological examples of covenant-making in the OT, and secular covenant-making in the OT in the light of the ANE parallels, then the relevance of the ANE parallels for OT covenant theology is undeniable. Indeed, many expressions occurring in the OT only in theological contexts, have parallels in Ancient Near Eastern accounts of inter-human covenants.[60]

Nevertheless, the concept of a covenant between a deity and a people is unique to the OT.[61] It must, therefore, be submitted that although most of the terms used in OT covenant theology were borrowed from secular covenant terminology in vogue in the ANE, they underwent an important transformation.[62] On this point, the scholars who attempt to explain covenant theology as a development peculiar to the OT are partly correct: the biblical notion of a covenant between YHWH and Israel must be studied in its own right, though not in isolation from the ANE context.

The main political concept that was transposed into the human/divine sphere to produce the covenant theology of the non-priestly sources is that of the vassal-treaty. YHWH is viewed as the great overlord, comparable to the Hittite or Assyrian kings, and Israel as the vassal state; a treaty document—called "Book of the Covenant" ($s\bar{e}per$ $habb^e r\bar{\imath} t$)—is established, the contours of which can still be recognized in the OT law collections (see in Chapter 2 above); both parties take on certain obligations: the overlord promises to protect his vassal and give

---

[60] Weinfeld, TWAT I, 781-808.

[61] For some possible parallels from the Ancient Near East, see K. Kitchen, "Egypt, Ugarit, Qatna and the Covenant", *UF* 11(1979), 453-464, pp. 462 and 463; J. C. de Moor, *The Rise of Yahwism*, BEThL 91 (Leuven, 1990), 257-259.

[62] See, for Deuteronomy, N. Lohfink, "Die Wandlung des Bundesbegriffs im Buch Deuteronomium", in H. Vorgrimler, Hsg., *Gott in Welt*, Fs K. Rahner, Bd I (Freiburg, 1964), 423-444.

him land, the vassal promises unwavering loyalty and obedience to all the suzerain's commandments. Disloyalty on Israel's side might take the form of political reliance on other, earthly powers, or more particularly of religious apostasy.[63] It has rightly been remarked that the underlying theological idea is that of monolatry rather than monotheism: many gods exist, but Israel's covenant is with this particular god. This complex of notions is found in several passages, particularly in Ex 19-24; 34:10-26 and Josh 24. In Deuteronomy it is adapted to the monotheistic outlook of its authors, in which process the concept of a covenant is changed almost beyond recognition.[64]

For it to be received and transformed by the Deuteronomic school, covenant theology had to be part of Israel's older theological traditions. An early date for the concept of a covenant between YHWH and Israel has been cogently argued from detailed exegesis of OT passages where *berīt* plays an important part,[65] as well as from comparisons with ANE terminology and practices.[66]

Covenant theology in P

Scholarly discussions of the *berīt* in priestly literature have not centred on questions of background and provenance of the concept,[67] but on a different problem. Whereas the other pentateuchal sources, and especially the book of Deuteronomy, situate the covenant in the wake of the Exodus, the priestly code makes no reference to a covenant established in the time of Moses.[68] Rather, it accentuates the covenant with Abraham (Gen 17),[69] and recounts the making of a covenant about which the other sources are silent, namely that between God and Noah and "every living creature of all flesh" (Gen 9:1-16). Why is the "cov-

---

[63] These two forms would often coincide, see, e.g. Ex 34:15f, where a covenant with the original inhabitants is said to lead to apostasy.

[64] Lohfink, "Wandlung"; Rofé, *Introduction*, 276.

[65] For Ex 19:3-6 see J. C. de Moor, *The Rise of Yahwism* (Leuven, 1990), 164-168; for Ex 34, see J. Halbe, *Das Privilegrecht Jahwes Ex 34,10-26. Gestalt und Wesen, Herkunft und Wirken in vordeuteronomischen Zeit*, FRLANT 114 (Göttingen, 1975); for Josh 24, see W. T. Koopmans, *Joshua 24 as Poetic Narrative*, JSOTS 93 (1990), esp. 128-141. See also, more generally, N. Lohfink, art. "Bund", in M. Görg, B. Lang, Hsg., Neues Bibel-Lexicon, Bd I (Zürich, 1991), 344-348, in part. coll. 345-346.

[66] Weinfeld, TWAT I, 781-808.

[67] See, however, the interesting study of Külling on the covenant in Gen 17, in S. R. Külling, *Zur Datierung der "Genesis-P-Stücke". Namentlich des Kapitels Genesis XVII* (Kampen, 1964).

[68] For Ex 31:16, see above, n. 51.

[69] Cf. Gen 15, which is not easily attributable to one of the sources.

enant at Sinai" absent from P? Zimmerli provided an answer that has remained uncontested almost to this day.[70] In his view, the covenant at Sinai was omitted from P's account of the history of Israel because its author wanted to eliminate the idea, dominant in the earlier sources (among which Zimmerli counts H), that the relationship between YHWH and Israel was conditioned by Israel's obedience to the commandments. Instead of the covenant at Sinai, with its proclamation of laws followed by blessings and curses, it is the covenant with Abraham—a covenant of promise (*Verheißungsbund*), of pure grace (*Gnadenbund*)—which is given pride of place in the priestly version of the history of the people of Israel; what then follows is no more than the fulfilment of the promises made to Abraham.[71] By thus shifting the theological accent from the law to God's grace, the priestly authors attempted to provide a response to the preaching of the prophets and the catastrophe of exile: the foundation of Israel's existence is not its obedience to the law, but God's eternal grace.[72]

In his dissertation, Knohl has proposed a different approach to this problem.[73] He criticizes Zimmerli for distorting the data: firstly, in P's account the covenant with Abraham was not merely a promise of God, but implied an obligation on Abraham;[74] and secondly it is wrong to ascribe to P a theology of pure grace when it so much emphasizes the need for exact observance of YHWH's commandments. In Knohl's view, the relationship established between Israel and YHWH after the Exodus was meant by P to be complementary to the covenant between God and Abraham. What God demanded of Abraham when he established his covenant with him was to "walk before him and be blameless"

---

[70] W. Zimmerli, "Sinaibund und Abrahambund. Ein Beitrag zum Verständnis der Priesterschrift", in idem, *Gottes Offenbarung. Gesammelte Aufsätze*, Theologische Bücherei, AT 19 (München, 1963), 205-216. On pp. 213f, Zimmerli discusses some earlier solutions to this problem.

[71] Cf. J. J. P. Valeton, "Bedeutung und Stellung des Wortes ברית im Priestercodex", *ZAW* 12 (1892), 1-22.

[72] A very different view has been advanced by Crüsemann, who ascribes all mentions of the covenant in the Sinai pericope to a late, post-priestly, deuteronomistic redaction: if the notion of the covenant at Sinai didn't yet exist in his time, the priestly redactor could not have omitted it from his work. Cf. Crüsemann, *Tora*, 63-65. Elsewhere in his book (*Tora*, 343), however, Crüsemann contradicts his earlier statement and says that the conception of a covenant was found in the pre-priestly passage Ex 34:10ff.

[73] Knohl, *Sanctuary*, 143-144, n. 80.

[74] The words *hithallēk lᵉpānāy wehyēh tāmīm wᵉʾettᵉnāh bᵉrītī bēnī ubēnekā* (Gen 17:1f) imply that "to walk before YHWH and to be blameless" are covenant conditions imposed on Abraham.

(Gen 17:1), i.e. to be morally irreproachable—in the image of Noah
(Gen 6:9). On the other hand, the relationship established at the Exodus
was not centred on morality but instead served a different purpose: the
laws of P confront the Israelites with the numinous presence of YHWH.
Not morality, but awe of the holy is the rationale of the laws given at
Sinai and from the tent of meeting. Characteristic for the new relationship is the term ʿēdūt, which—unlike the bilateral bᵉrīt—refers to an
obligation imposed by a stronger party on its weaker ally. In this view of
P, the tradition of the covenant at Sinai was not omitted or passed over
but transformed in a particular, typically priestly way.

Knohl's reconstruction of P's thought-world is in places quite hypothetical and tentative. He does, however, lay bare some real weaknesses
in Zimmerli's theory. The absence of the word bᵉrīt from P's account of
events at Mount Sinai does not imply a denial that any new relationship
was established at that time. The numerous innovations, such as the revelation of the name YHWH, the establishment of an earthly dwelling-
place for the godhead and the institution of a system of sacrificial worship, cannot be viewed solely as a continuation of the covenant with
Abraham. On the positive side, Knohl does well to introduce the notion
of the holy presence of YHWH, for the fact that YHWH dwells among
his people is indeed central to P.[75] Moreover, in Zimmerli's construction, no place is left in P for an imposition of moral laws on the people of
Israel: the covenant with Abraham was based on pure grace, and its fulfilment in the time of Moses leads to the institution of the cult. It is
preferable to share Knohl's view that in P's vision, the requirement of
morality—though not expressed in a collection of laws—was imposed
once and for all at the time of the Patriarchs, leaving the time of Moses
free for demands of a different order.

The covenant in H

Where does H stand in all this? In order to confront the data in H with
the covenant theologies of the priestly and non-priestly passages, we
need to take a close look at the passages mentioning the term. Most
relevant are the five passages in Lev 26 where the word clearly refers to
the relationship instituted after the Exodus. In one verse the word bᵉrīt
is explicitly connected with the Exodus:

---

[75] This point is somewhat controversial, see the discussion in 5.1. below.

26:45 וזכרתי להם ברית ראשנים אשר הוצאתי אתם מארץ מצרים
לעיני הגוים להיות להם לאלהום אני יהוה

But I will for their sake remember the covenant with their forefathers,
whom I brought forth out of the land of Egypt in the sight of the
nations, that I might be their God: I am the LORD.

At the end of the list of curses in 26:16ff, a number of verses are added
which affirm the continuing faithfulness of YHWH towards his people
even after the most severe of punishments (26:42, 44f). The mention of
the Exodus is expected in this context: when YHWH acquired the Israelites to be his slaves, this was meant to be a permanent arrangement; one
does not release a slave because he is disobedient. Moreover, the honour
of YHWH is at stake. This last thought is expressed by the words "in the
sight of the nations", which correspond to a well-known motif in the
Books of Exodus and Ezekiel (e.g. Ex 32:12; Ez 20:44). YHWH is still
entitled to occupy himself with his people after he has punished them;
moreover, his honour obliges him to do so. Both notions are rooted in
the Exodus event.[76]

Less evident is the use of the term *rī'šōnīm* "former persons, men of
old" to refer to the Exodus generation.[77] In the fiction of H, the generation of the Exodus is the one standing in front of Moses, so strictly
speaking "men of old" designates the audience. Even if we take account
of the use of the third person—the discourse shifts from "you" (up to v
35) through "those of you that are left" (vv 36 and 39) to "they" (vv
40ff)—which presumably refers to a later generation than the ones addressed, this designation is odd. It seems that we have here one more
instance of the "contemporizing" tendency which we found elsewhere
in H (see above, pp. 46-47). The fiction is abandoned and the generation
of the Exodus is revealed for what it really is in the eyes of the author
and the audience of H, namely their ancestors.

What is most striking, however, is that the relationship instituted at
the Exodus is here called *bᵉrīt* . According to our description in 4.1.

---

[76] This train of thought implies that 26:39-45, describing Israel's plight and YHWH's
continued sollicitude in exile, need not be a later addition; even barring direct inspiration, the notion might well have been arrived at by deduction: the relationship instituted
at the Exodus could not be definitively perturbed by disobedience of the Israelites.

[77] The term occurs in the same form (without definite article), with the same meaning
and involving the same anachronism in Deut 19:14 "You shall not remove your neighbour's landmark, which the men of old have set." The contexts, however, are very different.

above, the relationship resulting from the Exodus event is viewed, meta-
phorically, as a social bond between a master and his slaves, and realistically as a sacral bond between a God and his worshippers. The image
of an overlord and his vassal does not fit into that picture. In view of our
earlier considerations, therefore, we must suppose either that the conception of the relationship between YHWH and Israel emerging in this
verse diverges from the conception described in 4.1, or that H's conception of the *bᵉrīt* is not that of the non-priestly sources. Support for the
former view, that the covenant between YHWH and his people is modelled on political treaties, may perhaps be found in 26:25 "And I will
bring a sword upon you, that shall execute vengeance for the covenant"
(*wᵉhēbē'ti ᶜᵃlēkem ḥereb nōqemet nᵉqam bᵉrīt*), an expression that is
usually taken to call up the punitive actions executed by the suzerain on
his vassal in case of treason.[78] Unfortunately, however, this meaning is
less than certain,[79] though one is hard-pressed to find an alternative interpretation.

Three other verses in Lev 26 tip the scales in favour of the other possibility, however. They show that the term *bᵉrīt* does not imply the image of the vassal treaty.

26:9   ופניתי אליכם והפריתר אתכם והרביתי אתכם
                                                      והקימתי את בריתי אתכם

And I will have regard for you and make you fruitful and multiply
you, and will establish my covenant with you.[80]

26:15   ואם בחקתי תמאסו ואם את משפטי תגעל נפשכם לבלתי
                                      ...עשות את כל מצותי להפרכם בריתי

If you spurn my statutes, and if your soul abhors my ordinances, so
that you will not do all my commandments, but break my covenant...

---

[78] See the extensive discussion of this passage in H. G. L. Peels, *The Vengeance of
God. The Meaning of the Root NQM and the Function of the NQM-Texts in the Context
of Divine Revelation in the Old Testament*, OTS 31 (Leiden, 1995), 103-109.

[79] In the Aramaic treaty from Sfire (see KAI 224), the root *nqm* occurs twice, first in
a call to Mati'el of Arpad to avenge his overlord should he be murdered (Sefire II, 11f),
and then in the asseveration that if Mati'el becomes involved in murdering his overlord,
the latter will be avenged (Sefire III, 22). These instances accord with the biblical use of
the root *nqm*. They do not, however, throw much light on Lev 26:25.

[80] RSV "and will confirm my covenant with you."

26:44   ואף גם זאת בהיותם בארץ איביהם לא מאסתים
ולא געלתים לכלתם להפר בריתי אתם

Yet for all that, when they are in the land of their enemies, I will not
spurn them, neither will I abhor them so as to destroy them utterly
and break my covenant with them.

Note that in all these verses the covenant is defined not by reference to
the human partner (as in *bᵉrīt rī'šōnīm*) but, by the use of the first person
suffix, to YHWH.

The expression used in 26:9, *hēqīm bᵉrīt*, is typical of priestly writings though it occurs elsewhere as well (Gen 6:18; 9:9, 11; 17; 17:7, 19,
21; Ex 6:4; Ez 16:60, 62; Deut 8:18). It has been variously interpreted as
"to establish", "to keep" or "to fulfil" a covenant, and indeed each of
these renderings seems to be justified.[81] In the precise terminology of
the priestly writings, however, the meaning of the expression seems to
be more narrowly defined. An interesting terminological parallel is
found in the laws on vows by women:

Num 30:14   כל נדר וכל שבעת אסר לענת נפש
אישה יקימנו ואישה יפרנו

Any vow and any binding oath to afflict herself, her husband may
establish, or her husband may make void.

Here the verb *qwm* (hiphil) refers neither to the making nor to the keeping of the vow, both of which are done by the woman. Rather, the meaning seems to be "to ratify, to validate": a woman may take a vow, but it is
left to her husband to make it officially binding. On this analogy, we
may interpret the expression *hēqīm bᵉrīt* in the sense: "to ratify a covenant" or, seeing that when YHWH is the subject no separate ratification
is necessary, "to make a covenant that is officially binding". This meaning fits all the occurrences in P.[82] There is no reason to suppose that a
different meaning is intended in Lev 26:9. If the Israelites obey, YHWH
will establish his binding covenant with them. The future tense must be

---

[81] For "establish" see Gen 9:9, and with *'ēdūt* instead of *bᵉrīt*, Ps 78:5; for "keep" see
Ez 16:60, 62; for "fulfil", Deut 8:18. It is not necessary to postulate that the different
meanings point to a semantic development, or that P did violence to the Hebrew language (against N. Lohfink, "Abänderung", 166f, n. 10).
[82] It may be that P preferred the expression *heqīm bᵉrīt* to *kārat bᵉrīt* because it made
it possible to accentuate the initiative of YHWH, see S. Amsler, THAT II, 640.

interpreted as for the covenant formula discussed above: even though the covenant is already official and binding, YHWH will bring it to fruition if Israel observes the commandments.[83]

The antonym of *hēqîm bᵉrît* occurs in 26:15 and 44: *hēpēr bᵉrît*, "to break, violate the covenant". On the analogy of Num 30:14 quoted above, and in opposition to the priestly understanding of *hēqîm bᵉrît*, the priestly attestations of this idiom may be rendered "to go back on, to annul the covenant". Whereas YHWH's intention is to bless his people, and to "really establish" his covenant with them if they obey his commandments, the Israelites, by not heeding his voice, may annul the covenant (26:15). He himself, however, will not annul the covenant even if his people are rebellious (26:44). Thus these three verses play an important part in structuring Lev 26. Obedience will lead to the covenant being established; disobedience implies the contrary, the annulment of the covenant; human disobedience, however, does not lead to divine unfaithfulness: YHWH will not annul his covenant.

The fact that these statements containing the term *bᵉrît* are so well seated in the general discourse inclines one to the view that the term does not import the image of a vassal-treaty into H, but refers to the god/people relationship discussed above in 4.1. A contextual interpretation of the statements on the covenant confirms this impression. In 26:9-12, the declaration "I will establish my covenant with you" is followed first by a description of material blessings (v 10), and then by the promise "I will make my abode among you" (v 11) and "I will walk among you" followed by the covenant formula (v 12). These promises may be regarded as the content of the covenant, or more exactly as the explicit setting-out of the divine commitments attached to it. The underlying idea is not one of political dependence, but of sacral correlation. In 26:15, the annulment of the covenant at the hands of the Israelites is the result of their disobedience (*lᵉbiltî ᶜᵃśôt ʾet kol miṣwōtāy* "so that you would not do all my commandments"). Not a word is said about treason, neither in the form of worship of other gods,[84] nor of reliance on covenants with wordly powers.[85] In their capacity as YHWH's worshippers, his "slaves", they must do what he commands them; refusing this obedi-

---

[83] Cf. Gen 17:19 where God promises to establish his covenant with Isaac (*wahᵃqîmōtî ʾet bᵉrîtî ʾittô*), although from the start the covenant with Abraham included his descendants (v 7).

[84] Worship of other gods is an important theme in H, see n. 282 in Chapter 3. It is never mentioned, however, in the context of the covenant.

[85] Contrast Deut 7, etc.

ence means invalidating the relationship. Conversely, the annulment of the covenant by YHWH would mean that he would exterminate the Israelites (*lᵉkallōtām* "so as to destroy them").

These considerations cast doubt on the view of Lohfink, who, on the basis of 26:9, 11-13, has advanced the claim that H presents a synthesis of the priestly and the Deuteronomic theologies of the history of Israel.[86] As he points out, these verses take up the most important concepts from such key texts in P as Gen 17, Ex 6:4-7 and Ex 29:43-46: the covenant, the covenant formula, the promises to increase the people and to dwell among them, and the Exodus. However, according to Lohfink, the unconditional promises of P are made in H to depend on the fulfilling of the commandments; the phraseology comes from P, but the theology is that of Dt. In this way, H integrates the older priestly *Grundschrift* into the Deuteronomic theology.[87]

Lohfink's theory is rife with difficulties. To begin with, it depends very heavily on Zimmerli's thesis of P's idea of the covenant, which has been criticized above. Moreover, his delimitation of Pg is today problematic.[88] More specifically, however, it would seem in the light of the our study of the term *bᵉrīt* in Lev 26 that the "Deuteronomic" nature of H's covenant theology is quite doubtful. In spite of a number of apparently Deuteronomic characteristics—the word *bᵉrīt* itself, the introduction of moral commandments in the framework of the covenant at Sinai, the blessings-and-curses chapter following these commandments—it would seem that the notion of covenant in H is wholly its own, and typically priestly at that. When YHWH took the Israelites as his servants, his intention was to settle them on his land and to dwell among them in his sanctuary. The success of the whole undertaking depended on the sanctity of the earthly dwelling of God. Up to this point, the view of H concurs with that of P.[89] Where H goes further than P is the extension of the demand for sanctity to the entire land, and the entire people.[90] Unless this sanctity is respected, and even actively pursued, by the Israelites, it will be impossible for YHWH to remain with them; and since the dwelling of the godhead among his people is an essential part

---

[86] Lohfink, "Abänderung".

[87] Lohfink's proposals have been rejected by Blum, *Komposition*, 325-29.

[88] Cf. Lohfink, "Abänderung", 161, n. 5. If Knohl's view is correct that Ex 6 and Ex 29:42-45 stand under the influence of H, the literary relationship would be the reverse of that suggested by Lohfink. See also Blum, *Komposition*, 328.

[89] For an extensive comparison between P and H on this point see Knohl, *Sanctuary*.

[90] See also below in section 4.3. and Chapter 5.

of the plan, the whole arrangement will thus be jeopardized. It is in this conceptual framework that we must understand the "pseudo-Deuteronomic" elements in H. The moral commandments are aimed at bringing about the sanctity of the people. The blessings and curses also directly proceed from the same doctrine: the presence of the godhead among his people leads to material and spiritual blessings; however, when the people will not obey the commandments this will lead to disruption and eventually to the godhead's departure (26:31) and the undoing of every single provision contained in the original arrangement (notably the provisions for freedom and possession of land). Thus, although that arrangement is called $b^e r\bar{\imath}t$, it seems that this term is given a content entirely in keeping with priestly thought. Influence from, or even polemic against, Deuteronomic ideas are not in evidence.

On a different plane is the mention of the covenant with the Patriarchs at the end of Lev 26:

26:42   וזכרתי את בריתי יעקוב ואף את בריתי יצחק
                        ואף את בריתי אברהם אזכר והארץ אזכר

Then I will remember my covenant with Jacob, and I will remember my covenant with Isaac and my covenant with Abraham, and I will remember the land.

This verse is anomalous on several accounts. The syntactical structure of the phrases $b^e r\bar{\imath}ti$ $ya^{ca}q\bar{o}b$ etc. is not clear; the best solution probably being to take it as an elliptic expression meaning "my covenant with Jacob".[91] The order Jacob—Isaac—Abraham is unique in the entire OT; the reason for the inversion of the normal order is obscure. The sudden mention of the Patriarchs is surprising in the context of H, since elsewhere it is the Exodus event that is looked upon as the origin of the Israelite nation. In 26:45, "the ancestors" are the generation of the Exodus. Some have taken this verse as a later addition, pointing to the fact that v 43 ("...and they shall make amends for their iniquity") links up with verse 41 ("...if then their uncircumcised heart is humbled and they make amends for their iniquity").[92] Note should be taken of the last two words of v 42, however; if the verse is an addition, care was taken to

---

[91] See the comprehensive discussion in König, *Syntax*, 231-236.
[92] E.g. Zimmerli, "Heiligkeit", 509.

anchor it in the context by returning to the theme of v 43 ("But the land...").

Although the reference to the Patriarchs is surprising in H, it is entirely at home in P, where the covenant with the Patriarchs plays an important part (see above). The priestly account of the Exodus is set in motion by the remark "And God remembered his covenant with Abraham, with Isaac and with Jacob" (Ex 2:24).[93] In other traditions, the promises to the Patriarchs are also invoked when Israel has proven unfaithful—often in conjunction, as in Lev 26:42-45, with the motif of the honour of God (Ex 32:13; Deut 9:27; an appeal to the *covenant* with the Patriarchs is made in 2 Ki 13:23). Even if 26:42 is an addition, therefore, it is an appropriate one.

Yet a third usage involving the term *bᵉrīt* is found in the pericope on the shewbread (24:5-9). After the instructions concerning the baking and the piling-up of the bread, and the placing of frankincense upon it as a "memorial portion" (*'azkārāh*), it is stated:

24:8   ביום השבת ביום השבת יערכנו לפני יהוה תמיד
מאת בני ישראל ברית עולם

Every sabbath day Aaron shall set it in order before the LORD continually on behalf of the people of Israel as a covenant forever.

The sense of the word *bᵉrīt* in this verse is not entirely clear.[94] Neither is it apparent—if the word means "covenant"—to which covenant it refers. The expression "eternal covenant" (*bᵉrīt 'ōlām*) also occurs in the priestly account of the covenants with Noah (Gen 9:16) and Abraham (Gen 17:7, 13, 19), in the institution of the sabbath as a "sign" (Ex 31:16), and a number of times outside the Pentateuch (2 Sam 23:5; Isa 24:5; 55:3; 61:8; Jer 32:40; 50:5; Ez 16:60; 37:26; Ps 105:10; 1 Chr 16:17). In light of the priestly attestations, it is tempting to interpret the word *bᵉrīt* in Lev 24:8 metonymically as "sign of the covenant". This meaning is clearly attested in Gen 17: God first institutes circumcision as "a sign of the covenant between me and you" (v 11), and then states "so shall my covenant be in your flesh an everlasting covenant" (v 13). In Ex 31:12-17, the sabbath is first called "a sign between me and you"

---

[93] This verse does not prove that in P *bᵉrīt* is a covenant of pure grace, but merely that the covenant contained a divine promise of faithfulness.

[94] It seems to be paralleled by the word *ḥoq* in v 9. Cf. Ps 50:16; 105:10.

(v 12), then "a perpetual covenant" (v 16), and then again "a sign for ever between me and the people of Israel" (v 17). Moreover, in all three passages (Gen 9 and 17, Ex 31), the notion of the "sign of the covenant" (*'ōt bᵉrīt*) plays an important part. In Gen 9:16 the purpose of the sign is defined as follows: "I will look upon it and remember the everlasting covenant..."

A case could be made for the view that the shewbread fulfills a function similar to that of the "sign of the covenant" in Gen 9. The twelve loaves probably symbolize the twelve tribes of Israel; they are set "before the LORD" (*lipnē yhwh*) to remind him of the covenant.[95] Admittedly, none of these notions is made explicit in this passage, and the exegesis remains, therefore, entirely hypothetical. In any case, this occurrence of the word *bᵉrīt* does not do much to further our understanding of the term in H.

The generations of Israel

The importance in H of the genealogical element has been discussed in Chapter 3: the Israelites are viewed as descendants of a common ancestor, and it is the blood relationship which determines who is an Israelite. An additional manifestation of the genealogical interest is the accentuation of the validity of the relationship between YHWH and the Israelites throughout all their generations.[96] The most explicit statement to this effect occurs in the instructions concerning the feast of booths. "All that are native in Israel shall dwell in booths..." (23:42)

23:43   למען ידעו דרתיכם כי בסכת הושבתי את בני ישראל
                        בהוציאי אותם מארץ מצרים

...that your generations may know that I made the people of Israel dwell in booths when I brought them out of the land of Egypt.

Elsewhere, it is merely stated that a particular commandment is given as a "statute for ever throughout your/their generations" (*ḥuqqat ʿōlām*

---

[95] Cf. the "memorial portion' (*'azkārāh*) mentioned in v 7.
[96] Knohl has pointed to the frequent injunctions to recount the deeds of YHWH to the coming generations in the Holiness School (Ex 10:2; 16:32); see Knohl, *Sanctuary*, 174-175.

leḏōrōtēkem ; 23:14, 21, 31, 41; 24:3; *leḏōrōtām* 17:7).[97] Some laws concerning the priests are said to be valid for the descendants of Aaron throughout their generations (21:17; 22:3). Finally, this concept plays a role in the laws concerning the jubilee year: a house in the city will, after one year, "be made sure in perpetuity to him who bought it throughout his generations" (25:30); in the jubilee year a debt-slave will return to the possession of his fathers (25:41). The theological relevance of these latter examples is less immediate.

That YHWH's claim on the people of Israel should be valid throughout their generations is in keeping with the conception discussed above in 4.1. Since the Israelites have become YHWH's slaves, their children will also belong to him and so on for eternity (cf. 25:46). In view of the fictional nature of H—which is set in the desert period but addresses Israelites of a later generation—it is no exaggeration to state that this notion is ever-present throughout H, even where it is not made explicit.

Another motif that may be mentioned in this connection is that of the guilt of the fathers. The following passage comes towards the end of Lev 26:

26:39f
והנשארים בכם ימקו בעונם בארצת איביכם
ואף בעונת אבתם אתם ימקו
והתודו את עונם ואת עון אבתם
במעלם אשר מעלו בי

And those of you that are left shall pine away in your enemies' lands because of their iniquity; and also because of the iniquities of their fathers they shall pine away like them. But if they confess their iniquity and the iniquity of their fathers in their treachery which they committed against me...

Guilt resulting from disobedience to the divine commandment is transmitted from generation to generation; or rather, the guilt of each successive generation is accumulated until it is exorcised by confession.[98] The notion of guilt contaminating successive generations lies behind many

---

[97] This expression has been identified by Knohl as a mark of the Holiness School, see Knohl, "Priestly Torah", 107-115.
[98] For the function of confession in priestly theology, see J. Milgrom, "The Priestly Doctrine of Repentance", *RB* 82 (1975), 186-205.

OT texts.[99] Dubarle is certainly right to state that it was for the Israelites
"...une constatation qui s'impose et non une affirmation qui aurait un
besoin préalable de preuves."[100] In view of the stress placed on the solidarity of Israel's generations with regard to privilege and responsibility,
it is in no way surprising to find this notion expressed in H.[101] It is unnecessary to suppose, with Scharbert, that the principle of confessing
the sins of the fathers originated in the 7th century from an incorrect
understanding of the preaching of the prophets.[102]

The notion of the "guilt of the fathers" became the focus of an intense
debate during the exile: it seemed unfair to the generation of the exile
that they should be made to bear the punishment for the sins of their
dead fathers.[103] Whereas the deuteronomistic historians upheld the doctrine, and whereas Jeremiah was perplexed by it (Jer 31:28ff), the
prophet Ezekiel forcefully rejected it (Ez 18).[104] Since the idea expressed in Lev 26:39f is precisely what Ezekiel polemicizes against, it is
unlikely that these verses—which stand in the same tradition—[105]
should be later than Ezekiel.[106]

Admittedly, however, some of the latest of OT texts still echo the
motif of the sins of the fathers (Dan 9:16; see also Dan 9:6, 8; Neh
9:34).[107]

---

[99] See the review in A.-M. Dubarle, *Le péché originel dans l'écriture*, Lectio Divina
20 (Paris, 1967²), 25-29. Some Ancient Near Eastern parallels are collected by M.
Weinfeld, *Deuteronomy 1-11*, Anchor Bible (New York, 1991), 298.

[100] Dubarle, *Péché*, 25.

[101] Cf. 20:4f, where the sin of the father is said be visited on himself and on his family.
There is no reason, therefore, to excise the words $w^{e'}\bar{a}p\ ba^{ca}w\bar{o}n\bar{o}t\ {}^{'a}b\bar{o}t\bar{a}m\ {}'itt\bar{a}m$ in
26:39 as a gloss, as is proposed by M. C. A. Korpel, "The Epilogue of the Holiness
Code", in J. C. de Moor and W. G. E. Watson, eds., *Verse in Ancient Near Eastern Prose*,
AOAT 42 (Neukirchen, 1993), 123-150, p. 150.

[102] J. Scharbert, "Unsere Sünden und die Sünden unserer Väter", *BZ NF* 2 (1958), 14-
26.

[103] Cf. Lam 5:7 "Our fathers sinned and are no more; and we bear their iniquities".

[104] Cf. M. Greenberg, Prolegomenon to the reprint of C. C. Torrey, *Pseudo-Ezekiel
and the Original Prophecy* (New York, 1970), XXIV-XXIX.

[105] The expression "to pine away because of the sins of someone" (mqq [niphal] b^e +
$^caw\bar{o}n$ etc.), occurs only in these verses and in Ezekiel.

[106] Against Wellhausen, for whom the fact that Ezekiel reports the expression "to pine
away in one's sins" from the mouth of the exiled (Ez 33:10) is sufficient proof that H
borrowed the expression from Ezekiel; see Wellhausen, *Composition*, 172.

[107] These texts seem to have escaped the attention of L. Rost, "Die Schuld der Väter",
in idem, *Studien zum Alten Testament*, BWANT 101 (Stuttgart, 1974), 66-71, p. 71.

4.3 THE CALL TO HOLINESS

The god/people relationship instituted at the Exodus imposes certain demands on the people of Israel and on each Israelite individually. As has been stated above, the main consequence for the Israelites is that they are beholden to observe the commandments. From the point of view of H, this exigency—the calling of the people—is not so much conceived of in terms of obedience as in terms of holiness: by hearing and doing the commandments of YHWH the Israelites will be holy, as their God is holy.

What is holiness?

Studies on the notion of holiness—in biblical religion or elsewhere—are legion, and many different approaches to the problems connected with it have been essayed.[108] The most fruitful of these is that of R. Otto who defined "the holy" as a category *sui generis*, on a par with such categories as "the good" or "the beautiful". The holy is the divine in its "numinous", non-rational aspect, as real as it is unutterable.[109] Other notions which are sometimes used to define holiness, especially that of separation, do not touch the essence of the term. What is holy must be kept separate from what is not—for the sake of both domains[110]—and in order to approach the holy, a human being must keep himself separate from what is profane or impure; in all these cases, separateness is a secondary aspect.

In the OT, the notion of holiness is expressed by forms of the root *qdš*. Where holiness is attributed to God, this root refers to his unspeakable nature. It is often collocated with forms of the root *kbd* which expresses the glory of God.[111] When humans, objects, times or places are

---

[108] For a general overview, see J. Ries, "Le sacré et l'histoire des religions", in J. Ries et al., éds, *L'expression du sacré dans les grandes religions. I Proche orient ancien et traditions bibliques*, Homo religiosus 1 (Louvain-la-Neuve, 1978), 35-102. For the OT, see M. Gilbert, "Le sacré dans l'Ancien Testament", ibid., 205-289; H.-P. Müller, THAT II, 589-609; W. Kornfeld, H. Ringgren, TWAT VI, 1179-1204 (with bibliography).

[109] R. Otto, *Das Heilige. Über das Irrationale in der Idee des Göttlichen und sein Verhältnis zum Rationalen* (Breslau, 1921⁶; 1st ed. 1917). What is stated by Otto in a general way is true also for Hebrew *qdš* ; the articles in THAT and TWAT quoted in the preceding note follow Otto in all essential matters.

[110] THAT II, 590.

[111] E.g. Isa 6:3; Ex 29:23; Lev 10:3; Ez 28:22.

said to be holy, this puts them in the divine sphere.[112] In this sense, holiness is a relational term; it means "belonging to God, consecrated to God".[113]

In the priestly writings, including H, the notion of holiness is incorporated in a scheme consisting of the terms holy (*qdš*), profane (*ḥll*), pure (*ṭhr*) and impure (*ṭmʾ*). Distinguishing between these four is one of the main tasks of the priest:

Lev 10:10   ולהבדיל בין הקדש ובין החל ובין הטמא ובין הטהור

You are to distinguish between the holy and the common, and between the unclean and the clean.[114]

In order to determine the semantic relations between these terms, one must first distinguish two analogous privative oppositions: "profane" versus "holy", and "pure" versus "impure". The holy and the impure are dynamic qualities which may under certain circumstances extend their influence over the profane and the pure respectively; both holiness and impurity are "contagious".[115] On the other hand, the profane and the pure merely signal the absence of holiness and impurity respectively; they are static qualities, though by certain rites an object or a person may be transferred from the holy to the profane or from the impure to the pure. These two oppositions are related in a peculiar way: the profane may be either pure or impure, and the pure may be either holy or profane, but the holy and the impure are absolutely incompatible. What is impure may never be brought into contact with what is holy.[116]

The requirement to be holy

Although God is presented in H as the source and the absolute measure of holiness, a definition of divine holiness is nowhere to be found. The statement "I the LORD your God am holy" (*qādōš ʾᵃnī yhwh*

---

[112] For some exceptions, see THAT II, 589ff.

[113] Cf. TWAT VI, 1192, "nicht eine Beschaffenheit, sondern ein Verhältnis"; see also M. Buber, *Die Glaube der Propheten* (Zürich, 1950), 183f.

[114] Cf. Ez 22:26; 42:20 and 44:23.

[115] For holiness see Ex 29:37; Num 17:3; for impurity see Lev 21:1-4.

[116] For extensive discussion of the whole semantic field, see Milgrom, *Leviticus 1-16*, 729-732; P. P. Jenson, *Graded Holiness. A Key to the priestly Conception of the World*, JSOTS 106 (Sheffield, 1992), 40-55; Wenham, *Leviticus*, 18-25.

ʾᵒᵉlōhēkem) is a given which does not require explanation. In light of
what has been said above on the unutterable quality of holiness, this
reticence on the part of the authors of H is quite natural. On the other
hand, the requirement of holiness as extended to the priests and to all
Israelites does receive further definition, though much of it is implicit
and can only be recovered by patient reconstruction of the thought-complex underlying the text. We will presently attempt to explore some aspects of this part of H's conceptual universe.[117]

The importance of the sanctuary

The sanctuary plays an important part in H. Not only is it the centre of
the cult, the only legitimate place of worship (17:1-9) where various
rites are performed (24:1-9);[118] it is also the place where YHWH is
present among his people. Thus, one of the most important blessings in
Lev 26 is:

26:11   ונתתי משכני בתוככם

And I will make my abode among you.

This promise certainly refers to the presence of YHWH in the temple
which will be built in the land (Lev 26 speaks to the Israelites as if they
were already established in the land). The holy presence of the
godhead sanctifies the temple,[119] which is therefore called "sanctuary"
(miqdāš). Now, while it is by all means a blessing to have YHWH
dwelling among the people, his presence also implies certain demands
on the priests and the common Israelites, even on the resident aliens
among them. The aim of these demands is to maintain the holiness of
the sanctuary, which is in danger of profanation (desecration).

Profanation of the temple must be avoided at all costs. When one of
his relatives dies, the high priest may therefore not mourn them,

21:12   ומן המקדש לא יצא ולא יחלל את מקדש אלהיו

---

[117] On holiness in the holiness code, see Zimmerli, "Heiligkeit"; Mathys, *Liebe*, 98-
104 (with discussion of earlier literature).
[118] In Lev 23, the expression "before YHWH" (vv 11, 20) and other phrases also refer
to the sanctuary.
[119] This is stated explicitly in 21:23 (cf. Ex 29:43).

He must not leave the sanctuary, so that he does not profane the sanctuary of his God.[120]

Similarly, a priest with a physical deformity may not approach the veil or the altar for fear of desecrating the sanctuary ($w^e l\bar{o}$' $y^e hall\bar{e}l$ 'et $miqd\bar{a}\check{s}ay$,[121] 21:23). The root hll used in these verses probably implies the risk of impurity coming in contact with the holy abode of YHWH. This is at least very likely with regard to the restrictions on mourning imposed on the high priest, since corpses are among the strongest sources of impurity.[122] Strictly speaking, however, this verb means only that the holy is made, or treated as, profane; in other words, it describes only the first step towards impurity (since the profane may become impure).

Even more pernicious, therefore, is outright defilement. This is explicitly referred to only once:

20:3   ...כי מזרעו נתן למלך למען טמא את מקדשי

...because he has given one of his children to Molech, defiling my sanctuary.

Molech-worship generates such powerful impurity that it defiles the temple from afar.[123] Though this particular crime is singled out, it is likely that its connection with defilement of the sanctuary has an exemplary function: crimes of this sort all have the same ruinous effect. This interpretation receives support from the commandment "you shall reverence my sanctuary" ($umiqd\bar{a}\check{s}\bar{\imath}$ $t\bar{\imath}r\bar{a}$'$\bar{u}$) which is repeated twice in H, both times in contexts that are not specifically ritual (19:30; 26:2).[124] In their whole behaviour, the Israelites must show respect for the temple—the earthly abode of their God.

---

[120] This is the translation of Wenham. The RSV does not express the subordinate nature of the clause beginning with $w^e l\bar{o}$' $y^e hall\bar{e}l$.

[121] The plural may be taken to refer to the different parts of the sanctuary, cf. Jer 51:51.

[122] See, e.g., 21:1-4.

[123] See Milgrom, "Picture".

[124] Many scholars have been tempted to interpret the noun $miqd\bar{a}\check{s}$ in these verses in a different sense. Some opinions are collected by Schwartz, *Chapters*, 296, n. 7. Müller, THAT II, 592, takes it in the abstract sense of "holiness". In my opinion there is no valid reason to attribute a different meaning to the word here than in the five other attestations in H.

The ultimate consequence of not respecting the sanctity of the temple is that the godhead will depart from his earthly dwelling; for his holiness is incompatible with impurity. This consequence is spelled out explicitly in the climax to the curses sanctioning disobedience:

26:31   ונתתי את עריכם חרבה והשמותי את מקדשיכם
                                          ולא אריח בריח ניחחכם

And I will lay your cities waste, and will make your sanctuaries desolate,[125] and I will not smell your pleasing odors.

As is aptly remarked by Ehrlich, the verb *šmm* (hiphil), when its direct object is a locality, implies not so much destruction as doing away with the inhabitants.[126] Taken logically, therefore, the present verse states that YHWH will empty the sanctuaries of Israel of their inhabitant, who is of course none other than he himself. However, even if this exegesis be judged too far-fetched, the implication of the "desolation" of the sanctuaries will in any case be that YHWH will no longer dwell there, i.e. that he will no longer make his abode among the Israelites and walk among them (26:11f). The underlying idea, therefore, is that which dominates the first ten chapters of the book of Ezekiel: the sins of the people force the godhead out of his sanctuary.[127] The departure of YHWH from his earthly dwelling among them is the greatest catastrophe that could befall the Israelites, since in this way their whole relationship with their God—and the freedom and the possession of land connected with it—is called into question (cf. 26:32ff).

It is true that 26:31 does not allude to impurity resulting from the sins of Israel, nor does 20:3 specify that defilement of the sanctuary will lead to the departure of the godhead. Yet taken together, the seven passages in H which mention the sanctuary evince an idea that is as precise and logical as it is foreign to our modern ways of thinking. The Israelites who dwell around the tabernacle in the desert, and who are to be settled

---

[125] In this verse, the plural cannot well be interpreted otherwise than as a reference to multiple temples in the land of Israel. Cf. Am 7:9.

[126] Ehrlich, *Randglossen*, Bd 2, 101. See in particular 26:22 ("your ways shall become desolate"); 26:43 ("the land shall be left by them, and enjoy its sabbaths while it lies desolate without them").

[127] Cf. Milgrom, "Picture". Greenberg has collected some extra-biblical parallels, see M. Greenberg, *Ezekiel 1-20*, Anchor Bible (Garden City NY, 1983), 200f. A full study of the motif in ANE texts is provided by D. Bodi, *The Book of Ezekiel and the Poem of Erra*, OBO 104 (Freiburg, 1991), 183-218.

around YHWH's sanctuary in the land, are to respect the sanctity of the divine abode by observing certain rules. These rules are none other than the commandments given in H. Transgression of these commandments would lead to profanation or defilement of the sanctuary, which in turn would make it impossible for YHWH to maintain his presence among the Israelites. The departure of YHWH would mean utter ruin not only in the spiritual but also in the material realm; the observance of the commandments is therefore of extreme importance to the people.

If the ideas above are accurate, it is clear that the notion of holiness in H contains a strong spatial component.[128] It is the proximity of the godhead that obliges the Israelites to seek holiness. Of course, the personal dimension is important as well: YHWH can place this type of demands on the Israelites by virtue of his relationship with them. Yet it is probably no exaggeration to say that the personal dimension is projected into the spatial. When YHWH acquired for himself a people of worshippers, he intended them to dwell around his earthly abode; their obligation to be holy is a mere corollary of this arrangement.

YHWH the sanctifier

Holiness belongs exclusively to the divine nature, whence it may radiate outwards to human beings (or objects) who can thereby become holy in a derived sense. The call to "be holy" in H means no more than that the Israelites' behaviour should correspond to the holiness of their God. Through their appropriate behaviour, they will as it were absorb some of the holiness proceeding from the godhead in his sanctuary and thus become holy themselves.

This principle is expressly stated in the clause "I am the LORD who sanctify him/them/you" which occurs seven times in H. Where the direct object is expressed by a third person suffix, it usually refers to the priests.[129] The high priest may not marry any type of woman save a virgin of his own clan:

21:15   ולא יחלל זרעו בעמיו כי אני יהוה מקדשו

...that he may not profane his children among his people; for I am the LORD who sanctify him.

---

[128] Cf. Milgrom, *Leviticus 1-16*, 48.
[129] In 21:23 it refers to the sanctuary.

Though the precise meaning of the verse is obscure,[130] the implication is clear that the high priest and his offspring are holy, and therefore in danger of being desecrated (*ḥll*). The holiness of the high priest stems from YHWH who sanctifies him, a reference to the hallowing influence of the godhead on those working in his sanctuary. The same idea underlies the provisions concerning the purity of the priests; they may not eat of the holy things of the people of Israel while they are in a state of impurity:

22:9 ושמרו את משמרתי ולא ישאו עליו חטא ומתו בו כי יחללהו
אני יהוה מקדשם

They shall therefore keep my charge, lest they bear sin for it and die thereby when they profane it: I am the LORD who sanctify them.

Although the exegesis of this verse is again somewhat problematic,[131] the general meaning is clear: through his holy presence in the temple, YHWH hallows the priests.[132]

The priest is, therefore, intrinsically holy, at least from the point of view of the other Israelites. Every Israelite is called upon to respect the priest's holiness, to treat him as holy:

21:7b,8a כי קדש הוא לאלהיו וקדשתו כי את לחם אלהיך הוא מקריב

For the priest is holy to his God;[133] you shall consecrate him for he offers the bread of your God.

The holiness of the priest is not innate, however; it derives from his function and his position, and its ultimate source is YHWH. As a result, the priest needs actively to pursue holiness, i.e. to accord his behaviour with the holiness of YHWH: "They shall be holy to their God, and not profane the name of their God" (*qᵉdōšīm yihyū lēʾlōhēhem wᵉlōʾ yᵉhallᵉlū šēm ʾoᵉlōhēhem*, 21:6). Concretely, this means that the priests must observe stricter rules of purity than the other Israelites, as is made

---

[130] See Wenham, *Leviticus*, 292.
[131] The antecedent of the third person masculine singular suffixes (...bear sin for *it*, ...die for *it*) is not clear.
[132] Cf. also 22:16.
[133] Schwartz distinguishes *qādōš l-* "consecrated to" from *qādōš* "separate", see Schwartz, *Chapters*, 112f. However, as was stated above, *qādōš* is always a relational term and the notion of separateness is secondary.

clear in the provisions regarding mourning and marriage of the priests
(21:1-7) and, in particular, in the provision that the priests may not eat
$n^e b\bar{e}l\bar{a}h$ and $t^e r\bar{e}p\bar{a}h$ (22:8), which are permitted to common Israelites
(17:15f).

The clause "I am the LORD who sanctify you", with the direct object
expressed by a second person plural suffix, refers to YHWH's hallowing
influence on the Israelites. It occurs in a ritual context in 21:8 "The
priest shall be holy to you; for I the LORD, who sanctify you, am holy."
The import of this verse seems to be that YHWH's sanctity reaches the
Israelites through the sanctified priest.[134] Quite a different turn is taken
in a passage making the transition from laws on Molech-worship and
necromancy (20:1-6) to laws on sexual behaviour (20:9-21):

20:7f   והתקדשתם והייתם קדשים כי אני יהוה אלהיכם
                        ושמרתם את את חקתי ועשיתם אתם אני יהוה מקדשכם

Consecrate yourselves therefore, and be holy;[135] for I am the LORD
your God. Keep my statutes and do them; I am the LORD who sanctify you.

The synergy between YHWH who sanctifies and the Israelites who must
seek holiness is to be understood in the same way as for the priests: the
source of holiness is God and the way to appropriate it is to adapt one's
conduct to the divine demands. What is very different in the present
passage, however, is the content of the rules ensuring the attainment and
preservation of holiness. The statutes of YHWH which the Israelites are
to keep and do are certainly to be identified with the laws given in Lev
20. These are not rules of ritualistic cleanliness, at least not in the narrow sense of the rules which the priest has to observe in order to preserve his holiness (21:1-22:16); they concern a much wider area of
life.[136] Nevertheless, their rationale is the same as that of the rules concerning the priests: the transgression of these commandments will bring
impurity to the sanctuary (20:3, compare 21:12, 23, and see above).
What we observe here is the transposition of religious and social laws
into the ritual sphere. Or, conversely, we could say that the ritual cat-

---

[134] Cf. Knohl, *Sanctuary*, 191.
[135] For the nuance expressed by this double expression see Elliger, *Leviticus*, 263 ("So
heiligt euch und bleibt heilig"). Cf. Lev 11:44.
[136] The call to holiness in 22:32 may also be interpreted in a wider sense; it is to be
noted, however, that it occurs at the close of rules on sacrifice.

egory has undergone a mutation so that it now includes social and religious ethics.[137]

The most complete expression of this mutation is found in Lev 19. The call to holiness functions here as a title; it is the general command of which the following provisions are the concrete elaboration:[138]

19:2   קדשים תהיו כי קדוש אני יהוה אלהיכם

You shall be holy; for I the LORD your God am holy.

One could paraphrase this verse in the following way: you shall do everything that is in your power to attain holiness, namely observe all the commandments of YHWH; you will then be hallowed by his sanctity,[139] and thus be rendered fit to live in his proximity. Some scholars have sought to deny that these words imply a call to imitate God.[140] To my mind, this is a misjudgment of the plain meaning of the verse. Holiness is not a fruit of the Israelites' observance of the law (though that is necessary too), nor does their holiness imply that the Israelites become divine themselves; none the less, by their sanctification they will indeed become like YHWH, fit to be with him.[141]

The concrete application of this call to holiness is then elaborated in the miscellany of commandments which follows, and recapitulated in 19:37 "And you shall observe *all* my statutes and *all* my ordinances, and do them." In order to attain the state of holiness which will permit them to dwell around YHWH's sanctuary, the Israelites must submit every domain of their lives to him.[142]

Thus the spatial dimension of holiness described above is set into sharper relief. The space surrounding the sanctuary is divided in two distinct domains, like concentric circles. Nearest to the sanctuary are the priests, whose holiness is therefore more immediate. In order to realize

---

[137] Knohl, *Sanctuary*, 183-184, has pointed out that the antonym of *qdš*, *ḥll* (piel), also takes on an ethical meaning.

[138] On the function of 19:2aαb, see Schwartz, *Chapters*, 113.

[139] Cf. H. J. Kraus, "Das heilige Volk", in idem, *Biblisch-theologische Aufsätze* (Neukirchen-Vluyn, 1972), 37-49, p. 42: "Jahwes Heiligkeit ist kein Zielbild, kein Vollkommenheitsideal, sondern machtvoll gegenwärtiges Wirken des gebietenden und Heiligenden."

[140] See Zimmerli, "Heiligkeit", 511f; Mathys, *Liebe*, 103; Schwartz, *Chapters*, 112.

[141] For early Jewish exponents of this interpretation, see Schwartz, *Chapters*, 264, n. 25. See also Buber, *Glaube*, 183f; Wenham, *Leviticus*, 25.

[142] Cf. 20:26.

their holiness, the priests must observe stricter rules of ritual purity. The second circle is that of the common Israelites. They are sanctified through the holy presence of YHWH in the temple and among the priests (21:8), which means concretely that they are called upon to achieve their holiness by observing the commandments expounded in H.[143]

The holiness to which the Israelites are called is therefore a dynamic quality, both existential and relational.[144] By an ongoing process of putting the commandments into practice, they will adjust their lives to the requirements of YHWH's holiness: they will be holy as he is holy. Thus will they be capable of living in proximity to his sanctuary. The Deuteronomic notion that Israel, because it has been chosen by YHWH, is a holy people is very far from the thought of H.[145] Of course, H recognizes the special relationship between Israel and YHWH (20:24, 26); the Israelites are his slaves, his people. This particular status, however, is not called holiness in H. The idea of holiness underlying H is different again from that of P, which is almost entirely limited to ritual purity.[146] The difference between H and P on this point has been treated extensively by Knohl and need not occupy us here.[147]

The call to holiness as it is presented in H can be integrated without difficulty into the wider conceptual framework regarding the relationship between YHWH and the Israelites. The people that were liberated from slavery in Egypt in order to become YHWH's slaves and be settled around his sanctuary on his land must respect the holy presence of their God among them. They must also obey him. The notions of obedience to the commandments and striving for holiness are practically synonymous in H. It is through his commandments that YHWH calls his people to sanctity, and indeed actually sanctifies them. Transgression of the

---

[143] This scheme must not be taken to imply that the priests are not subject to the wider demands of holiness. Since the priests are also "sons of Israel", Lev 19 is addressed to them as well.

[144] This opposes the view that holiness in the priestly writings is an abstract idea, see e.g. Wellhausen, *Prolegomena*, 441; W. Houston, *Purity and Monotheism. Clean and Unclean Animals in Biblical Law*, JSOTS 140 (1993), 249.

[145] Against Mathys, *Liebe*, 104 (with literature); Knohl, *Sanctuary*, 183.

[146] In Lev 15:31, defilement of the sanctuary is the result of the non-observance of purity regulations; contrast 20:3.

[147] According to Knohl, H differs from P in two respects: holiness is made to include ethics, and the call to holiness is extended to the entire people; see Knohl, *Sanctuary*, 180-186.

commandments desecrates the bond between the people and their God,[148] and leads to defilement of the sanctuary.

Holy gifts, holy times and holy places

The 66 occurrences of the root *qdš* in H have not so far all been covered above. The remaining usages, however, are much less significant theologically. Particularly frequent is the noun *qodeš* or the phrase *qodeš qodāšim* referring to different types of offerings (19:8, 24; 21:22; 22:2, 3, 4, 6, 7, 10, 12, 14, 15, 16; 23:20; 24:9). This use of the root *qdš* is not problematic.

A moot point is the precise meaning of the phrase *miqrā' qodeš* which occurs 11 times in Lev 23.[149] In modern commentaries, this expression is usually translated as "holy assembly" or the like,[150] and the inference is that this chapter dates from a period during or after the exile when the Jews developed the habit of assembling on the sabbath and on feast-days.[151] This interpretation has a very narrow basis, however. From the context, it is merely possible to say that the days on which there is (or which are called) *miqrā' qodeš* are set apart, in that no laborious work may be done on them. Etymology does not favour the interpretation "assembly". Since one of the meanings of the verb *qr'* is "to summon", the translation "convocation" for *miqrā'* is possible (cf. Num 10:2), but many other renderings could be thought of.[152] Nor is there any old tradition according to which *miqrā' qodeš* would mean "holy assembly": none of the versions translates it in this way,[153] and in post-Biblical Hebrew the noun *miqrā'* carries a very different meaning (cf.

---

[148] This seems to be what is implied by the expression "to profane my holy name" (20:3; cf. 18:21; 19:12; 21:6; 22:2, 32): the "name of YHWH" is probably to be connected with the frequent use of the formulas "I am YHWH (your God)".

[149] The expression occurs also in Ex 12:15; Num 28-29; *miqrā'* alone in Isa 1:13; 4:5.

[150] Cf. Elliger, *Leviticus*, 313 (Versammlung).

[151] Wenham (*Leviticus*, 301) has suggested that it means "a national gathering for public worship". In view of the designation of the sabbath as a *miqrā' qodeš* (23:3), this seems unlikely (compare, however, Ez 46:3; Isa 66:23).

[152] Another possibility is that the root is not *qr'* I, "to call etc.", but *qr'* II, "to happen, to befall"; the translation would then be something like "holy event, holy occasion". The expression has been rendered in this way in the Targums (Onkelos: *m'r'* ; Neofiti: *'yrw'*).

[153] The LXX has κλητη αγια; the Vulgate *vocabitur sanctus* (and other expressions); the Peshitta, *qaryā wqaddīšā* ; for the Targum, see the preceding note. For the LXX and the Vulgate, see P. Katz, "מִקְרָא in der griechischen und lateinischen Bibel", *ZAW* 65 (1953), 253-255.

Neh 8:8).[154] In view of this lack of data, it is not possible to draw any telling conclusions from the expression; it may not be used to postulate a late date, nor should it be taken as a reference to a type of synagogue worship.[155] On balance, the most likely meaning of the term is "holy festal day, holiday".[156]

In 25:10, 12 the Israelites are called upon to sanctify the jubilee year, it is to be holy for them. Like the sabbath and the feasts, the jubilee year is consecrated to God: no secular work will be done.

Finally, in 24:9 the expression "holy place" (*māqōm qādōš*) occurs. It refers to a place in the court of the tabernacle where all the priestly portions are to be eaten (cf. Lev 6:9).[157]

4.4 CONCLUSIONS

Since H never systematically expounds its underlying thought-complex, the analysis presented above in 4.1. to 4.3. cannot presume to be more than a tentative reconstruction. Nevertheless, every step in our research has confirmed the impression that the various and sundry elements— terms, phrases, ideas—expressing H's concept of the people of Israel in its ideal aspect exhibit a high degree of coherence. The vision for the Israelite nation is entirely subordinated to the notion of its relationship with YHWH. Important social and material privileges are guaranteed to Israel: personal freedom, possession of land, prosperity—but these exclusively proceed from the stipulated god/people relationship; they will, therefore, cease if it is violated.

At the basis of this vision for the people lies a sacral scheme: a god acquires a group of people—his "slaves"—to serve him in his sanctuary; these servants are settled on land surrounding the sanctuary and belonging to the god; since they are the god's personal possession, they

---

[154] See for exhaustive discussion, E. Kutsch, "מִקְרָא", *ZAW* 65 (1953), 247-253. Kutsch arrives at the meaning "Feiertag" and denies that the noun has any connotation of "assembly". The only criticism that may be levelled at Kutsch is that he does not mention earlier scholars who argued a similar thesis: see the references in Dillmann, *Exodus und Leviticus*, 122f; and Eerdmans, *Alttestamentliche Studien IV*, 110-112.

[155] Dommershausen has suggested that the expression implies that the Israelites are called holy when they are assembled for the cult; see W. Dommershausen, "Heiligkeit, ein alttestamentliches Sozialprinzip?", *Theologische Quartalschrift* 148 (1968), 153-166. In my opininon this exceeds the available evidence.

[156] See n. 152.

[157] Cf. Milgrom, *Leviticus 1-16*, 392-394 (with literature).

may not be enslaved to any human master, and since the land they live on belongs to the god, it can never be sold. The arrangement involving the god YHWH, the people of Israel, and the land which will be given to them is called a "covenant" (*b⁰rīt*). The basic scheme is also attested in extra-biblical literature,[158] but its elaboration here exhibits some elements peculiar to H. Whereas elsewhere the acquisition of slaves for the godhead is the work of a wordly lord, who makes them over to the god, in H it is YHWH himself who led the Israelites out from slavery in Egypt and thus took possession of them. Another difference—connected to the first—is that in the other instances, the temple with its slaves would still be integrated in a secular empire, whereas in H the arrangement is seen as the foundation of an independent state. The slaves acquired by YHWH are the people of Israel.

The ubiquitous call to holiness, from which H took its name, is a necessary corollary of the way the god/people relationship was conceived of. Since all the Israelites were acquired by YHWH to serve him in his temple, they are as it were temple slaves who must observe the holiness of the sanctuary.[159] The practical elaboration of this exigency, whereby the demands emanating from YHWH's holiness are made to encompass all aspects of individual and national life, is a theological achievement of the highest order. It appears that this achievement was almost entirely the work of the authors of H; nowhere else in the Old Testament do we find this comprehensive interpretation of holiness. Traditio-historically, this concept is firmly planted in the priestly school, which of old accentuated the demands issuing from the holy presence of YHWH in his earthly dwelling.[160]

The *strength* of H's concept of the relationship between YHWH and Israel lies in the fact that this relationship was from the start seen as an arrangement between a god and a people. The "covenant-theology" of H is not based on a more or less remote analogy. Israel is not viewed as YHWH's vassal, or his adoptive son, or his wife, or his family, but: "I will be your God, and you shall be my people"—the formula hides nothing and implies nothing. In this way, all the negative implications of

---

[158] See above, at n. 23.
[159] In Knohl's view, texts originating in the Holiness School liken the Israelites to priests, see Knohl, *Conception*, 190.
[160] The "liturgies of the gate" (e.g. Psalms 15 and 24) may also have played a part in the preparation of the theology of H. See also Isa 5:16; 6:3-7; Ex 19:3-6.

reasoning by analogy are avoided.[161] Both the transcendence of YHWH and his attachment to the people are secured. The call to imitate God can freely be made in this framework, since both emulation and assimilation are excluded.

The *weakness* of the scheme was exposed by history. Even before the Israelites attained full nationhood, they split into two nations, one of which later went into exile and disappeared from the scene while the other led a precarious existence for somewhat longer before it too came to an end as an independent state. At no point in the history of the people of Israel did circumstances allow the vision of H to materialize. After the loss of the Temple, the land and political independence, the vision lapsed definitively. The promise of continuing faithfulness on the part of YHWH (26:42-45), though a necessary part of H, now became anomalous and vague: the vision had passed, what did the future hold?

---

[161] For some of these implications and the way they were dealt with in Deuteronomy, see Lohfink, "Wandlung".

CHAPTER FIVE

PERSPECTIVES ON THE LAND

The notion of land is central to H, second in importance only to the notion of peoplehood. Time and again reference is made to "the land"— the land of Canaan, the land of the Israelites, the land of YHWH. In order to gauge the theological quality of the "land consciousness" exhibited by H, it is useful first to evaluate the different perceptions of the land. Three different perspectives will be briefly discussed in the present chapter. The picture of the Israelites' camp in the desert contains features paradigmatic of their settlement in the land; several passages speak globally of the land as a well-defined territory; finally, throughout H a provincial outlook on the land may be observed.

5.1 THE CAMP IN THE DESERT

In several passages in H, the Promised Land remains seemingly outside the reference frame of the text. The realities of the desert period dominate the discourse: the assembly, the tent of meeting, the camp, the open field... Occurring as they do in the context of H, however, even these passages shed some light on the notion of the land. Indeed, in H the sojourn in the desert is seen as a period of preparation for entry into the land.[1] Laws that are given in the context of the camp in the desert are meant to remain operative in the context of the land. One might say that the camp is presented as a temporary arrangement with a view to definitive establishment in the land. Since certain features of the camp will therefore also characterize the land, it is important briefly to review the description of the camp in H.

---

[1] For the desert as a transitional stage between Egypt and Canaan in P, see E. Cortese, *La terra di Canaan nella storia sacerdotale del Pentateuco*, Supplementi alla Rivista Biblica 5 (Brescia, 1972), 68.

The camp

The camp (*maḥᵃneh*) of the Israelites is mentioned explicitly only in 17:3; 24:10, 14, 23. Yet throughout H, the picture of Israel encamped in the desert remains the constant backdrop. Where prescriptions are laid down with a view to life in the land (e.g. 19:9, 23; 25:2), this happens in a prospective manner; establishment in the land is represented as something belonging to the future. It seems that H's concept of the camp is essentially similar to that of the other priestly texts, where however more information about it is provided (see, in particular, Num 1-3). The notion of the camp of the Israelites journeying from Egypt to the Promised Land is found in the earlier sources of the Pentateuch as well;[2] it is all but absent from Deuteronomy.[3] Grammatically, the noun is derived from the verb *ḥnh*, "to encamp"; it may designate different types of encampment and most often refers to military camps.

It is sometimes supposed that the camp of the priestly writings is an image of the Jewish exilic community in Babylon.[4] On this view, P created the picture of the Israelites camping in the desert and awaiting entry into the land of Canaan in order to encourage the Jews in exile aspiring to return to their motherland. A slight variation of this theory is that the priestly camp is a model for the return and the post-exilic community.[5] An altogether different view has been expressed by Kaufmann, who argues that the camp in P is a representation of any city in (pre-exilic) Israel in which there was a sanctuary.[6] Laws given with regard to the camp were therefore meant to be operative in every Israelite city;[7] P is the law code of the cult on the high places (*bāmōt*).[8] A third hypothesis is that the priestly description of the camp is modelled on pre-exilic

---

[2] Cf. F. J. Helfmeyer, TWAT III, 4-20, p. 11.

[3] The term occurs three times in the framework of the laws, Deut 2:14f, 29:10. The camp mentioned in Deut 23:10-15 is not that of the Israelites in the desert.

[4] See e.g. K. Elliger, "Sinn und Ursprung der priesterlichen Geschichtserzählung", in idem, *Kleine Schriften zum Alten Testament*, Theologische Bücherei, AT 32 (1966), 174-198.

[5] Cf. TWAT III, 14.

[6] J. Kaufmann, "Probleme der israelitisch-jüdischen Religionsgeschichte", ZAW 48 (1930), 23-43, 34.

[7] Kaufmann points to Lev 14:1-3 and 14:33-34 where the camp and the city are viewed as co-extensive entities. Moreover, two of the priestly laws regarding the camp are known to have been applied to Israelite cities: those sentenced to death are executed outside the camp (Lev 24:14f; Num 15:35; outside the city: 1 Ki 21:10, 13); lepers are excluded from the camp (Num 5:2f cf. Lev 14:2f; from the city: 2 Ki 7:3).

[8] Kaufmann, "Probleme", 32.

pilgrims' camps.[9] The sacral view of the camp and the preoccupation with holiness could then be explained as temporary measures characteristic of a festal assembly, that have been made permanent in the priestly picture of the Israelites in the desert.[10]

A critical evaluation of these theories exposes them as being rather unnecessary and far-fetched. In view of the fact that the older pentateuchal sources mention the Israelite camp in the desert, it may be submitted that the camp played a part in the traditional account of the people's history. Several of the features in the priestly description of the camp link up with elements occurring in the earlier sources.[11] The focus on sacral matters and the preoccupation with holiness are in keeping with the general character of the priestly texts in the Pentateuch. Such features merely attest to the fact that these writings do indeed proceed from a priestly milieu, as is generally recognized. Priests in any period and any locale may be trusted to manifest a high sensitivity to the sacred and the conditions it imposes on its surroundings.

Not all the laws contained in H are meant for life in the camp. Many of the prescriptions are stated to be given with a view to life in the land (Lev 18-20), while others could only become operative there (Lev 23 and 25). The only passages which explicitly lay down rules for life in the desert camp are the laws on slaughter and the disposal of blood in Lev 17, the ritual prescriptions concerning the furnishing of the tabernacle in 24:1-9 and the laws attached to the narrative on the blasphemer in 24:10-23. The mere enumeration of the different regulations operative in the camp is not itself illustrative of H's conception of the Israelites' settlement in the desert. These same passages, however, define two general qualities of the camp which merit full attention. The first of these is that within the camp the word of YHWH has force of law. The commandments given by YHWH to Moses, and transmitted by him to the sons of Israel, are meant to regulate the life of all those who are in the

---

[9] This view was first mooted by Kuschke and then developed by Kraus. See A. Kuschke, "Die Lagervorstellung der priesterschriftlichen Erzählung. Eine überlieferungsgeschichtliche Studie", *ZAW* 63 (1951), 74-105, 105; H. J. Kraus, *Gottesdienst in Israel* (München, 1954), 23-37; see also Helfmeyer, TWAT III, 11-16.

[10] Yet another view is expressed in the Midrash, where the camp is seen as an image of Jerusalem, see EM IV, 801-805.

[11] The camp is essentially a military camp, see Kaufmann, "Probleme", 28; the ark is the sign of YHWH's presence in the camp (Num 1-3 for P, Num 10:33-36 for the older sources); lepers are excluded from the camp (Num 5:2f for P, Num 12:15 for the older sources).

camp. Whereas disobedience is taken into consideration, and sanctions are provided for, the possibility to "opt out", i.e. to sojourn in the camp without being subjected to the commandments of YHWH, is not envisaged. Moreover, in the representation of H, the law given through Moses is the only rule of the Israelite camp. Admittedly, it is never stated explicitly that no law other than that of YHWH may be followed;[12] however, in view of the fact that YHWH's commandments cover the domain of what we would call civil and criminal law, as well as that of ritual, the existence of other legislative authorities in the conception of H is highly unlikely. When the Israelites are in doubt as to a specific point of juridical procedure, their only recourse is to consult YHWH, through the office of Moses.[13]

The principle that YHWH's word is the only law for the Israelite camp is to be connected with H's conception of the Exodus as it was described above. The Israelites have exchanged their former, Egyptian masters for YHWH, to whom they belong as slaves. They must, therefore, obey him and him alone. This implies, on the human plane, that the people of Israel as pictured in H are politically independent. Although they have not yet taken possession of the land their God promised to give them, they have already received the status of a free nation, enfranchised from foreign domination.

A particularly salient expression of the subordination of the camp to the word of YHWH is the fact that the prescriptions of H apply to the resident alien (gēr) as well as to the Israelites. As we have seen above in 3.2., the resident alien is to be viewed as a non-Israelite sojourning among the people, to whom certain rights are granted and who must in turn observe certain rules. As presented in H, the resident alien is not only a type of person Israel will have to deal with once they have occupied their land: the camp also counts its non-Israelite residents. As a matter of fact, almost all the laws given in the setting of the camp are stated to be valid for resident alien and for Israelite alike.[14] The only exception is the stipulation in 17:3, which seems to imply that profane slaughter was allowed to resident aliens, whereas to Israelites it is expressly forbidden. As was argued above in 3.2., this testifies to a tolerant attitude towards non-Israelites who are not forced to comply with the positive commandments connected to Israel's religion, although they

---

[12] The principle that no other law than YHWH's may be followed is stated explicitly with regard to the land, see 18:3f; 20:22f, see below.
[13] See 24:11f.

must observe the negative commandments lest the sanctuary be polluted.

Another point underscoring the absoluteness of YHWH's word as a rule of life in the camp is the fact that disobedience may be sanctioned by death. The *krt* formulas in Lev 17 may be referred to here, even though it is difficult for our modern minds to conceive of their terrifying force. More specific is the mention of the death penalty by human agency in 24:14, 16, 17, 21, 23. Both blasphemy and manslaughter are here stated to be punishable by the death penalty, and the narration of the stoning of a blasphemer shows that these are not philosophical statements. The absolute authority of the divine law is a matter of life and death.

The second quality of the Israelite camp expressing an essential element in the conception of H is the presence of YHWH in the midst of it. In order to understand the notion of the presence of the godhead we must take a closer look at the single most important component of the camp, namely the tabernacle or tent of meeting.

The tent of meeting

The expression "tent of meeting" (*'ohel mō'ēd*) occurs in 17:4, 5, 6, 9; 19:21 and 24:3, and the synonymous "tabernacle of the LORD" (*miškan yhwh*) in 17:4.[15] The same expressions are used throughout the priestly writings in reference to the tent-sanctuary which YHWH commanded Moses to build at Mount Sinai. The term "tent of meeting" occurs also in non-priestly parts of the Pentateuch,[16] although a different institution seems to be meant.[17] The questions concerning the origin of the term *'ohel mō'ēd*, the original nature of the institution thus designated, and the tradition history leading up to the priestly description of it, are extremely complicated. They are not, however, very relevant for

---

[14] See 17:8, 10, 13, 15; 24:16-22.
[15] The term *miškān* occurs once more in 26:11, where it is probably to be taken in the general sense of "dwelling". For the relationship between the "tent of meeting" and the "tabernacle", see Kuschke, "Lagervorstellung", 82-89; Milgrom, *Leviticus 1-16*, 36.
[16] See Ex 33:7; Num 11:16; 12:4; Deut 31:14; see also 1 Sam 2:22 and 1 Ki 8:4.
[17] Cf. M. Haran, "The Nature of the «'Ohel Mo'ed» in Pentateuchal Sources", *JSS* 5 (1960), 50-65; M. Görg, *Das Zelt der Begegnung*, BBB 27 (Bonn, 1967); Milgrom, *Leviticus 1-16*, 140.

an understanding of the conceptual universe of H and need not be reviewed here.

Because the priestly tabernacle is generally supposed to be entirely fictitious, scholars have tended to view it as the image—either a reflection or a model—of another sanctuary:[18] Solomon's temple,[19] the second temple,[20] any Israelite "high place",[21] the sanctuary in Shiloh,[22] a projected sanctuary to be erected in exile,[23] or a symbolic sanctuary among the exiles.[24] Although some of these views have been well argued and may well contain a grain of truth, it must also be stressed that the priestly picture of the tabernacle is to a large extent determined by the narrative context: the structure simply had to be collapsable and movable if it was to serve during the wandering in the desert. Furthermore, the fact that there was only one sanctuary in the camp must not necessarily be interpreted to mean that the priestly texts envisage a centralization of the cult,[25] or already presuppose the Deuteronomic centralization.[26] In the context of the camp, a plurality of sanctuaries would be absurd; but what the arrangement of the cult in the land will be is left open.[27]

The nature of the priestly tent of meeting is subject to controversy. Von Rad has argued in many studies that the desert sanctuary is the place where YHWH reveals himself intermittently.[28] YHWH does not dwell in the tent, but manifests himself—or rather, manifests his glory (*kābōd*) perceived in the image of a cloud—to Moses and the people of Israel on different occasions; it is a constantly recurring event.[29] He finds irrefutable proof of his theory in a text which may indeed be

---

[18] Milgrom has suggested that the tabernacle is an image of Mount Sinai, see Milgrom, *Leviticus 1-16*, 142f.

[19] Cf. M. Haran, *Temples and Temple Service in Ancient Israel* (Oxford, 1978), 189.

[20] See, e.g., V. Fritz, *Tempel und Zelt*, WMANT 47 (Neukirchen, 1977).

[21] Kaufmann, "Probleme", 34.

[22] Cf. M. Haran, "Shiloh and Jerusalem: The Origin of the Priestly Tradition in the Pentateuch", *JBL* 81 (1962), 14-24; Milgrom, *Leviticus 1-16*, 29-34.

[23] Elliger, "Sinn", 197f.

[24] J. G. Gammie, *Holiness in Israel*, Overtures to Biblical Theology (Minneapolis MN, 1989), 17.

[25] As against the view of M. Haran, *Temples*, 145.

[26] As against Wellhausen, *Composition*, 151.

[27] With regard to H, it is not easy to know what its stand is on the question of the centralization of the cult. In 26:31 the existence of several sanctuaries of YHWH in the land of Israel is clearly presupposed.

[28] See G. von Rad, *Die Priesterschrift im Hexateuch*, BWANT 65 (Stuttgart, 1934), 182f; idem, *Old Testament Theology I*, transl. by D. M. G. Stalker (London, 1975), 238f.

[29] See Ex 16:10; 40:34; Lev 9:6, 23; Num 14:10; 16:19; 17:7; 20:6.

viewed as the explicit priestly definition of the function of the tent of meeting:

Ex 29:42f   ‏...פתח אהל מועד לפני יהוה אשר אועד לכם שמה‏
      ‏לדבר אליך שם ונעדתי שמה לבני ישראל‏

... at the door of the tent of meeting before the LORD, where I will meet with you, to speak there to you. There I will meet with the people of Israel.

The tent of meeting is the place where YHWH will "meet" Moses and the Israelites: the same root is used in the verb y'd (niphal), "to meet by appointment", and in the name of the tent (mō'ēd).[30] In Von Rad's view, the statement that YHWH will meet the Israelites at the tent of meeting would be meaningless if he were thought of as dwelling in the tent.[31] The tent is rather the one and only place of meeting, where YHWH reveals his word to Moses. On this point, according to Von Rad, P links up with the older conception of the tent of meeting as a place where oracles were given.[32] This theory has been taken up and elaborated by many.[33] The conclusion has often been drawn that the particular manifestation-theology of P reflects a period when the presence of God among his people had become problematic, i.e. after the destruction of the Temple in Jerusalem.[34]

A criticism of this view must be that it neglects part of the evidence. In contradistinction to the passages where the glory of YHWH is said to appear (Num 14:10; 16:19; 17:7; 20:6), other priestly passages clearly speak of a constant presence of the glory and the cloud (Ex 40:34-38; Num 9:15-23). Moreover, the frequent statement that ritual acts are performed "before YHWH" (lipnē yhwh) implies that YHWH is indeed present in the sanctuary. Finally, it is stated explicitly in a number of passages that it is YHWH's intention to dwell (škn) among the Israelites (25:8; 29:45f) or that he does so (Num 5:3; 35:34).[35] On the other hand,

---

[30] See also Ex 25:22; 30:6, 36; Num 17:19.
[31] Von Rad, *Theology I*, 239.
[32] See Ex 33:7; Num 11:16f; 12:4f; Deut 31:14.
[33] See, e.g., Kuschke, "Lagervorstellung"; Görg, *Zelt*, 172.
[34] See, e.g., Helfmeyer, TWAT III, 14.
[35] These passages have been explained either as witnessing an older concept, against which P was struggling, or as later passages no longer representative of P's theology, see, e.g., Von Rad, *Theology I*, 239, n. 115. Such hypotheses are unnecessary, however, since the different statements concerning the presence of YHWH in the tent of meeting can be integrated into a meaningful picture.

the positive arguments advanced by Von Rad are not strong: even if YHWH dwells in the tent, he can still establish it as the exclusive place of meeting. Nor do the passages recounting the appearance of the glory at various occasions exclude the possibility that YHWH is continually present in his sanctuary.

For all these reasons, several scholars have rejected the theory argued by Von Rad, adopting instead the position that in the priestly understanding, the tabernacle is indeed conceived of as the dwelling-place of the godhead.[36] It has been pointed out that the entire cult and worship service as commanded in the priestly parts of the Pentateuch are implicitly motivated by the fact that YHWH does indeed dwell in the tent-sanctuary.[37] Yet, most of these scholars admit that the priestly writings exhibit a certain reticence on the matter of YHWH's indwelling. On this point, P is at one with many other parts of the OT where the immanence of God—as expressed by the fact that he dwells on earth—generates a certain amount of tension with regard to his transcendence.[38]

As to H, although it does not give much information on the nature of the tent of meeting, the available evidence indicates that the concept is indeed that of YHWH's permanent indwelling. In H, no mention is made of YHWH's meeting with Moses,[39] nor of the cloud's appearing to the Israelites. On the positive side, the terms "the tabernacle of YHWH" (17:4) and "the altar of YHWH" (17:6) tend to show that the tabernacle was really thought of as his dwelling-place, where sacrifices were brought "to YHWH" (17:4, 5, 9) for a "pleasing odor to YHWH" (17:6). The same idea is implied by the expression "before YHWH" (*lipnē yhwh*): the continually burning lamp and the shewbread are to be set in the tent of meeting, before YHWH (24:3, 4, 8; cf. also 19:22). On other points, the idea of the divine presence in the camp is more implicit: the purpose of the purity rules, which must be observed by Israelites and resident aliens alike (e.g. 17:15f) is to safeguard the purity of the camp and, ultimately, of the sanctuary. Defilement of the camp is to be avoided because of YHWH's presence, as is expressly stated in Num 5:2f, a passage closely akin to H in style and ideology. Here it is stated

---

[36] See R. E. Clements, *God and Temple* (Oxford, 1965), 110-122, who cites earlier literature on p. 115 n. 1; Milgrom, "Picture"; Knohl, *Sanctuary*, 131.

[37] Clements, *God and Temple*, 115; Knohl, *Sanctuary*, 131.

[38] See, e.g., 1 Ki 8:12f, 27, 29.

[39] In 24:12f Moses consults YHWH on the case of the blasphemer, but the procedure is not described.

that every leper, and every one having a discharge, and every one that is unclean through contact with a corpse must be sent from the camp:

Num 5:3   ולא יטמאו את מחניהם אשר אני שכן בתוכם

... that they may not defile their camp, in the midst of which I dwell.

In H, this principle is set out more explicitly in the context of the land (see in 3.2. above, pp. 64-70). There is no indication, however, that the rules obtaining in the camp have a different rationale from those given with a view to life in the land (see below).[40]

The camp as a paradigm

Above in 3.1. it has been argued that the functional equivalence of the "assembly" (as described in 24:10-23) and the "people of the land" (as viewed in 20:2, 4) may be interpreted to mean that the first of these institutions is paradigmatic with regard to the second: the people of the land—the real audience of H (however they are to be identified histori-cally)—are reminded that they "are" the assembly, i.e. that what had been imposed on the assembly in the desert is now their responsibility (pp. 45-47). The same paradigmatic relationship may be observed be-tween the camp and the land, at least with regard to the two aspects that have been reviewed above.

The first paradigmatic aspect is that, as in the camp so in the land, the word of YHWH has force of law. Moreover, the laws dictated by YHWH are to be the only law for the people of Israel as is stated explicitly in the following passage:

18:3f   כמעשה ארץ מצרים אשר ישבתם בה לא תעשו וכמעשה ארץ
                כנען אשר אני מביא אתכם שמה לא תעשו ובחקתיהם לא תלכו
                את משפטי תעשו ואת חקתי תשמרו ללכת בהם

You shall not do as they do in the land of Egypt, where you dwelt, and you shall not do as they do in the land of Canaan, to which I am

---

[40] The doctrine of YHWH's presence in the sanctuary does not deny his transcend-ence. "Yahweh himself does not cease to be the transcendent lord of the universe and to dwell in heaven, but he sends forth his glory to be with his people", Clements, *God and Temple*, 113.

bringing you. You shall not walk in their statutes. You shall do my ordinances and keep my statutes and walk in them.[41]

This passage should not be taken to mean that when the Israelites come into the land, the previous inhabitants will continue to live there according to their own laws—which Israel may not adopt. The rest of the chapter makes it perfectly clear that the original inhabitants will have (or have already) gone from the land: the land will vomit (has vomited) them out (18:24, 25, 28; cf. 20:23).[42] The Israelites will not have to share their land with another people whose laws could interfere with theirs. Neither does H ever mention other legislative instances than the word of YHWH. In view of the all-encompassing nature of the laws contained in it (see 4.3. above, pp. 130-133), there seems to be no place for such an instance in the underlying conception.[43] The law given to them by YHWH will therefore be the only law of the land. This principle underlies all the laws which envisage life in the land. It is particularly apparent, however, from the laws on the sabbath and jubilee years and on the redemption of property and persons in Lev 25. The sabbath and jubilee years are national events, to be observed by all the inhabitants of the land; similarly, the laws on redemption are to be operative throughout the land of the Israelites. Consequently, it is obvious that the Israelite settlement in the land is viewed as a politically independent entity. While with regard to their God the Israelites are beholden to absolute obedience, with regard to other nations and their subjects, they constitute a free nation.

It is logical, therefore, that the resident alien is included in the laws laid down with a view to life in the land (as in the rules for life in the desert camp).[44] The subjection of the *gēr* to the laws of YHWH is stipulated in very general terms in the context of Lev 18:

---

[41] The same ideas are expressed in 20:22f.

[42] Whereas in 18:24, the casting out of the peoples from the land is represented as belonging to the future, in 18:25 it is related in the past tense, betraying that the real historical perspective is that of the Israelites' already being established in the land.

[43] Mathys has argued that H contains mostly general principles and laws that could be applied in exile, see Mathys, *Liebe*, 108. However, the regulations concerning homicide (24:17, 21), buying and selling of real estate (25:13-34), redemption of slaves from non-Israelites (25:47-54), sacrifice (17:1-9; 22:17-33), and the cultic calendar (23:4-44) seem to contradict this view.

[44] The very fact that the resident alien is included in laws regarding the camp may indicate that the camp was meant as a paradigm for the land. Indeed, as can be seen from the discussion in 3.2. above, there is usually a territorial component in the meaning of the term: the *ger* is the landless person granted the right to live on another people's land. In view of this territorial aspect, the picture of *gērīm* in the camp is somewhat odd.

18:26 ושמרתם אתם את חקתי ואת משפטי ולא תעשו מכל התועבת
האלה האזרח והגר הגר בתוככם

But you shall keep my statutes and my ordinances and do none of
these abominations, either the native or the stranger who sojourns
among you.

As we have seen above, this rule is not an indication of the resident
alien's adhesion to the religion of Israel; rather, it flows from the fact
that he, as a non-Israelite sojourner, must respect the purity of the land
(see 3.2. above, pp. 64-70). This principle is operative throughout the
laws of H as has been sufficiently demonstrated above in 3.2. The inclusion of the resident alien in the laws of the land is particularly striking in
25:47-55, where the rich resident alien is subjected to a rule that is definitely to his disadvantage (see the exegesis in 3.2. above, pp. 62-63). In
the land as in the camp, observing the law of YHWH is not an option
applicable solely to those who wish to adore this particular God; the law
is binding on everyone. However, as in the camp, this does not mean that
resident aliens are forced to embrace the Israelite religion: the positive
demands of the worship of YHWH (such as observance of the feasts) are
not enjoined upon the resident aliens.

Finally, as in the camp, disobedience to the divine law in the land is in
many cases punishable by death, for Israelites and resident aliens alike
(e.g. 20:2, 9-16).

The second paradigmatic aspect of the camp is that, as in the camp so in
the land, the godhead is constantly present. The idea of YHWH's dwelling in the sanctuary is evinced by many characteristic expressions. The
temple is called "my sanctuary" by YHWH (19:30; 20:3; 26:2; cf.
21:23), and the "sanctuary of his God" (21:12); the sacrifices are termed
"the food of your God" (21:8, 17, 21, 22, 25); sacrifices and rites are
executed in the sanctuary "before YHWH" (*lipnē yhwh* ; 23:11, 28, 40),
and this expression is used once in a *krt* formula with regard to a disobedient priest: "that person shall be cut off from my presence" (*wᵉnikrᵉtāh
hannepeš hahī' millᵉpānāy* ; 22:3, cf. 3.3. above, p. 82, n. 261). The
words "I will make my abode among you" (*wᵉnātattī miškānī
bᵉtōkᵉkem* ; 26:11), far from implying that YHWH was not previously
present among the Israelites, are shown in the context of 26:9-12 to be
YHWH's promise to maintain his presence and to bring the covenant to
fruition (see in 4.2. above, pp. 106, 115-116). Even more significant

than these expressions is the fact that the notion of the divine presence, hallowing the sanctuary (21:23), the priests (21:15) and all the Israelites (20:8), is the central idea upon which all the laws in H are based. The related thought-complex has been reviewed extensively above in Chapter 4 (see, in particular, 4.3.) and need not occupy us further here.

The point of all these considerations is not to argue that the camp symbolically represents the land. One should be extremely cautious in using the picture of the camp to draw inferences with regard to the land as envisaged in H.[45] However, what has been demonstrated in the present section is a functional equivalence between the camp and the land on two essential points. Firstly, rules laid down for life in the camp are to remain operative in the context of the land,[46] and the principle itself that YHWH's word constitutes the law will abide after the occupation of the land. Secondly, the ultimate rationale of the rules given to the Israelites is the need to accord their behavior with the holy presence of YHWH among them in his earthly abode. On these points the Israelite settlement in the land is represented as being on a par with the desert camp.[47] Thus it appears that even the picture of the camp contains important information on the view of the land underlying H.

5.2 THE LAND AS A DELIMITED TERRITORY

As represented in H, the Israelites are in the desert, in the camp, preparing for entry into the land. The land YHWH will give to the Israelites is viewed as a space for living and a source of sustenance. The noun *'ereṣ* (land, earth), may refer to land in general, as in the expression "people of the land" (*'am hā'āreṣ*, 20:2, 4), or in the prohibition that "the land shall not be sold in perpetuity" (*wᵉhā'āreṣ lō' timmākēr liṣᵉmitūt*,

---

[45] Thus it is sometimes supposed that H was written at a time when the Israelites' territory was small: otherwise, the prohibition of slaughter except at the central sanctuary would have been impracticable (17:3-7). See, e.g., the discussion in Reventlow, *Heiligkeitsgesetz*, 17f. Such an inference is unnecessary if we take account of the fictional nature of H.

[46] Several laws laid down in the context of the camp are explicitly stated to be valid throughout the generations of the Israelites (*ḥuqqat 'ōlām lᵉdōrōtām //ᵉdōrōtēkem*, 17:7; 24:3).

[47] Or perhaps it would be better to say that the notions of the camp and the land blend into one another, they are not consistently distinguished.

25:23). More often, however, the land is spoken of in a global way as a well-defined geographic entity. One enters into the land (19:23; 23:10; 25:10; 18:3), and goes out from it (18:24; 20:23; cf. 26:33); the land may become full (of wickedness, 19:29), or empty (of its inhabitants, 26:43).

This global view of the land finds expression in the passages in which the land is defined as the place where the law must be put into practice (cf. above, 5.1.).[48] In "your land" (*'arṣᵉkem*),[49] the Israelites must remember the poor during the harvest (19:9f; 23:22f), respect the resident alien (19:33f), proclaim the jubilee year (25:9); they may, in their land, take slaves from among the non-Israelite residents (25:45), but they may not castrate animals (22:24), or erect a graven image or pillar (26:2). In "all the country you possess" (*bᵉkol 'ereṣ 'ᵃḥuzzatkem*), the Israelites must institute the possibility of redeeming land (25:24). In these passages, where the Israelites are exhorted to apply in their land the laws given to them by YHWH, the term *'ereṣ* (land) designates the territory of the Israelite state.

The land is not, however, defined simply as the domain occupied by the Israelites. Where a specific designation is used, we find the name "land of Canaan", which contains no indication of the relationship between Israel and their land. Moreover, on occasion it seems as though the land is ascribed a personality entirely distinct from that of its inhabitants. These two aspects will now be briefly reviewed.

The land of Canaan

The expression "the land of Canaan" (*'ereṣ kᵉnaᶜan*) occurs twice in H, both times designating the land YHWH will give to the Israelites (18:3 "...the land of Canaan, to which I am bringing you" and 25:38 "...to give you the land of Canaan"). As a designation of the Promised Land this term is fairly frequent in the priestly texts in the Pentateuch.[50] In this sense, the expression is used also in older pentateuchal texts, especially in the Joseph story.[51] Finally, the term is found a number of times in the account of the occupation of the land in the books of Joshua and

---

[48] See 19:23; 23:10; 25:2; 18:3. Cf. Chapter 6 below.
[49] On the significance of the second person plural suffix, see above, pp. 47-54.
[50] Cf. Cortese, *Terra*, 69-74.
[51] Cf. Cortese, *Terra*, 69, 71.

Judges.[52] It is virtually absent from the book of Deuteronomy.[53]

The etymology and origin of the name Canaan are obscure and need not occupy us here.[54] Of more relevance is the question of the extent of the land of Canaan as it is defined in the OT. The fullest definition of the borders of Canaan is found in Num 34:1-12, a text usually ascribed to the priestly school.[55] The border-list laid down in this passage is striking on two accounts: firstly, the land of Canaan is defined as including all the territory west of the river Jordan, from the Brook of Egypt (the Wadi el Arish) in the south to an unidentified point north of Sidon in the north; secondly, no territory on the eastern side of the river Jordan is included. A similar circumscription of the land of Canaan underlies several other passages in the Pentateuch and the Book of Joshua.[56] This definition of the borders of Canaan is puzzling because in no period of the history of Israel did the Israelites occupy such a territory: the "land of Israel" never extended so far north, and it ususally included part of Transjordan.[57] Scholars have found the answer to this conundrum in the El Amarna letters.[58] In these letters the land of Canaan is represented as an Egyptian province which seems to be defined in similar terms as in the OT.[59]

---

[52] The only other places where the expression is found as a designation of the Promised Land are Ps 105:11 (= 1 Chron 16:18); Ps 106:38; 135:11. Ps 105 and 106 appear to reflect knowledge of the entire Pentateuch in its finished form.

[53] The occurrence in Deut 32:49 is usually ascribed to P. The concept of the Promised Land being limited to Cisjordan is contrary to the idea in Deuteronomy, where the Promised Land includes Transjordan, see M. Weinfeld, "The Extent of the Promised Land—The Status of Transjordan", in G. Strecker, ed., *Das Land Israel in biblischer Zeit*, Jerusalem-Symposium 1981 (Göttingen, 1983), 59-75. The expression 'ereṣ hakkᵉna'anī in Deut 1:7; 11:30 does not refer to the entire Promised Land.

[54] For the etymology, see H.-J. Zobel, TWAT IV, 224-243, pp. 227-229.

[55] Partial parallels to this list are found in Josh 15:1-4 and in Ez 47:15-20; 48:1, 28. Tuell has argued that the list in Ez 47f describes the Persian province Abar-Nahara, see S. S. Tuell, *The Law of the Temple in Ezekiel 40-48*, HSM 49 (Atlanta, 1992), 152-174. However, his theory is entirely based on some scanty remarks in Herodotus and fails to convince. He does not discuss the connection between the list in Ez 47f and the one in Num 34.

[56] The brief description of the land of the Canaanites in Gen 10:19 is essentially in accord with the list in Num 34. For other parallels see Y. Aharoni, *The Land of the Bible. A Historical Geography* (London, 1967), 69f.

[57] See the discussion in Aharoni, *Land*, 68.

[58] The original discovery was made by B. Maisler (Mazar), "Lebo Hamath and the Northern Boundary of Canaan", *BJPES* 12 (1945-46), 91-102; in agreement is R. de Vaux, "Le pays de Canaan", *JAOS* 88 (1968), 23-30. See also TWAT IV, 231f; Weinfeld, "Extent", 65f; Milgrom, *Leviticus 1-16*, 11.

[59] The existence of an Egyptian province called Canaan has been doubted by N. Lemche, *The Canaanites and their Land. The Tradition of the Canaanites*, JSOTS 110 (Sheffield, 1991), 29-40, see also pp. 63-73. The hypothesis has been upheld, however, by Thiel in his review of Lemche's book, cf. W. Thiel, *Biblica* 74 (1993), 112-117. Detailed criticism of Lemche's position will be found in N. Na'aman, "The Canaanites and their Land. A Rejoinder", *UF* 26 (1994), 397-418.

This has led to the hypothesis that at the occupation of the land, the Israelites adopted the name and geographical definition which had been in use previously.[60]

It has been argued that the abundant use of the term "land of Canaan" in the priestly texts is a sign of exilic provenance: if the priestly writers had been working in the land, they would not have felt the need to be so precise.[61] On closer inspection of the attestation of the term, however, this view turns out to be highly problematic. The expression "land of Canaan" is almost entirely absent from the OT outside the books of Genesis-Judges. Moreover, where the name Canaan appears in the prophetical books, it usually carries a different meaning, either the Phoenician coast (Isa 23:11; cf. Zeph 2:5), or merchants (Hos 12:8; Zeph 1:11; Ez 16:29; 17:4).[62] This is an indication that in the later period, the term "land of Canaan" had become obsolete as a designation of the land occupied by the Israelites. In defence of an exilic date for the priestly writings, one might raise the possibility that the priestly writers were reviving an old tradition when they used the term to designate the lost territory of the Israelite State, but such a view is not supported by the facts. In the Book of Ezekiel—at least part of which may be dated to the exile—the theme of the land is central, yet the land from which the Israelites have been exiled and to which they will return is never called 'eres kᵉnaᶜan ;[63] moreover, when the term 'eres kᵉnaᶜan is used, it apparently means "land of merchants" and refers to Babylonia. In view of all the above it is preferable to say that the priestly writers link up with an old tradition according to which the Promised Land was the land of Canaan as defined in the second millennium BC. If this conclusion is correct, the expression cannot be used to date the priestly texts exactly, since the said tradition may have been alive for centuries; however, it is more likely to be indicative of a date before rather than after 587 BC.[64]

---

[60] Cf. De Vaux, "Le pays", 30: "[il est] vraisemblable que les Israélites ont d'abord reçu le terme avec le sens qu'il avait à la veille de leur établissement." Weinfeld, "Extent", 65: "The land of Canaan, as fixed in the Egyptian empire, that is, without Transjordan, was taken over by the Israelites in very early times. It is possible that an oracle on this matter was current from the beginning of the the conquest and this could not be changed."

[61] Cortese, Terra, 71f.

[62] Note also Isa 19:18, "the language of Canaan".

[63] In Ez 47:15ff, the borders of the land are defined in the same terms as in Num 34:1-12, yet the land thus circumscribed is not called land of Canaan, but "the land" (Ez 47:15) and "the land of Israel" (Ez 47:18).

[64] Cf Thiel, Biblica 74, 117: "Ihre (the Canaanites') Darstellung wird mit jedem Jahrhundert wahrscheinlicher, das man von 500 v. Chr. an zurückgeht."

In H no specifications are given with regard to the extent of the territory designated as the "land of Canaan". Nevertheless, in light of the
geographical definition discussed above, which recurs in fairly consistent terms in priestly and non-priestly texts, it is likely that the term refers to the same territory in H. No specifications need to be given since
the term itself is well-known and unambiguous: it refers to the land to
the west of the River Jordan, stretching out from the border of Egypt
northward to the mountains of the Lebanon.

The land personified

In a few passages in H, the land is not considered in its practical, geographic sense, but seems to be represented as a living being with its own
personality. The most remarkable passages are those where the land is
said to vomit out its inhabitants:

18:25   ותטמא הארץ ואפקד עונה עליה ותקיא הארץ את ישביה

And the land became defiled so that I punished its iniquity, and the
land vomited out its inhabitants.

18:28   ולא תקיא הארץ אתכם בטמאכם אתה כאשר קאה את הגוי
                             אשר לפניכם

...lest the land vomit you out, when you defile it, as it vomited out[65]
the nation that was before you.[66]

In these verses the land is clearly pictured as an entity distinct from its
inhabitants.[67] Moreover, it is represented as an independent agent.
While it is stated in the same context that YHWH will cast out the nations dwelling in the land (18:24; 20:23), in the present verses the casting out is done by the land itself. A similar personification of the land

---

[65] The form *qā'āh* has the accent on the last syllable as if it were the feminine participle, which would lead to the translation: (it) is about to vomit out. However, the participle usually requires the subject to be explicitly represented, which makes it likely that
the form should be taken as a third-person feminine singular perfect, with a past tense
meaning.

[66] Cf. also 20:22.

[67] The word is sometimes used as a metonym, designating its inhabitants; see, e.g.,
18:3 where the practices of the land of Canaan (*ma'ăśeh 'ereṣ kᵉna'an*) means the practices of its inhabitants. This is not the use of the word in 18:25, 28.

may perhaps be found in the notion that the land will enjoy its sabbaths when the Israelites have gone into exile:

26:35   כל ימי השמה תשבת את אשר לא שבתה בשבתתיכם
בשבתכם עליה

As long as it lies desolate it shall have rest, the rest which it had not in your sabbaths when you dwelt upon it.[68]

Here again, the land appears as an entity distinct from its inhabitants, to which certain actions are ascribed.

A closer parallel to 18:25, 28 and 20:22, however, is found in the priestly account of the inspection of the land in Num 13f. One of the many calumnies of the land adduced by the spies is:

Num 13:32   הארץ אשר עברנו בה לתור אתה ארץ אכלת יושביה היא

The land, through which we have gone, to spy it out, is a land that devours its inhabitants.[69]

Although there is certainly no direct literary relationship between the picture of the land devouring and that of the land vomiting out—the ideas expressed in them are mutually exclusive—the same stylistic mode lies at the basis of both. The land is presented as an animate being far more powerful than its inhabitants. Some have thought that such a sharp distinction between the land and its inhabitants could only have arisen among the Israelites after they were severed from their land;[70] before the experience of exile, an organic unity existed between people and land which would not have permitted such modes of speech.[71] Against this point of view, it must be pointed out that all the major strands of tradition contained in the OT stress that the Promised Land

---

[68] Cf. also 25:2; 26:34, 43.

[69] An exact parallel to the motif in Num 13:32 is found in Ez 36:13. It is usually supposed that P depends on Ezekiel at this point, see, e.g., N. Lohfink, "Die Priesterschrift und die Geschichte", in J. A. Emerton et al., eds., *Congress Volume. Göttingen 1977*, SVT 29 (1978), 189-225, p. 212. This dependence has never been demonstrated, however. The motif itself does not necessarily point to an exilic context, see the biblical and Akkadian parallels collected by U. Rütersworden, *Dominium terrae*, BZAW 215 (Berlin, 1993), 6.

[70] Cf. Wellhausen, *Composition*, 153; Gerstenberger, *Leviticus*, 234.

[71] Perlitt speaks about the "Geist der ungebrochenen, der quasi natürlichen Einheit von Gott und Volk und Land" in the time of Jeremiah, see L. Perlitt, "Anklage und Freispruch Gottes", *ZThK* 69 (1972), 290-303, p. 293.

did not and does not intrinsically belong to the people of Israel: it was promised to the patriarchs, who came from elsewhere; the patriarchs themselves sojourned in the land as strangers; the Israelites were led out of Egypt to receive the land of the promise, and it had to be won by the conquest of other peoples by the help of God.[72] Whether or not these traditions arose from historical circumstances is immaterial to our purpose. What counts is that the people of Israel conceived of their land as being a gift from their God, and of themselves as not being, *sensu stricto*, autochthonous.[73] Since the land had not always been theirs, a time might come when it would again no longer belong to them;[74] if their God had the power to give it to them, he had the power to take it away again. Against the backdrop of these traditions it is possible to imagine the personification of the land even in the pre-exilic period. The Israelites were commanded to thank YHWH for the gift of the land (e.g. Deut 26:5-10); but in periods of distress they may well have been tempted to curse his gift, the land that was eating them instead of feeding them. And a preacher, seeking to instil respect for the land because of the divine presence in the midst of it, may well have been inspired with the poetical image of the land itself being intolerant of ethical and religious impurity.

The fact that 18:25, 28 and 20:22 seem to contain a menace of exile cannot be used to argue for exilic provenance of these passages.[75] This point has already been discussed above and need not occupy us here (see Chapter 1, note 30).

5.3 THE PROVINCIAL OUTLOOK OF H

In Chapter 3 above, we have discussed the significance of the expression "people of the land" for the determination of the real addressees of H. In the historical books, the group thus designated is sometimes defined as the inhabitants of the provinces, as opposed to the urban popu-

---

[72] For this complex of notions, see H. Wildberger, "Israel und sein Land", *EvTh* 16 (1956), 404-422.

[73] It is at any rate impossible to explain this consciousness of Israel only from the experience of the Babylonian exile, as it surfaces already in the books of Amos and Hosea.

[74] Cf. Kaufmann, *Toledot* I, 199.

[75] Another question is whether the text refers to exile at all. After all, the previous inhabitants of the land of Canaan did not go into exile, see Heinisch, *Leviticus*, 88.

lation of Jerusalem. An audience made up of the people of the land therefore tends to indicate that H originated in the countryside. Moreover, a provincial milieu would account for the simple power structure presupposed in H (see the discussion in 3.3. above). Of course, if the use of the expression "people of the land" and the simplicity of the power structure were the only arguments, the hypothesis of provincial provenance would be very weak indeed. However, a whole series of other considerations reveal that the outlook of H is distinctly provincial. This circumstance is particularly striking when H is compared to Deuteronomy, which evinces a more urban background.[76] These considerations lend strong support to the hypothesis that H originated in the provinces.

The attitude toward cities

In H, cities are very rarely referred to, in contradistinction to the Deuteronomic law code, where they are frequently mentioned.[77] Moreover, whereas in Deuteronomy the cities appear as the given social matrix,[78] in H they are treated rather as exceptions. This is especially clear in the treatment of immovable property within the walls of a city in the redemption laws in 25:25-55. The object of these laws is to assure that an impoverished Israelite will not forever continue to slide down the social ladder. In four paragraphs, clearly marked by the expression "If your brother becomes poor..." ($k\bar{\imath}$ $y\bar{a}m\bar{u}k$ $\,^{\prime}\bar{a}\hbar\bar{\imath}k\bar{a}...$; $um\bar{a}k$ $\,^{\prime}\bar{a}\hbar\bar{\imath}k\bar{a}...$), different degrees of destitution are treated: the case of an Israelite having to sell part of his property (25:25-28), the case where he sells all of his property and becomes dependent for his livelihood on a fellow Israelite (25:35-38), the case where he has to sell himself to a fellow Israelite (25:39-43), and finally the case where he sells himself to a resident alien (25:47-55). In the first and the last paragraph (25:25-27, 48-52) the remedy of redemption, by the person himself or by a member of his family, is proposed. In all four cases the jubilee is presented as the ulti-

---

[76] See Weinfeld, *Deuteronomy 1-11*, 36f.

[77] In H cities are mentioned in two passages only, in 25:29-34 (7 times); 26:25-33 (3 times). In the Deuteronomic law-code, cities are mentioned very often, see Deut 13:13, 14, 16, 17; 19:1, 2, 5, 7, 9, 11, 12; 20:10, 14, 15, 15, 16, 19, 20; 21:2, 3, 3, 4, 6, 19, 20, 21; 22:15, 17, 18, 21, 23, 24, 24; 25:8; 28:3, 16.

[78] Cf. the Deuteronomic expressions $b^{e}kol$ $\check{s}^{e\,\varsigma}\bar{a}rek\bar{a}$ and $b^{e\,\flat}a\hbar ad$ $\check{s}^{e\,\varsigma}\bar{a}rek\bar{a}$ (in all your gates, in one of your gates: e.g. Deut 15:7; 16:5).

mate solution: in the jubilee year every Israelite regains his freedom and his property.[79]

In this context, the verses treating the sale of real estate in a walled city look a little out of place:

25:29

ואיש כי ימכר בית מושב עיר חומה
והיתה גאלתו עד תם שנת ממכרו ימים תהיה גאלתו

If a man sells a dwelling house in a walled city, he may redeem it within a whole year after its sale; for a full year he shall have the right of redemption.

The implication of this provision is that if the house has not been redeemed after a year, it will belong in perpetuity to the buyer (25:30). The provision is then hedged in two ways: houses in unwalled villages are reckoned with the fields, i.e. they may be redeemed and will be released in the jubilee (25:31), and houses in the Levitical cities may always be redeemed, since they are as it were the landed property ($^{a}huzz\bar{a}h$) of the Levites (25:31-33). As to the fields surrounding their cities, they may not be sold at all (25:34). The legal reasoning behind these verses is manifest: laws valid for the countryside are not applicable in an urban setting; the different status of real estate in cities—although defined within strict limits—has to be recognized in order to prevent abuse of the law.[80] The main concern, however, of vv 29-34 is entirely different from that of the four paragraphs on the impoverished Israelite discussed above. These verses have been described as a later addition, or an amendment to the main text of the law.[81] At any rate, it is clear that the realities of the city are looked upon as an exception. Although the author acknowledges the existence of cities and the different rules obtaining there, his real concern is with life in the countryside, and it is to that reality that the main thrust of the law is addressed.

---

[79] As is remarked by Wright, more often than not the jubilee would benefit the posterity of the impoverished Israelite rather than the impoverished person himself (cf. 25:41, 54). "It was *not* provided that an Israelite who, for whatever reason, failed to maintain his property should automatically and immediately have it restored to him, but that a person's descendants should not have to suffer in perpetuity the consequence of the economic collapse of his generation." Wright, *God's People*, 124.

[80] These verses have been interpreted as a concession of Israelite law to the earlier Canaanite system of land tenure which persisted in the cities, see Wright, *God's People*, 125 and 44f (with exhaustive literature).

[81] See S. E. Loewenstamm, "Law", in B. Mazar, ed., *The World History of the Jewish People, Vol. 3. Judges* (Tel Aviv, 1971), 231-267, p. 245.

A very similar attitude towards cities is evinced by Lev 26. In the catalogue of curses waiting to befall Israel in case of disobedience, their
cities ('*ārēkem*, 26:25, 31, 33) are mentioned three times. As in Lev 25,
however, it appears that the cities are not part of the direct environment
of the addressees, as is implied at least by the verse in which they are
first mentioned:

26:25   והבאתי עליכם חרב נקמת נקם ברית ונאספתם אל עריכם
               ושלחתי דבר בתוככם ונתתם ביד אויב

And I will bring a sword upon you, that shall execute vengeance for
the covenant; and if you gather within your cities I will send pestilence among you, and you shall be delivered into the hand of the
enemy.

In this passage, the cities are presented as a means of last resort. The
Israelites to which H is addressed are not dwelling in cities in times of
peace, and only the menace of foreign troops will force them to find
refuge there. However, even their cities cannot protect them from the
wrath of their God: after suffering different types of catastrophes within
the city wall (26:25-29), the cities themselves will be destroyed (26:31,
33).

Both of the passages in H which mention cities contain clear indications that the author is not concerned with city life. He knows about
cities, and acknowledges their distinct status as well as their partial use-
fulness in case of war. Moreover, the cities are certainly not exempt
from the law. The author's own outlook is provincial, however, and his
interest is the life of the Israelites in the countryside.

Agriculture and country life

Another indication of the provincial outlook of H is the relative domi-
nance of the themes of agriculture and country life. An interest in agriculture is manifest in the following passages: 19:9f and 23:22, provisions for the poor during the harvest; 19:19, prohibition on mixed
breeding and mixed sowing; 19:23-25, provisions concerning the plant-
ing of fruit trees; 20:24, the Promised Land is characterized as a land
overflowing with milk and honey; 23:10 and 23:39, the feasts are defined after the attendant agricultural activities. Perhaps the verses where

animals are mentioned are relevant as well: 18:23 and 20:15f, on bestiality; 24:18, 21, on killing another man's domestic animals. For Lev 25
and 26, see below. It is not the quantity, nor the content of these passages
which permits us to claim that the theme of agriculture is particularly
important in H: most of these rules and themes, including the ones occurring in Lev 25 and 26, are found in the Deuteronomic law-code or in
the Book of the Covenant as well. What remains striking, however, is
the absence of themes going beyond the provincial framework. Roughly
speaking, the only other themes treated in H are those of ritual (sacrifices: 17:1-16; 19:5-8; 22:17-33; purity of the priests: 21:1-22:16;
feasts: 23:1-44; appurtenances of the tabernacle: 24:1-9), human relationships (18:6-23; Lev 19 and 20), idolatry (17:7; 18:21; 19:4; 20:2-5;
26:1, 30) and respect for the name of YHWH (24:10-23). In H, one finds
no information on a central court of justice (contrast Deut 17:8-13), on
the king (Deut 17:14-20), on military service (Deut 20:1-9), warfare
(Deut 20:10-20; 23:9-14) or captives of war (Deut 21:10-14), nor on the
attitude to be adopted towards the neighbouring peoples (Deut 23:1-8;
25:17-19). Whereas Deuteronomy bears the mark of an urban, cosmopolitan outlook, H reflects a provincial mentality.[82] This may be further
illustrated by a closer look at Lev 25 and 26, where the essential importance of agriculture and country life in the conception of H is particularly clear.

Sabbath year and jubilee year

The sabbath year is presented in H as a sacral institution which touches
the land: "the land shall keep a sabbath to the LORD" ($w^e\check{s}\bar{a}b^e t\bar{a}h$
$h\bar{a}$'$\bar{a}re\d{s}$ $\check{s}abb\bar{a}t$ $layhwh$, 25:2). The practical application and consequences of this commandment are all about agricultural practices like
sowing, pruning and reaping (25:3-7). In this, H departs from the provisions for the seventh year in Deut 15.[83] In Deuteronomy, nothing is said
about the land or about agriculture; the seventh year is a year of debt-
release between Israelites. Although it is unlikely that either of the codes
knew or used the other, the different treatment of the seventh year is

---

[82] Another indication of the different backgrounds of H and the Deuteronomic code
is the important function of the written word in Deuteronomy (Deut 17:18; cf. 6:8f;
24:1; 27:3, 8; 30:10; 31:9-11, 19, 24) as opposed to the absence of any reference to the
practice of writing in H.

[83] By the same token, H stands closer to the Book of the Covenant, see Ex 23:10.

telling: in Deuteronomy the seventh year signifies an interruption of the money economy, in H the suspension of agricultural activities.

The rest of Lev 25 deals with the jubilee year. Again this year is defined as a sacred institution (25:10, "you shall hallow the fiftieth year"), and again all of its implications touch the use of the land: every Israelite shall return to his property (25:10); no sowing or reaping is allowed (25:11); the price of land must be set in accordance with the Jubilee (25:13-18); extraordinary fertility is promised (25:19-22); the land cannot be sold in perpetuity, not even when its original owner has become enslaved (25:23-55). On the matter of slavery, a comparison with Deut 15 is again instructive. In Deut 15:12-18, Hebrew slaves and bondwomen are viewed strictly from the perspective of personal bondage and personal freedom; not even a hint is given that these persons will recover their landed property, or even that they ever owned any land. In H, on the other hand, the Israelite brother is consistently viewed as a land-owner, even though he may have lost his land and his personal freedom. The purpose of the entire section on the Jubilee is that even if he has become enslaved, he will eventually go free and recover his property.[84] Again we may suppose that the two law codes constitute independent developments of the same legal tradition, yet the difference between them reveals something of their underlying conception.[85] Whereas Deuteronomy accentuates the independent value of personal freedom, the conception of H is that without land no man is entirely free, since he will not be able to support himself.[86] Deuteronomy's outlook is urban, that of H provincial.

Blessings and curses

Both the blessings and the curses in the final chapter of H show that the point of view of the author and his audience is that of the countryside.

---

[84] See 25:10, 28, 41. In 25:54 the provision that he shall return to his property is lacking. *De jure*, the implication that he shall return to his property is nevertheless clear, since the legal principle has already been well established in what precedes. It is not impossible, however, that this omission signifies that even if an Israelite, for whatever reason, has no property to go back to, he will go free from his non-Israelite master at the jubilee. In this latter case, the Israelite would *de facto* fall into the same category as the liberated Hebrew slave of Deut 15.

[85] The laws do not, in point of fact, contradict one another, as is often thought. See the remarks of H. M. Wiener, *The Origin of the Pentateuch* (London, 1912), 79f, and the full discussion of Wright, *God's People*, 248-259.

[86] Cf. 25:35-38: the Israelite who has sold all his land becomes dependent on his "brother".

The blessings promise fertility and abundant harvests (26:4f, 9f) and peace from wild animals (26:6). The promise of peace from foreign troops is formulated in a way which shows that the perspective is that of the provinces: "the sword shall not go through your land" (*weḥereb lōʾ taʿăbōr beʾarṣekem*, 26:6); admittedly, this promise is then developed over several verses (26:7f), showing that the absence of war is important to the audience of H. The only other promises are the more spiritual ones discussed above in Chapter 4 (26:9b, 11f). In Deut 28, on the other hand, the blessing in the fields is juxtaposed with the blessing in the cities (Deut 28:3); instead of the promise of peace from foreign incursions, comes an assurance of victory (Deut 28:6); moreover, stress is laid on the fact that Israel's blessings will impress all the peoples of the earth (Deut 28:10), and that Israel will be first among the nations (Deut 28:12f). The local, provincial outlook of H stands in contrast to the more urban and cosmopolitan perspective of Deuteronomy.

With regard to the curses, H is again quite provincial. Curses include different kinds of diseases, infertility (26:16, 20), incursions of foreign troops (26:17), lack of rain (26:19), wild animals attacking children and animals (26:22a) and deserted roads (26:22b). The following verses of Lev 26 speak of war and the population crowding into the cities, whereupon the discourse becomes more "urban": pestilence, famine, cannibalism, destruction of the cities and exile. Nevertheless, the entire catalogue of curses in H remains quite provincial when compared with Deuteronomy. The Deuteronomic curses juxtapose the city and the field at the outset (Deut 28:16); furthermore, they seem to paint the picture of foreign occupation (Deut 28:30-34); Israel will become a byword among all the peoples (Deut 28:37). Elements like these are absent from H. Furthermore, it has been demonstrated that the Deuteronomic curses draw on motifs and formulas current in Assyrian suzerainty treaties, whereas these are absent from Lev 26.[87] Weinfeld finds here an indication that the authors of Deuteronomy belong to the school of wise men, instructed in international politics and diplomacy; the setting of H, on the other hand, is distinctly provincial.

A final detail in the discourse confirms the view that Lev 26 addresses a rural audience. The only law to which explicit reference is

---

[87] Cf. Weinfeld, *Deuteronomy*, 124f, with literature. See, however, the recent study by H. U. Steymans, *Deuteronomium und die* adê *zur Thronfolgeregelung Asarhaddons. Segen und Fluch im Alten Orient und in Israel*, OBO 145 (Freiburg/Göttingen, 1995), 284-291.

made in these blessings and curses, is the law on the sabbath year (26:35 quoted above, see also 26:34, 43). As we have seen above, this law, and the formulation it receives in H, concerns specifically the Israelites living in the countryside.

The dwelling-places of the Israelites

We have seen above that cities play a marginal role in H. A more central notion is that of the dwelling-places (*mōšābōt*).[88] The term occurs five times in H, all of them in the festal calendar (23:3, 14, 17, 21, 31).[89] In the plural, and referring to the dwelling-places of the Israelites, the term is also found a few times in priestly texts outside of H (Ex 12:20; 35:3; Lev 3:17; 7:26; Num 15:2; 35:29),[90] in Ezekiel (Ez 6:6, 14),[91] and in Chronicles (1 Chron 4:33; 6:39; 7:28).[92] It is not entirely certain whether the plural *mōšābōt* is derived from the singular *mōšāb*, or from a feminine *mōšābāh* otherwise unattested in Biblical Hebrew; in any case, the general sense of "dwelling-places" is unproblematic.

On the supposition that the priestly texts of the Pentateuch date from the time of the exile or later, several scholars have advanced the view that this term refers to, or alludes to, the Jewish Diaspora.[93] The main argument in favour of such a view is that some of the laws prescribed for "all your dwellings" concern principles that might be applied in the Diaspora: eating unleavened bread (Ex 12:20), not lighting fire on the sabbath (Ex 35:3), not eating blood or fat (3:17; 7:26). This argument is seriously weakened, however, by the fact that other priestly occurrences of the term cannot be viewed as an allusion to the Diaspora. In Num 35:29, the provision that the law will be valid in all Israel's dwellings concludes the rules on the cities of refuge; in Num 15:2 the term occurs in the clause "when you come into the land of your dwelling-places..."

---

[88] This term does not refer to cities, as is manifest from such examples as Ez 6:6 and Num 31:10, where cities are said to be located within the dwelling places.

[89] The singular *mōšāb* occurs in 25:29, but since singular and plural have a different meaning, it is better to keep them apart.

[90] See also Ex 10:23, which is usually attributed to the older sources (E?).

[91] See also 34:13, where a different plural is used. In 37:23 the MT is problematic, see BHS.

[92] Cf. also Num 31:10 (dwelling places of the Midianites); Gen 36:43 (of the Edomites).

[93] P. Grelot, "La dernière étape de la rédaction sacerdotale", *VT* 6 (1956), 174-189, pp. 178f; Elliger, *Leviticus*, 313; Van Houten, *Alien*, 137f.

(*kī tābōʾū ʾel ʾereṣ mōšᵉbōtēkem...*).[94] The occurrences in the book of
Ezekiel also refer to dwelling-places in the land of Israel. In view of
these facts, it is better to drop the theory that *mōšābōt* alludes to the
Diaspora. The intention of the phrase "in all your dwellings" stresses
that a law must be put in practice all through the land, and not only in
and around the temple. This is illustrated by a comparison between one
of the priestly texts and a verse from Deuteronomy:

Ex 12:20   בכל מושבתיכם תאכלו מצות

In all your dwellings you shall eat unleavened bread.

Deut 16:4   ולא יראה לך שאר בכל גבלך

No leaven shall be seen with you in all your territory.[95]

In different formulations the same rule is laid down: the Israelites shall
not eat leavened bread in their entire land; the priestly expression "in all
your dwelling-places" is equivalent to Deuteronomy's "in all your territory".

In H, the expression "in all your dwellings" occurs four times in the
chapter on the Feasts (23:3, 14, 21, 31). It is not easy to determine
whether the phrase refers each time to the entire paragraph or only to the
rule that immediately precedes it, i.e. that no work shall be done on that
day (23:3, 21, 31), or that no produce of the new season may be eaten
until that day (23:14). The same chapter contains the expression "from
your dwellings":

23:17   ממושבתיכם תביאו לחם תנופה שתים שני עשרנים סלת תהיינה
           חמץ תאפינה בכורים ליהוה

You shall bring from your dwellings two loaves of bread to be waved,
made of two tenths of an ephah; they shall be of fine flour, they shall
be baked with leaven, as first fruits to the LORD

It is not easy to interpret this verse. Does it mean that the first fruits have
to be offered by the priests in the central sanctuary,[96] or in the local

---

[94] RSV: "When you come into the land you are to inhabit..."
[95] The same expression is found in Ex 13:7.
[96] Cf., e.g., Knohl, "Priestly Torah", 85.

sanctuary,[97] or that each farmer has to bring them to the local sanctuary?[98] Fortunately, the determination of the meaning of the term *mōšābōt* does not depend on the solution of these historical problems. The expression "(all) your dwellings" does not refer to individual cities or villages, but functions as a *plurale tantum* designating the entire Israelite territory. The expression cannot possibly be viewed as an allusion to the Diaspora in 23:14, 17, which speak of sacrifice, and it is therefore unlikely that it was meant as such an allusion in the three other occurrences.[99]

Excursus: Priests in the provinces

It has been observed by Knohl that H tends to give an important place to ideas and practices of popular religion.[100] In contrast to the Priestly Torah, which reflects the ritual of the Temple in Jerusalem, the Holiness School integrates several elements of popular worship in its treatment of the festivals.[101] Furthermore, whereas the Priestly Torah is entirely focused on the sanctity of the dwelling place of YHWH, the Holiness School yields to the popular idea that worship is meant to elicit blessing. Knohl hypothesizes that the blending of priestly and popular worship came about when the priests reached out to the people in reaction to prophetic criticisms directed at the Temple.[102] The considerations brought forward in the preceding sections suggest a different explanation, namely that H is the product of a priestly school located in the countryside. The historical presupposition of such a suggestion is that the priests attached to the Temple in Jerusalem were not necessarily living there permanently. This is indeed attested in several places in the OT: a priest might have his home in the countryside while executing his

---

[97] See Weinfeld, *Deuteronomy*, 218.

[98] See Kaufmann, *Toledot I*, 124.

[99] Furthermore, it is generally unlikely that H should contain any prescriptions for the Diaspora. The fundamental idea is that the Israelites must obey the laws because of the holy presence of YHWH in their midst; this idea is not applicable in exile.

[100] Cf. Knohl, "Priestly Torah", 104.

[101] For Knohl's definition of "Priestly Torah" and "Holiness School", see above in Chapter 1.

[102] Cf. Knohl, *Sanctuary*, 222-224.

priestly duties in the capital.[103] We are not well informed about this arrangement and do not know whether these priests had public duties in the countryside as well and, if so, what kind of duties.

This hypothesis may seem excessively speculative. Admittedly, much is left blank in the picture it paints since the sources do not offer the information necessary to fill it out. On the other hand, the hypothesis does not force the facts into a straitjacket, but integrates them into a meaningful picture. The priestly tradition was most probably developed at an important sanctuary, and its connection with the first Temple has been cogently argued.[104] H certainly stands in this tradition, meaning that it must be connected to the Temple in Jerusalem in some way or another. However, the provincial outlook of H, identified above, could not have arisen in the capital. At this point, the circumstance of priests residing in the countryside establishes a link between the priestly tradition and the popular, provincial preoccupations evinced by H. Moreover, this view ties in well with the historical reconstruction attempted in 3.3. above: H is addressed to a provincial audience, called "people of the land", far removed from the realities of the capital and its preoccupations; the political organization of the state does not touch it directly. Nevertheless, the priest is an important figure in this environment, not because of his power, but because of his holiness resulting from the fact that he approaches YHWH.

These historical considerations merit more ample evaluation, which cannot however be provided in the present exegetical study.[105]

---

[103] Cf. M. Haran, "Studies in the Account of the Levitical Cities. I Preliminary Considerations", *JBL* 80 (1961), 45-54; idem, "Studies in the Account of the Levitical Cities. II Utopia and Historical Reality", *JBL* 80 (1961), 156-165, esp. p. 51f. The arguments put forward by Haran are (a) that Abiathar is seen to own a plot of land in Anatoth, see 1 Ki 2:26 (and compare Jer 32:6-25), and (b) the fact that the Levitical cities destined for the Aaronites are located in Judah, see Josh 21:4, 9-19. Hoffmann brings some material which tends to show that the 24 priestly classes officiating in the second Temple were also settled each in their own city (cf. Luke 1:5-9, 39), and advances the hypothesis that this arrangement corresponded more or less to that of the first Temple. See D. Hoffmann, *Die wichtigsten Instanzen gegen die Graf-Wellhausensche Hypothese* (Berlin, 1904), 151.

[104] Cf. the list of arguments in Milgrom, *Leviticus 1-16*, 13-35.

[105] An additional argument in favour of the view that H originated in the Judean countryside are the points of contact between H and the book of Amos. For Amos 4 and Lev 26, see the literature in Chapter 1, n. 35. Compare also Amos 7:9 with Lev 26:30f; Amos 5:21 with Lev 26:31b.

5.4 CONCLUSIONS

A certain tension exists in H between the fictional framework of Israel in the desert on the one hand, and the importance of the theme of the land on the other. In several points of the discourse, the fiction moves far into the background and the Israelites are addressed as if they are already in the land (particularly in Lev 25 and 26). This tension has generated a variety of pictures and points of view concerning the land. In the present section we will draw some general conclusions. The results of the present chapter will be confronted with those of Chapter 3, and questions of date and the historical referent of the land in H will be taken up.

The land and the people

Above in 3.3. it has been established that the people of Israel are viewed in H as a group constituted along ethnic lines. That observation accords well with the notion of the land as an entity distinct from the people of Israel. In H it is made clear that the Israelites were originally outsiders, whose entry into the land had been prepared in the desert (see 5.1. above). The name of the land, Canaan, has nothing to do with the people of Israel, another indication that people and land do not originally belong to one another. Moreover, even after they have settled, the land preserves, as it were, a distinct personality; establishment in the land can never be taken for granted, and in the event of disobedience it may come to an end (see 5.2. above). All these elements show that what holds the Israelites together is not, in the view of H, the fact that they live together in the same land. A stronger tie binds them together, that of the blood.

Another notion defined in 3.3. is that of the national perspective in H: the Israelites are called upon to become a nation; the laws set forth concern the entire people. This national perspective also finds expression in the view of the land obtaining in H. The word of YHWH will be the only law in the land to which he will bring the Israelites. On the political level, this implies that Israel in their land will be an independent nation (see 5.1. above). The territory of this nation will be the land of Canaan, apparently a fairly well-defined geographical unit stretching out from the Brook of Egypt in the South to the Lebanon range in the North (see 5.2. above). On the other hand, however, the facts brought to light in section 5.3. tend to relativize this national perspective. The outlook of H is seen to be distinctly that of the countryside. Although the laws and the teaching it transmits are certainly meant to be authoritative for the whole nation, its main preoccupations are those of the rural population. The scope is national, but the outlook is provincial. The provincial outlook explains why H, although it purports to address the whole nation, nevertheless lacks regulations for several domains indispensable for the functioning of a state (such as central government and military organization). On these points, the national design of the Deuteronomic code with its urban and cosmopolitan outlook is much more adequate than H.

The internal organization of the people as it has been described in 3.3. is in accord with the results of 5.3. concerning the provincial provenance of H. The two levels in the power structure are the individual family and the assembly (which in the land becomes the assembly of the 'am hā'āreṣ). This structure may have corresponded quite closely to the one found in the Israelite countryside.[106] In this social framework, the priest represents the Temple viewed as the dwelling place of YHWH. His presence in the countryside may be explained from the fact that priests working in the sanctuary in Jerusalem did not necessarily live there, but might have had their homes in the provinces.[107]

The land in historical terms

With regard to the land as viewed in H, the historical question may be posed in the same terms as with regard to the people. The text itself does not intend to give any historical information, which would have been well known to its original audience. Present-day scholars are left, therefore, to divine the date and milieu of the text from indications betraying its historical background. The precariousness of this procedure cannot be exaggerated. Nevertheless, since the historical approach may assist exegesis by providing additional relief to the text, we will briefly review the results of the present chapter in that light.

All three of the preceding sections contain indications that the text reflects a historical situation before the year 587. The paradigmatic di-

---

[106] See 2 Ki 4:13 and the commentaries to that verse.

[107] Alternatively, the presence of priests in the countryside might be explained on the supposition that they were attached to a provincial sanctuary. This was the idea of Kaufmann, see notes 6 and 8 above. This would not explain, however, the connection between H and the other priestly texts, which probably originated in Jerusalem.

mensions of the camp, and the resultant conclusions with regard to the land, reveal that the Israelite state is viewed as politically independent and YHWH as dwelling in its midst. Both of these principles are applicable to pre-exilic Israel,[108] but neither of them finds a place in any later period. With the loss of political independence, the possibility of applying the commandments of YHWH as state law had vanished. The autonomy granted to the Jewish citizen-temple community in the Persian period is a far cry from the outright freedom envisaged in H. As to the notion of the divine presence, during the exile it never was more than a tantalizing vision,[109] whereas after the exile it remained largely an unfulfilled prophecy.[110] It is perhaps not impossible to spiritualize the paradigmatic qualities of the camp, or to explain them as idealistic features, but it is doubtful whether such approaches do justice to the evidence.

The use of the name Canaan to refer to the territory of the Israelite state is another indication of an early date. The evidence suggests that this usage goes back to the second millennium when Canaan was an Egyptian province. In the OT, it disappears after the account of the conquest of the land. In the prophetical books, including Ezekiel, the name Canaan occurs as a geographical term with a different meaning. Admittedly, the author of H probably received this name from tradition, a tradition which may have spanned hundreds of years. However, the foregoing considerations make it unlikely that it could have been used in such a self-evident way as in H (where no specifications are laid down) in the exilic or post-exilic periods.

Finally, the provincial outlook informing much of the discourse may be used as an argument against an exilic or post-exilic date. After 587, the Jews lost their country and hence their countryside. The social matrix of the Books of Ezekiel and Jeremiah, of Haggai, Zechariah and Malachi, of Ezra and Nehemiah is decidedly different from that of H: although agriculture and country life may play a role, varying in importance from book to book, the main outlook of these books is nevertheless that of a group with strong connections to the city and a concern for international relations.

None of the arguments advanced in the present chapter is capable of proving a pre-exilic date for H, nor does their cumulative weight decide

---

[108] The schism between the Northern tribes and Judah did not jeopardize the political independence of either state, nor the idea that YHWH actually dwelt in the sanctuaries.
[109] See, e.g., Ez 40-48.
[110] Cf. Clements, *God and Temple*, 123-134.

the matter. However, in conjunction with similar arguments advanced above in 3.3, and in the absence of indications of a later date, these considerations strengthen the hypothesis of an historical background in the pre-exilic period.

CHAPTER SIX

YHWH'S LAND AND ISRAEL'S LAND

The preceding chapter discussed the different perspectives from which the land is contemplated in H. In the present chapter we will turn our attention to the theological and ideological value of the notion of the land. What is the status of the land in the conception of H? The answer to this question can be condensed into the words which form the title of this chapter: it is YHWH's land, while at the same time it is the land of the Israelites. These two statements and the relationship between them will presently be evaluated.

6.1 YHWH'S LAND

In the view of H, the ultimate owner and lord of the land is YHWH. This idea is expressed explicitly in 25:23 and implicitly in a series of laws regarding the produce of, and behaviour in, the land. The underlying concept is a cultic one: the land belongs to YHWH because he dwells there.

YHWH as owner and lord of the land

The notion that the land on which the Israelites are settled really belongs to YHWH is explicitly expressed in many places in the OT, in highly diverse formulations.[1] Moreover, this notion is implicit in several other

---

[1] It is called "the land (*'ereṣ*) of YHWH", Hos 9:3, or with suffixes, "my/your/his land": 1 Ki 8:36; Isa 14:25; Jer 2:7; 16:18; Ez 36:5, 20; 38:16; Joel 1:6; 2:18; 4:2; Ps 10:16; 85:2. Using a different Hebrew noun, it is designated as "the land (*'ªdāmāh*) of YHWH", Isa 14:2, or with a suffix my land (*'admātī*) 2 Chron 7:20. In Ex 15:17 it is referred to as "the mountain of your inheritance" (*har naḥªlātᵉkā*); the expression "the inheritance of YHWH" refers to the land in 1 Sam 26:19; Jer 2:7; 50:11; Ps 68:10; 79:1; (cf. also 2 Sam 14:16). More exceptional phrases are "the pastures of God", Ps 83:13; "the land-holding of YHWH", Jos 22:19; "the house of YHWH" Hos 9:15; "my vineyard and my portion" Jer 12:10f (cf Isa 5:1-7); see also Ps 78:54.

passages.[2] The wide spread of the OT attestations, as well as the fact that
the motif is attested in other Ancient Near Eastern texts, makes it seem
probable that it belonged to the oldest theological traditions of Israel.[3]
An influential essay on the theological significance of this motif is that
of Von Rad.[4] Von Rad distinguishes the *historical* conception of the land
as promised to the patriarchs and given to their descendants, from the
cultic conception of the land as YHWH's possession. In Von Rad's view,
these conceptions originally existed separately, as is shown by the fact
that the first one dominates the historical account of the Hexateuch
stretching from the promises to the patriarchs to the fulfillment under
Joshua, while the second conception prevails in the law-codes with their
emphasis on first-fruit offerings and Sabbath years. Only at the latest
stage of the history of tradition were the two conceptions connected
with one another. Whereas several scholars have adopted and elaborated
Von Rad's approach,[5] others have criticized the separation of the "historical" and the "cultic" views of the land. The latter hold that it is unnecessary to suppose that these conceptions originated in different circles and continued for a long time to exist separately.[6] The two
conceptions of the land are not mutually exclusive but rather complementary: in order for YHWH to promise and give the land, it had to be
his in the first place. The occasional mention of other peoples as owners
of the land before it was given to Israel (Ex 3:17; Deut 4:38; 9:5) does
not contradict this view, since it lies on a different level.[7] The fact that

---

[2] Von Rad has pointed to the legislation of the seventh year (Ex 23:10f; Lev 25:1ff)
and to the different commandments regarding the harvest: first fruits, tithes, etc. See G.
Von Rad, "Verheißenes Land und Jahwes Land im Hexateuch", in idem, *Gesammelte
Studien zum Alten Testament*, Theologische Bücherei, AT 8 (München, 1961), 87-100,
pp. 92-94. See also the discussion below.
[3] For Ugaritic attestations, see Clements, *God and Temple*, 51ff. Cf. also the Mesha
Stone, lines 5-9. The presence of this motif in other Ancient Near Eastern texts makes it
unlikely that it was first introduced into Israelite thought by Hosea (cf. Hos 9:3) in the
8th century, as is argued by Köckert. See M. Köckert, "Gottesvolk und Land. Jahve,
Israel und das Land bei den Propheten Amos und Hosea", in A. Meinhold und R. Lux,
Hsg., *Gottesvolk*, Fs S. Wagner (1991), 43-74, p. 51 and note 35.
[4] Von Rad, "Verheißenes Land"; for a discussion of later literature, see Wright,
God's People, 5-9.
[5] To the representations of the land identified by Von Rad, Lohfink wishes to add a
third one in which YHWH is represented as a king who gives certain territories in fief to
his subjects; see TWAT III, 958-985, cols. 972-973. Köckert extends Von Rad's theory
to four different conceptions, see Köckert, "Gottesvolk", 44-51.
[6] See in particular Wright, *God's People*, 10-43, with discussion of the relevant literature.
[7] In the same way, the later occupation of the land by the Israelites does not contradict the fact that it ultimately belongs to YHWH.

the conception of divine ownership of the land is not made explicit in most of the historical passages relating the promise or the gift of the land is insignificant: in many of the law-texts operating on this principle, too, the conception is implicit.[8]

Moreover, the complementarity of the two ideas is expressed explicitly in Ex 15:17, usually considered to be one of the oldest texts preserved in the OT:

Ex 15:17   תבאמו ותטעמו בהר נחלתך מכון לשבתך פעלת יהוה

Thou wilt bring them in, and plant them on thy own mountain, the place, O LORD, which thou hast made for thy abode.[9]

The motifs of the Exodus and the giving of the land are here combined with the idea that the land of the promise is YHWH's holy mountain. This combination shows that the two conceptions distinguished by Von Rad are neither incompatible nor historically unconnected.

The connection of the two conceptions in H, which will be reviewed below, is therefore not indicative of a relatively late stage in the tradition history.

The land is mine

In H, the sole explicit reference to the notion of divine ownership occurs in the context of the jubilee year legislation:

25:23   והארץ לא תמכר לצמתת כי לי הארץ כי גרים ותושבים אתם
עמדי

The land shall not be sold in perpetuity, for the land is mine; for you are strangers and sojourners with me.

The primary object of this verse is not to make a theological point, but to ensure that the redemption and jubilee laws will be observed.[10] This does not, however, preclude the possibility that the theological principle enunciated in this verse is of great importance to the author of H. The

---

[8] See the examples contained above in note 2; see also below.
[9] Cf. Ps 68:10. See the discussion in Clements, *God and Temple*, 51-54; Wright, *God's People*, 61.
[10] See the discussion in 3.2. above.

statement *lī hā'āreṣ* ("the land is mine") is constructed as a regular non-verbal clause in which *lī* is the predicate—i.e. the new information—and *hā'āreṣ* the subject—i.e. the known element.[11] In the context in which it appears, it is clear that the definite noun *hā'āreṣ* refers to the land of the Israelites, where the jubilee will be proclaimed (25:9) and where the redemption laws are operative (25:24).[12]

As has already been established in 3.2. above (pp. 58-59), YHWH is here represented as the great landlord with the Israelites as his tenants. Further light is thrown on the underlying concept by the second half of the verse: "for you are strangers and sojourners with me", but the discussion of that statement will be reserved for the second part of the present chapter (see 6.2. below). For additional information regarding YHWH's ownership and lordship of the land, we must turn to passages where these notions are implicit.

"When you come into the land"

On three occasions in H, a law is introduced by the words "When you come into the land" (*wᵉkī tābō'ū 'el hā'āreṣ*, 19:23) or "When you come into the land which I give you" (*kī tābō'ū 'el hā'āreṣ 'ᵃšer 'ᵃnī nōtēn lākem*, 23:10; 25:2).[13] Similar introductions are found at various points in the Pentateuch.[14] In H, the tenor of the laws following these introductions is identical in all three cases. Verses 19:23-25 stipulate that when the Israelites plant a fruit tree, its fruit may not be eaten during the first three years, while in the fourth year the yield of the tree is to be holy (probably meaning that it must be given to the priest); from the fifth year on, its produce may be eaten by the owner. The ordinance in 23:10 is to bring a sheaf of first fruits at the harvest for waving before YHWH, and to abstain of the new produce until that day (23:14). Fi-

---

[11] See F. I. Andersen, *The Hebrew Verbless Clause in the Pentateuch* (Nashville and New York, 1970), 91, #388 and #389.

[12] Taken in isolation, a possible translation would be "the earth is mine", cf. Ex 19:5.

[13] For Jagersma, the fact that the relative clause "which I give you" is lacking in 19:23 is an argument to date this text in exilic times. See Jagersma, *Leviticus 19*, 123f. It is methodologically unsound, however, to consider the formula in 19:23 in isolation from the two other attestations in H, where the relative clause is expressed.

[14] See Ex 12:25; 13:5, 11; Lev 14:34; Num 15:2, 18; 35:10; Deut 17:14; 18:9; 26:1. In my opinion, this spread of attestations does not prove that H borrowed the formula from Deuteronomy, as is advanced by Jagersma and others (see Jagersma, *Leviticus 19*, 123). In any case, the significance of this expression in H should first be established on the basis of the attestations in H.

nally, 25:2 introduces the legislation concerning the sabbath year. What is common to these three passages is that the rules prescribed can only be executed when the people of Israel will be settled on their land. More significantly, however, each one of these rules expresses the ownership of YHWH over the land which the Israelites will occupy. To him are given the first fruits as a token that the entire harvest is his; to him the land will rest in the seventh year in expression of YHWH's right over it.[15]

The significance of the introduction "When you come into the land…" is that when the Israelites come into the land and take possession of it, they must be mindful that its ultimate owner is and remains YHWH. The occurrence of the same introduction in combination with similar provisions in three different passages in H attests to the relative unity of H as a corpus. While it is difficult to say at what stage of the redaction of H these passages were added to it,[16] they clearly are representative of the conceptual universe of H. They are entirely consonant with the explicit statement in 25:23. Other provisions, although not introduced by the clause "When you come into the land…", carry the same implications as the three earlier passages: the prescription to bring a cereal offering of new grain (*minḥāh ḥᵃdāšāh*, 23:16) and the laws of the jubilee year (in particular 25:11f).[17] These also give expression to the idea that the ultimate owner of the land is YHWH, and that he must be honoured as such. It is therefore no exaggeration to say that the notion that YHWH is the ultimate owner of the land permeates the entire discourse.

Laws expressing YHWH's lordship over the land

The statement made in the opening verses of Lev 18 is on a different level, implying not so much ownership as lordship. The Israelites may not follow the practice of Egypt, nor the practice of the land of Canaan, to which YHWH will bring them; rather they are told:

---

[15] Hamilton compares the sabbath year to the closing of private streets in North America one token day a year in order to maintain legal claim to the right of way. See J. M. Hamilton, *Social Justice and Deuteronomy. The Case of Deuteronomy 15*, SBLDS 136 (Atlanta, 1992), 95.

[16] For discussion, see Elliger's commentary.

[17] Cf. also the allusions to the commandment on the sabbath year in 26:34, 35, 43.

18:4   את משפטי תעשׂו ואת חקתי תשמרו ללכת בהם

You shall do my ordinances and keep my statutes and walk in them.

It is strongly suggested by the context that this statement applies specifically to the time when the people of Israel will be settled in the land.[18] In
particular the latter part of the chapter shows that the land is the domain
within which the ordinances and statutes of YHWH need to be put into
practice (18:26-28: "You shall keep my statutes and my ordinances...
lest the land vomit you out..."). No indication is given that the ordinances and statutes referred to are limited to rules pertaining to the land
or its produce, as in the laws discussed in the preceding section. Most
probably the statement refers to all the laws of YHWH.[19] Thus the land
is pictured here as the space in which the commandments ought to be
put into practice. This recalls what was said in the preceding chapter on
the paradigmatic function of the camp (cf. 5.1. above, pp. 145-148),
where we saw that in H the land is pictured as the domain in which the
word of YHWH has force of law for all inhabitants. Conversely, the
implication of this principle is that compliance with the law of YHWH
is an expression of his lordship over the land. Lordship in this case does
not primarily mean ownership, as in 19:23; 23:10 and 25:2, but takes on
a political sense: YHWH's commands are to be obeyed there.

Further expression of the notion of YHWH's lordship over the land is
given by the verses which stipulate that a certain law must be done "in
the land", or "in your land" (19:9f; 23:22f;19:33f; 25:9; 25:45; 22:24;
26:2; 25:24, see 5.1. above, pp. 145-147). Even though the land is not
explicitly referred to as YHWH's land, and even though it is at times
explicitly termed the land of the Israelites, it always represents the domain in which the laws of YHWH are operative. Thus, the notion of
YHWH's lordship over the land is fundamental to the conception of H,
being even more dominant than the notion of ownership.

The notion of the land as the space in which the laws are to be put into
practice is found also in Deuteronomy.[20] However, whereas in H this

---

[18] Cf. also 20:22f.
[19] See above in Chapter 3, n. 235.
[20] Deuteronomy exaggerates this principle to the point of implying that in the desert
the law was not observed at all, see Deut 12:8. In H, the camp in the desert and the land
are not distinguished in this respect, see above in 5.1.

notion flows from the conception of YHWH's lordship over the land,
Deuteronomy is careful never to imply any special relationship between
YHWH and the land.[21] While in H the land is presented as *imposing* the
application of the law, in Deuteronomy it is presented as *rendering possible* the application of the law:

Deut 12:8f

לא תעשון ככל אשר אנחנו עשים פה היום
איש כל הישר בעיניו
כי לא באתם עד עתה אל המנוחה ואל הנחלה
אשר יהוה אלהיך נתן לך

You shall not do according to all that we are doing here this day,
every man doing whatever is right in his own eyes; for you have not
as yet come to the rest and to the inheritance which the LORD your
God gives you.[22]

The expression "the rest and the inheritance" refers to the land, which is
here presented as providing the freedom and the space necessary for
lawful behaviour, as opposed to the desert, which seems to imply anarchy. The land is the gratuitous gift of YHWH to his people, the precondition for the well-being which will come about through their observance of the law. The land is not represented as the sphere of YHWH's
lordship, where all his commandments must be observed for fear of being cast out from it.[23]

Moreover, in Deuteronomy one also finds the motif that fulfilling the
commandments is a condition for receiving and possessing the land
(6:18; 11:8f; 16:20).[24] This motif is absent from H. Wrongdoers will be
"cut off", and a disobedient Israel will be cast out from the land; but
nowhere in H is it stated, or even intimated, that entry to the land is
reserved for those who practise the commandments.[25] The continuity

---

[21] See the perceptive comments of Rofé, *Introduction to Deuteronomy*, 277.
[22] The statement in Deut 12:8f is characteristic for Deuteronomy in general. For the
land-theology of Deuteronomy, see Von Rad, "Verheißenes Land", 97-100, and L.
Perlitt, "Motive und Schichten der Landtheologie im Deuteronomium", in G. Strecker,
ed., *Das Land Israel in biblischer Zeit*, Jerusalem-Symposium 1981 (Göttingen, 1983),
46-58.
[23] Although, of course, exile is one of the punishments listed in Deuteronomy.
[24] See Von Rad, "Verheißenes Land" 98; Perlitt, "Motive" 54.
[25] Cf. Von Rad, 98: "Jedenfalls spiegelt sich im Deuteronomium eine wesentlich
fortgeschrittenere Situation als in der Priesterschrift, in der das Land eine reine Gabe
von Jahwe bleibt."

between the camp and the land as regards the need for obedience to
YHWH's commandments flows from the divine presence in the earthly
sanctuary, which is found in both.

These divergences warn us once more not to view H in the light of
Deuteronomy, even where both codes contain elements that at first sight
may be thought to be identical.

The land as YHWH's dwelling place

Although 25:23 explicitly states that the land of the Israelites ultimately
belongs to YHWH, and although other texts show this idea to underlie
the entire discourse, the term "the land of YHWH" is nowhere to be
found in H.[26] The absence of this term is all the more striking because it
does occur in other sources.[27] The reason may well be that in H, the term
"the land of YHWH" was avoided lest it be inferred that there was a
natural relationship between YHWH and the land, or that his power was
limited to a specific territory.[28] A limitation of YHWH's power or influence to a specific territory is nowhere implied in H. On the contrary,
YHWH intervenes in Egypt, whence he brings out the Israelites; he is
lord over the camp in the desert; when the Israelites are in their land, he
has the power to drive them out again and to harm them even in the lands
of their enemies. These facts seem to indicate that for H, YHWH is lord
over all the earth. However, if there is no natural relationship between
YHWH and the land, and if his power is not limited to a particular domain, what is the sense of the statement that the land is his?

The land as an extension of the sanctuary

The answer to the question of the relation between YHWH and the land
is provided by our earlier discussions in Chapters 3, 4 and 5 (see 3.2.,
4.3. and 5.1. above). One of the theological axioms of H—in fact, the
most fundamental of its theological axioms—is that YHWH is present
in the midst of his people, in the camp and, later, in the land.[29] YHWH's

---

[26] This recalls the fact that the Israelites are never referred to as "the people of
YHWH" in H. See above in Chapter 4, n. 46.
[27] See the examples above in n. 1.
[28] For this inference, see Wright, *God's People*, 61; Köckert, "Gottesvolk", 49f.
[29] In this respect, the camp functions as a paradigm of the land, see above in 5.1.

holy presence radiates outward from the sanctuary throughout the entire land and imposes its demands on all the inhabitants. This fundamental axiom explains the notions of YHWH's ownership and lordship over the land. The land occupied by the Israelites is his because he dwells there in his sanctuary.

That the entire land should be viewed as an extension of the temple may seem strange to our modern understanding. The idea, however, is not at all unusual in the OT context. In several passages from the Psalms and the prophetical books the temple and the land are viewed as being co-extensive (e.g. Ps 78:54; 23:6; Isa 11:9; 57:13; Hos 9:15; cf. Ex 15:17 quoted above). Clements has shown that in some texts, the temple is representative of the whole land, and that worship in the temple is connected with dwelling in the land:

> An Israelite who participated in the worship of Yahweh on Mount Zion was maintaining his obligations and responsibilities as one who dwelt on Yahweh's land. He was rendering due homage to the one to whom the whole land belonged and who held the right to give or withhold the land from its inhabitants. When therefore, the poet proclaimed, "Who shall dwell on thy holy hill?" (Ps. 15:1), not only was the right to enter the temple at stake, but through that the right to continue as an Israelite.[30]

This thought-complex is certainly relevant for the understanding of H. The conception of YHWH's ownership and lordship over the land is a cultic one, revolving around the notion of the land as the abode of God.[31] The entire territory promised to the Israelites—the land of Canaan—is viewed from the perspective of the temple.

The notions of YHWH's presence in the land and hence his lordship over it are entirely absent from Deuteronomy. Indeed, for all its importance in Deuteronomic theology, the land is there entirely desacralized.[32] The Temple—far from being his earthly dwelling from

---

[30] R. E. Clements, "Temple and Land: A Significant Aspect of Israel's Worship", *Transactions of the Glasgow University Oriental Society* 19 (1961-62), 16-28, p. 23.

[31] In his discussion of Lev 25:23, Wright has rejected the view that YHWH's ownership of the land is conceived of in cultic terms, because the verse does not contain a reference to the temple. However, whereas in Lev 25 the sanctuary is not explicitly mentioned, in other parts of H its significance is such that we are justified in supposing that it is present in the underlying ideas even where it is absent in the text (see, in particular, above in 4.3).

[32] Cf. Rofé, *Introduction to Deuteronomy*, 277. The only distinction of the land in Deuteronomy is that "the eyes of the LORD your God are always upon it" (Deut 11:12).

which his holiness radiates outward—is merely the place where YHWH has made his name to dwell.[33] Neither the land nor the sanctuary are represented as imposing any demands on Israel. The commandments are viewed as a function of the personal relationship obtaining between YHWH and Israel.[34]

The purity of the land

The conception of H is more precise, however, than that of the poetic and prophetic texts discussed by Clements. In these other texts the distinction between the Temple and the land is blurred: the two domains are co-extensive. In the conception of H the land and the sanctuary are consistently distinguished, although both stand under the influence of YHWH's immanent presence. The difference maintained in H between the land and the sanctuary is one of degree: whereas the sanctuary is holy, and therefore in danger of being profaned,[35] the land is merely pure and in danger of being defiled.[36] This is stated clearly in 18:24-28: the nations who occupied the land before the Israelites have defiled themselves and the land, wherefore they have been vomited out; the Israelites should beware not to defile themselves in the same way, by transgressing YHWH's commandments,

18:28   ולא תקיא הארץ אתכם בטמאכם אתה

...lest the land vomit you out when you defile it.

Although the positive term ṭāhōr is not applied to the land, the implication that the normal, and required, state of the land is one of purity is clear. The purity of the land as opposed to the holiness of the sanctuary should be interpreted, it seems, in the light of the idea of concentric circles of diminishing holiness discussed above in section 4.3. (pp. 131-

---

[33] For more ample discussion of the notion of divine presence in Deuteronomy, cf. J. G. McConville, J. G. Millar, *Time and Place in Deuteronomy*, JSOTS 179 (Sheffield, 1994), 114-116.

[34] As a result, the resident alien is not required to observe ritual purity in Deuteronomy, see Deut 14:21 (contrast Lev 17:15f).

[35] The sacredness of the sanctuary is indicated by its name *miqdāš* ; in 21:23 it is stated that YHWH sanctifies his sanctuary; being holy, the sanctuary can be desecrated (*ḥallēl*), see 21:12, 23. In 20:3 defilement (*ṭammēʾ*) of the sanctuary is referred to, probably because of the gravity of the crime in question.

[36] For the definition of the terms holy and profane, pure and impure, see above in section 4.3. pp. 123-124.

132). Whereas the priests are positively holy, the common Israelites should merely strive to be so; in the same way the sanctuary is sacred while the demand for the land surrounding it is merely that it should be pure. Impurity of the land would imperil the holiness of the sanctuary located in its midst. Although the land thus stands under the influence of YHWH's holy presence in its midst, it is not itself hallowed by this presence. Nowhere in H, nor in other priestly texts, do we find the idea of the holiness of the land.[37]

The notion of the purity of the land occupied by the Israelites can be detected in a number of other passages in the Old Testament.[38] Several texts implicitly oppose the purity of the land of Israel to the impurity of foreign lands (Am 7:17; Hos 9:3). The idea seems to be connected to the cultic notion that YHWH can be served only in the land of Israel (cf. 1 Sam 26:19; 2 Ki 5:17).[39] Other passages speak, like Lev 18:28, of defilement or pollution of the land (Deut 21:23; Jer 2:7; 3:1, 2, 9; Ez 36:17, 18; Ps 106:38).[40] The most illuminating parallels are two priestly texts explicitly stating that the demand for purity is connected to the idea of YHWH's dwelling in the land. Num 35 lays down the legal procedure for killings with and without intent; non-observance of the rules will lead to pollution of the land (Num 35:33). It is then stated:

Num 35:34   לא תטמא את הארץ אשר אתם ישבים בה
            אשר אני שכן בתוכה כי אני יהוה שכן בתוך בני ישראל

You shall not defile the land in which you live, in the midst of which I dwell; for I the LORD dwell in the midst of the people of Israel.

Bloodshed defiles the land. This must be avoided because of the divine presence in the midst of the land.[41] The notion of YHWH's dwelling in the land is more explicit here than in any passage in H. However, the

---

[37] The doctrine of the holiness of the land is found in Zech 2:16. It seems the first intimation of this idea occurs in Jer 16:18, which speaks of desecration (*ḥallēl*) of the land.

[38] A similar doctrine is attested in Hittite texts of the second millenium, e.g., TUAT II, 800: "Nur das Land Hatti (ist) euch, den Göttern, ein wahrlich reines Land." Such parallels show that the idea could be very old in Israel as well.

[39] Cf. Kaufmann, *Toledot*, vol. 1, 606-609. Kaufmann attempts to show that these ideas are representative of popular beliefs, whereas the prophetic faith was more universalistic.

[40] Cf. also Deut 24:4; Jer 23:15; Ez 22:24; 39:12, 14, 16; Ezra 9:11; 2 Chron 34:3-8; Zech 13:2; Mic 2:10

[41] See the discussion above in 3.2.

present passage clearly shares the conceptual universe of H: YHWH's earthly presence touches the whole land of Israel, imposing its demands on all the inhabitants; the transgression of the commandments leads to defilement of the land.

The second example, Jos 22, relates how the Transjordanian tribes built an altar by the Jordan. The other tribes accuse them of treachery, going on to say:

Jos 22:19   ואך אם טמאה ארץ אחזתכם עברו לכם אל ארץ אחזת יהוה
אשר שכן שם משכן יהוה והאחזו בתוכנו

But now, if your land is unclean, pass over into the LORD's land where the LORD's tabernacle stands, and take for yourselves a possession among us.

Transjordan, which according to the priestly texts falls outside the promised land,[42] is suspect of being unclean, even if it is inhabited by Israelites committed to YHWH. The territory on the western side of the Jordan, on the other hand, is called the land-holding of YHWH (*ʾaḥuzzat yhwh*) because of the tabernacle which "dwells" (*škn*) there; its purity is not in doubt. This passage shows even more explicitly than Num 35:34 that the presence of YHWH in his sanctuary in the midst of the land leads to the land's being designated as his possession. These are the very conceptions which underlie H.

Defilement of the land is referred to in two passages in Deuteronomy (Deut 21:23 in the law on the hanged man, and 24:4 in the law on divorce and remarriage). However, this motif does not seem to fit the general thought world of the book, and has often been ascribed to its sources.[43] More importantly, the phrase "(the land) which the LORD your God gives you for an inheritance" (*ʾašer yhwh ʾoelōhekā nōtēn lekā naḥalāh*), which occurs in both passages, makes it clear that the underlying conception is not that of God's dwelling in the land, but of respect for the gift of the great giver.

---

[42] Cf. the discussion on the extent of the land of Canaan, above in 5.2.
[43] See M. Weinfeld, "On 'Demythologization and Secularization' in Deuteronomy", *IEJ* 23 (1973), 230-233, p. 232; E. Otto, "Soziale Verantwortung und Reinheit des Landes. Zur Redaktion der kasuistischen Rechtssätze in Deuteronomium 19-25", in R. Liwak and S. Wagner, eds., *Prophetie und geschichtliche Wirklichkeit im alten Israel*, Fs S. Herrmann (Stuttgart, 1991), 290-306, p. 296.

6.2 ISRAEL'S LAND

Although the notions of divine ownership and lordship over the land dominate the conceptual universe of H, the land is also referred to as Israel's land. The expression "your land" occurs 13 times (19:9, 33; 22:24; 23:22; 25:7, 9, 45; 26:1, 5, 6, 19, 20, 33; cf. "the land of your property" 25:24). The conception of Israel's entitlement to the land links up with the cultic conception of divine ownership and lordship: the land is YHWH's because he dwells there, it is Israel's because of their relationship to YHWH and his temple.

The Israelites as YHWH's asylants

Above in 4.1, we noted the territorial implications of the Exodus motif in the conception of H. By the act of the Exodus, YHWH acquired the Israelites as his slaves, i.e. his worshippers. An integral part of his purpose was to settle these worshippers on land surrounding the temple and belonging to it. Being viewed entirely from the perspective of the sanctuary, the relationship between YHWH and his people contains a strong spatial component.

A very similar motif, but with even more emphasis on the territorial aspect, is expressed in the passage stating the principle of divine ownership:

25:23   והארץ לא תמכר לצמתת כי לי הארץ כי גרים ותושבים אתם
עמדי

The land shall not be sold in perpetuity, for the land is mine; for you are strangers and sojourners with me.

The statement that the Israelites are resident aliens and sojourners (gērīm wetōšābīm) with YHWH has already been discussed above in 3.2. On the realistic level, it was sufficient to observe that the Israelites are pictured as landless people granted the right to stay in the land of YHWH. In the present context, however, we must penetrate deeper into the meaning of the image used. For the notion of the Israelites as YHWH's gērīm and tōšābīm contains a further level of meaning, which is specifically religious. Although the religious use of the terms gēr and tōšāb is less current than that of the term 'ebed (see above in 4.1.), Bib-

lical and Ancient Near Eastern material allows us to define this use with
some degree of certainty.

In several Psalms, the Psalmist states that he is a *gēr* or intends to
gwr with YHWH. A good example is the following:

Ps 61:5   אגורה באהלך עולמים אחסה בסתר כנפיך

Let me sojourn in thy tent for ever![44] Oh to be safe under the shelter
of thy wings.[45]

The reference to the temple ("your tent") and to God's presence ("your
wings") show that at the basis of this prayer lies a conception of God's
temple as a place of refuge and asylum. In the religious context, the *gēr*
becomes a metaphor for the asylant seeking refuge in the temple.[46] The
notion of the temple as a place of refuge is attested also in other Psalms
as well as in some narrative and prophetical texts.[47]

The Ancient Near Eastern parallels to this notion have recently been
collected and discussed by Weinfeld. He has integrated the indications
from the OT with material from the Ancient Near East into a general
picture of the sanctuary as asylum.[48] All through the *Umwelt* of Ancient
Israel, we find accounts of persons having fled—for whatever reason—
to the sanctuary or the sanctuary city and being endowed with the right
to remain there as clients of the god. In Phoenician such a client seems
to have been referred to as a *gr*—using the same lexeme as Biblical
Hebrew—of the god, as is indicated by personal names of the type *gr* +
divine name.[49]

These parallels throw a new light on 25:23. The expression "you are
strangers and sojourners with me", where the speaker is the god, pictures the Israelites as asylants of YHWH. The terms "strangers and
sojourners", which primarily refer to resident aliens as has been estab-

---

[44] RSV: "Let me dwell in thy tent for ever."

[45] Cf. Ps 15:1; 39:13 and Isa 33:14.

[46] In Ps 61 and the other examples cited in the preceding note the expression is probably no more than a literary trope. At the basis of the expression lies a real religious
institution, however. Cf. Robertson Smith, *Lectures*, 77: "This notion of the temple-
client, the man who lives in the precincts of the sanctuary under the special protection of
the god, is used in a figurative sense in Psalm XV."

[47] See, e.g., J. Milgrom, "Sancta Contagion and the Altar/City Asylum", in J. A.
Emerton, ed, *Congress Volume. Vienna 1980*, SVT 32 (1981), 278-310; Weinfeld, *Justice*, 73-77.

[48] Weinfeld, *Justice*, 57-78.

[49] Cf. Robertson Smith, *Lectures*, 77-81; R. Martin-Achard, THAT I, 412.

lished above in 3.2, have a metaphoric function: the aliens residing with
a god are his clients, who have received the right to stay in the temple, or
more precisely, on the temple lands. In the narrow context of Lev 25,
this conclusion may seem unwarranted, since the temple is not at all
mentioned in this chapter.[50] However, the central place held by the sanctuary in the wider context of H gives ample justification for this interpretation. The land is YHWH's because he dwells in its midst, in the
sanctuary; the entire Israelite territory is viewed as temple land. In this
conceptual framework, the Israelites' status in the land is quite logically
viewed as that of allochthons who have been adopted as clients by the
godhead, and have therefore received his protection and the right to stay
in the vicinity of the temple. It is this status, granted to them by the
godhead, which—paradoxically—makes it possible to speak of the land
as belonging to the Israelites. Their entitlement to the land is that of
allochthons adopted as clients by the resident god.

The paradox involved in the notion that the Israelites are entitled to
the land because it does not belong to them but to YHWH, is reminiscent
of the notion that they are free because they are YHWH's slaves. Indeed,
the religious conception of the Israelites as *gērīm* with YHWH is entirely consonant with the conception of the Israelites as YHWH's slaves.
Whereas in social terms, the resident alien and the slave are different
categories, their projection in the religious domain proceeds from the
same underlying idea, namely that the entire lives of the Israelites are
oriented toward the divine presence in the sanctuary. When the social
aspect of the Israelite existence is being considered, the slave metaphor
comes into play. The Israelites are YHWH's slaves: whereas, on the one
hand, they are beholden to absolute obedience to the rules of the sanctuary (which extend all through the land), they are, on the other hand,
guaranteed freedom from bondage, both as a nation and individually.
Nobody has the right to enslave them, because they belong to God.
When, however, the focus is on the economic aspect, the metaphor of
the resident alien is used. The Israelites are resident aliens with YHWH:
they have obtained protection and sustenance in the temple, or rather on
the temple lands; the land they hold is therefore regarded as inalienable
property of the family throughout their generations. At the basis of both
conceptions lies the same intellectual procedure: institutions from the
sacral sphere ("slaves", who are in fact worshippers; "resident aliens",

---

[50] See above, note 31.

who are in fact asylants) are scaled up to encompass the whole of Israel's national existence. One might say that the rules of the temple are extended to the entire land, or, conversely, that the entire land of the Israelites is conceived of as temple land.

Although the conception of the Israelites as *gērīm* finds parallels in Ancient Near Eastern texts, it's scope in H is unique. Whereas in the parallels the client of the god is an individual, or in some cases a tribe,[51] in H the entire people of Israel is so represented. Moreover, the extent of the territory advocated in H is unique in that the entire Promised Land is viewed as belonging to the temple. What is expressed in 25:23 is a global vision for the Israelite nation.

Since the land belongs to the god, it is never to be treated as a mere commodity or an object of speculation. In order to enforce this principle, the land is entrusted to the family. Indeed, the people of Israel are not collectively settled on the land; rather, every individual family is assigned a part of it.[52] Moreover, since this assignment of property is done on divine authority, nobody can annul it, at least in principle. Every Israelite family is assured a share of landed property, which means in the terms of H a livelihood. Everything should be done to preserve the share of land (*'ᵃḥuzzāh*) for the family to which it was originally assigned—this is the object of the redemption laws (25:25-34). At the jubilee, all property is restored to the original occupants or to their descendants. The landholdings of the Israelites may not be sold in perpetuity.

The giving and taking possession of the land

In accordance with the narrative framework of H, the settlement of the Israelites in the land is presented as belonging to the future. It will come about through, on the one hand, YHWH's giving (*ntn*) of the land and, on the other, Israel's taking possession of it (*yrš*). The procedure may be illustrated by accounts of royal land grants, which employ the same terminology.

---

[51] Cf. Robertson Smith, *Lectures*, 79-80.
[52] Cf. Wright, *God's People*, 63.

The giving of the land

Four times in H, YHWH states that he will give the land to Israel (20:24; 23:10; 25:2, 38). The motif of the giving (*ntn*) of the land—to the patriarchs or to the people of Israel—is found in the non-priestly pentateuchal material (e.g. Gen 13:15, 17; 26:4),[53] in priestly texts (e.g. Gen 17:8; Ex 6:8) and very often in Deuteronomy. The Hebrew verb *ntn* has a wide field of meaning which differs somewhat from that of the English verb "to give". Even where the semantics of the verb imply the transfer of an object from one person to another, the implication is not always that of a gratuitous exchange; the verb *ntn* may imply selling (1 Ki 21:6), paying (Ex 21:19), or lending (Lev 25:37) as well as other nuances. With regard to the cases where the direct object is a plot of land or a territory, there is no unanimity among scholars as to the precise meaning of the verb. The great majority of examples involving the giving of land are precisely the ones speaking of YHWH giving land to Abraham or his descendants. Some have sought to explain YHWH's giving of the land in the light of inheritance practices.[54] The basis of this view is found in texts where the notion of inheritance is explicit, e.g.:

Deut 4:21   ...הארץ הטובה אשר יהוה אלהיך נתן לך נחלה

... the good land which the LORD your God gives you for an inheritance.[55]

These texts are said to clarify the meaning of the other texts, where "giving" is to be taken in the sense of "giving as an inheritance". The motif of the giving of the land, therefore, represents Israel as YHWH's heir,

---

[53] Albrecht Alt and his disciples have forcefully contended that the promise to give the land belongs to the hoariest traditions of Israel. In recent studies, however, these texts are often assigned a late date, because of their function in structuring the Pentateuch. In my opinion, the arguments for the lateness of the motif are dependent on a problematic use of literary criticism. There is no intrinsic reason why the promise and the gift of land could not have been recounted in early, pre-exilic or even pre-monarchic, traditions. For an evaluation of recent literature, see L. Schmidt, "Väterverheissungen und Pentateuchfrage", *ZAW* 104 (1992), 1-27

[54] See C. J. Labuschagne, THAT II, 117-141, col. 124; E. Lipiński, TWAT V, 693-712, cols. 704f. For the use of the verb in describing the practice of inheritance, see Gen 25:5; Deut 21:17.

[55] Similar phrases are frequent in Deuteronomy, see Deut 15:4; 19:10; 20:16; 21:23; 24:4; 26:1.

either as a son or as an adoptee.[56] A number of criticisms need to be made with regard to this theory. To begin with, it seems unnecessary to infer that Israel is represented as YHWH's heir even in the texts where *ntn* is combined with the noun *naḥᵃlāh*. It is more likely that Deut 4:21 etc. are to be taken in the sense that YHWH gives the Israelites a land which is to become their heirloom, which will be passed on from generation to generation. The significance of the term "inheritance" concerns the recipients in relation to the following generations, not the recipients in relation to YHWH. Secondly, although the verb *ntn* may in some contexts denote the giving of an inheritance, it does not by itself invite such an interpretation. One should not, therefore, interpret the cases of simple *ntn* in light of cases where the verb is accompanied by the noun *naḥᵃlāh*. And finally, the analogy of inheritance seems inadequate to explain the motif in the priestly texts, where every effort is made to dispel the impression that a natural relationship exists between YHWH and his people.[57] It is unlikely that in these texts the people of Israel should be represented as YHWH's heir.

A more felicitous approach, therefore, is that of Lohfink, who sees YHWH's giving of the land as modelled on royal grants of land.[58] Such grants are alluded to in 1 Sam 22:7, and a specific example is related in the same book:

1 Sam 27:6   ויתן לו אכיש ביום ההוא את צקלג
                           לכן היתה צקלג למלכי יהודה עד היום הזה

So that day Achish gave him Ziklag; therefore Ziklag has belonged to the kings of Judah to this day.[59]

As Lohfink remarks, such grants would normally imply that the territory which is the object of the "gift" continued to belong to the overlord. Such land might not, therefore, be sold to a third party.[60] These features

---

[56] Lipiński's theory is more involved. In his view, the basis of the motif is to be found in a formula of inheritance which implied that the deceased proprietor of a plot of land would be adored as a god (*ᵉlōhîm*, cf. 1 Sam 28:13) by his heir. See TWAT V, 704. This view seems to have very little to commend itself.

[57] See above in 4.2.

[58] See N. Lohfink, TWAT III, 953-985, cols. 972-973. Lohfink applies his theory only to Deuteronomy and the Deuteronomistic literature; it seems, however, that his considerations are valuable also for other passages.

[59] Cf. also Ez 46:16f.

[60] Lohfink points to Ancient Near Eastern parallels from which it appears that land may never be sold from one citizen to another, but must be constructed as a new grant from the king. See TWAT III, 972.

accord well with the ideas attached to the motif of the gift of land in the
Pentateuch.

In H, YHWH is viewed consistently as holy and divine; no royal features are attributed to him. Nevertheless, in his capacity as owner and
lord of the land, which he may give to whom he pleases, he resembles
the human king granting a fief to his subject.

Taking possession of the land

The action which Israel is to perform in complementarity to YHWH's
giving is "to take possession" (*yrš*) of the land, as is stated in one passage. The previous inhabitants of the land have done what was contrary
to the will of YHWH and will therefore be cast out from the land
(20:23), and the Israelites will settle there in their stead:

20:24   ואמר לכם אתם תירשו את אדמתם ואני אתננה לכם לרשת אתה

But I have said to you, 'You shall take possession of their land,[61] and
I will give it to you to possess'.

The semantic range of the verb *yrš* includes the meanings "to dispos-
sess", "to take possession of" and "to inherit".[62] With regard to land, the
verb is used both in military and non-military contexts.[63] The combination of the verbs *ntn* and *yrš* to describe the complementary actions of
YHWH and Israel with regard to the land is very frequent in Deuteronomy and in Deuteronomistic literature.[64] This has led Lohfink to the
claim that the combination arose in Deuteronomic circles whence it was
adopted in other types of literature.[65] If this were true, Lev 20:24 would
be a fragment of Deuteronomistic diction in H.[66] Lohfink's claim fails

---

[61] RSV: "You shall inherit their land…"

[62] Lohfink has argued that the meaning "to inherit" is a late specialization of the
earlier meaning "to take possession", see TWAT III, 960. In view of such texts as 2 Sam
14:7, however, it seems better to assume that the two meanings always existed alongside
one another.

[63] Although the verb is often used in military contexts, the fact that it is used in the
same sense in non-military contexts shows that the military aspect is not part of its
lexical meaning (as opposed to contextual meaning).

[64] Outside the Deuteronomic literature the pair is found in Gen 15:7 (where, however, Deuteronomic influence has been suspected), and in Num 33:53 (a text of the
priestly tradition).

[65] See TWAT III, 968f.

[66] On the claim for Deuteronomistic phraseology in H, see Thiel, "Erwägungen" (see
above in Chapter 1). Thiel does not list the word pair *ntn—yrš*, however.

to convince, however. The combination *ntn—yrš*, with land as the direct object, is attested also outside the context of YHWH's gift of the land to Israel:

Num 27:11   ואם אין אחים לאביו ונתתם את נחלתו לשארו הקרב אליו
                   ממשפחתו וירש אתה

And if his father has no brothers, then you shall give his inheritance to his kinsman that is next to him of his family, and he shall possess it.[67]

This then raises the possibility that the combination was not freely invented by Deuteronomistic theologians, but existed in legal terminology from whence it was taken over to describe what YHWH did for Israel.[68] In that case, different circles may have used the same legal expressions in a theological context, and Lev 20:24 is not necessarily to be ascribed to Deuteronomic influence.[69]

As to its meaning, Lohfink has suggested that *yrš* implied some sort of ritual, either marching around or physically entering into the land of which possession is taken.[70] However this may be, the verb designates the action complementary to the divine giving of the land. In the light of what was said above on the verb *ntn* in Lev 20:24, the verb *yrš* may therefore be interpreted as "to occupy land allocated by its royal or divine master". A profane parallel to this meaning is found in the account of the settling of other peoples on the territory of the ten tribes:

2 Ki 17:24   ויבא מלך אשור מבבל ומכתה ומעוה ומחמת וספרוים
                    וישב בערי שמרון תחת בני ישראל וירשו את שמרון וישבו בעריה

And the king of Assyria brought people from Babylon, Cuthah, Avva, Hamath, and Sepharvaim, and placed them in the cities of Samaria instead of the people of Israel; and they took possession of Samaria, and dwelt in its cities.

---

[67] Although the context is one of inheritance, neither *ntn* nor *yrš* express this aspect lexically.

[68] Note that in Jer 8:10 the word pair is employed in stating that YHWH will give Israel's fields to strangers.

[69] Another possibility is that the expressions existed in the older tradition, as may be suggested by their presence in Gen 15:7. Genesis 15 is itself difficult to date, however.

Although the verb *ntn* is absent from this account, having been replaced by the verb *yšb* (hiphil), "to settle", the procedure is entirely parallel to the one described in Lev 20:24: the master of the land sends forth its former inhabitants and settles a different group in their place.

Although the closest parallels to the giving and taking of the land as pictured in H are accounts of royal grants of land, the verbs *ntn* and *yrš* themselves do not specify the type of context involved.[71] It would be wrong to claim that by the use of these verbs, H pictures YHWH as a king granting land to a vassal or a group of subjects. One is justified, therefore, in interpreting the procedure described by *ntn* and *yrš* in light of what was said above on the relationship between YHWH and Israel and the land. YHWH is owner and lord of the land because he resides there in his sanctuary; he grants the Israelites the right to settle on land surrounding his sanctuary; the Israelites occupy the land in their capacity as worshippers and clients of YHWH.[72]

6.3 CONCLUSIONS

YHWH's land and Israel's land. On close inspection of the thought world of H, these phrases turn out to express two aspects of the same concept. The land is YHWH's because his sanctuary is located there. Since, however, the sanctuary is surrounded by the people of Israel— YHWH's fundamental intention was to take the people of Israel for his priests and worshippers and to dwell in their midst—one might say that the land is YHWH's because the people of Israel are settled there. Or formulated differently, the practical expression of YHWH's lordship over the land is the fact that Israel is (or will be) installed there.[73] Conversely, the people of Israel have no other title to the land than the religious one: they are represented in the image of asylants granted the right to settle on temple lands. The land is Israel's because its owner and lord

---

[70] Note in H the use of the verb *bw'* (hiphil), which implies actual entry into the land, see 18:3 and 20:22.

[71] In Num 27:11, they refer to the legal action undertaken by the community towards the kinsman of a deceased Israelite.

[72] For the use of *yrš* in a sacral context, reference may perhaps be made to Isa 61:7 (discussion in Lohfink, TWAT III, 985).

[73] In the event of exile, the land will nevertheless retain the attention of YHWH, as is stated in 26:42 ("and I will remember the land"). This will be a problematic and exceptional situation, however.

is YHWH. In other words, the sacral quality of the land as YHWH's possession guarantees Israel's entitlement to it. Central to this complex of notions is the conception of the land occupied by the Israelites as temple land. The entire territory settled by the Israelites—ideally the entire land of Canaan—stands under the influence of the divine presence in the earthly sanctuary. Anyone established in the land, even a non-Israelite, must know that he lives in proximity to the sanctuary. He must, therefore, adapt his actions, his words and his thoughts to the holy presence of the God of Israel. It is this conception which lends the notion of the land its critical value.

Several scholars have noted the central place of the notion of the land in the thought of H, although to my mind they have not always interpreted it correctly. For Jagersma, the mention of the land in 19:9, 23, 33 is a sure indication of the exilic period, when Israelites began to prepare for their return to the land.[74] Particularly striking is the fact that the law in 19:9 speaks of "the harvest of your *land* " while the parallel in Deuteronomy has "your harvest in your *field* " (Deut 24:19). Mathys has developed this idea further and collected a number of passages from H where the mention of the land is unparalleled in similar provisions in the Book of the Covenant and Deuteronomy,[75] or where it was not required by the context.[76] Like Jagersma, the conclusion he draws from this phenomenon is that H was composed during the exile by Israelites preparing for the return. In exile, the notion of the land acquired enormous importance precisely because it had become problematic: absence makes the heart grow fonder. For all its persuasiveness, however, the view advanced by Jagersma and Mathys falls short of proof. Indeed, while it is probable that the Israelites in exile longed for their lost land,[77] this probability does not imply, conversely, that every text in which the land plays a central role is necessarily to be ascribed to the exilic period. In light of the complex of notions which, as the preceding sections have attempted to demonstrate, underlies the discourse of H, a different explanation seems more likely. The frequent mention of the land as the space within which the laws must be put into practice, and the overall centrality of the notion of the land in H, do not reveal the historical

---

[74] See Jagersma, *Leviticus 19*, 123f.
[75] See Mathys, *Liebe*, 104f. He compares Lev 19:33 with Ex 22:20; 23:9; and Lev 26:1 with Deut 16:21f.
[76] Mathys lists 20:2-4; 22:24; 23:10, 22; 23:39; 25:24, 45.
[77] The importance of the theme of the land in the Book of Ezekiel points in this direction.

context of H, but flow from its internal logic. The land, in its capacity as the space surrounding the earthly sanctuary of YHWH,[78] imposes upon the Israelites and other inhabitants the need to obey the commandments of YHWH. Holiness, incorporated as it is in the different laws contained in H, is a relational term: it creates the possibility for the Israelites to live in the proximity of their God. The land is the specific extent of this proximity. On this understanding, the mention of the land in several of the laws amounts to a reminder that the proximity of the deity in his earthly sanctuary imposes certain demands. "In your land"—i.e. where YHWH has granted you the right to live as his clients—"you shall make no idols" (26:1), "you shall not do wrong to the resident alien" (19:33), "you shall not reap your field to its very border, you shall leave it for the poor" (19:9f). If the abundant references to the land, even in contexts where the notion seems to be superfluous, can thus be explained from the conceptual framework underlying H, they may no longer be used in arguing for an exilic date. If anything, the fact that the presence of YHWH in the midst of his people is treated as a given in H favours a pre-exilic date, as has already been argued above in 5.4.

The results of the present chapter have shown how central the notion of the land is to H. The land is not merely frequently referred to, it also plays a crucial role in the paraenetic strategy of the author. On the other hand, however, the conception embodied in the two phrases "YHWH's land—Israel's land" also shows that the notion of the land is ultimately subordinated to the notion of the people in the thought of H. This point needs to be made, since several earlier exegetes have affirmed the contrary. Wellhausen, one of the first to treat H as a separate corpus, writes of "...die durch Jahves Wohnung bewirkte Heiligkeit des Landes, welche zu respectieren die Religion der Bewohner ist. Das Land Jahves ist wichtiger als das Volk Jahves; es ist, als ob er das Land und nicht das Volk erwählt hatte."[79] The view of holiness of the land resulting from YHWH's presence in its midst goes beyond what is stated in H, where the land is never described as being holy.[80] It is the second part of the statement, however, which is really problematic. The reduction of H's religion to respect for the holiness of the land, and the further conclusion that the land is more important than the people—as if Israel's pres-

---

[78] The camp, which is characterized in the same way in H, functions as a paradigm of the land, see above in 5.1.
[79] See Wellhausen, *Composition*, 168-169 (n. 2).
[80] See above, pp. 178-180.

ence in the land were rather accidental—are contradicted by the results of the present chapter (and of Chapter 4). Therefore, although Wellhausen's views on this point have been endorsed by several authorities, it seems to me that they need to be rejected.[81] H never envisaged YHWH's land without the presence of the Israelites. Before the occupation of the land by the Israelites (18:24-28; 20:22-24), YHWH does not yet dwell in the land but in the camp. And after the expulsion of the Israelites (26:33-45), YHWH will no longer dwell in the land, for the sanctuaries will have been destroyed (26:31). This means that if the Israelites are not living in the land, YHWH's ownership and lordship over it are rendered problematic.[82] Moreover, the stated purpose of YHWH was to take the people of Israel as his "slaves" and settle them around his sanctuary, on his land (25:38, see above 4.1).[83] YHWH dwells in the land, which thus has become the domain within which his holiness imposes its demands on all; however, his dwelling in the land is inseparably connected to the fact that he dwells in the midst of the Israelites (see Num 35:34 quoted above), whom he has acquired as his people. The arrangement involving YHWH, Israel, and the land was considered a package deal.

---

[81] See P. Grelot, "La dernière étape", 177: "Les juristes se placent non au point de vue du *peuple* saint (comme précédemment), mais à celui de la *terre* sainte, où certains membres du peuple sont enracinés depuis longtemps, indigènes, autochtones (*ezrah*), tandis que d'autres sont qualifiés de *gerim* , soit parce qu'ils n'y sont jamais que des *hôtes* de passage, soit plutôt parce qu'ils *séjournent* dans les pays étrangers." Weinfeld, *Deuteronomy*, 228 "As opposed to the deuteronomic concept of the 'holiness of the people', P promulgates the concept of the 'holiness of the land'."

[82] See above, note 73.

[83] Moreover, as has been established above in 3.2, the religion of the resident alien is not necessarily the same as that of the Israelites. This is an indication that the land is not the only, nor even the main factor in the motivation of the law in H.

CHAPTER SEVEN

CONCLUSIONS

It may seem strange that an exegetical study devoted to the Holiness Code should contain so little discussion of the actual prescriptions and commandments it contains. Indeed, the aim of the present study was not to make a contribution to the interpretation of the individual laws, but to inquire into the underlying principles of the law such as they are presented in this corpus, into the ideational framework regulating the whole discourse. In order to achieve this aim, the research has been focused on literary elements that are marginal to the legal passages, in particular on those elements which serve to express the concepts of people and land.

The approach essayed in the preceding chapters, although it will have to be complemented by exegesis of the legal passages, and cannot answer all the questions it raises, has turned out to be both viable and fruitful. The viability of the approach flows from the fact that the hypothesis of the Holiness Code as a distinct corpus, exhibiting—despite the undoubted incorporation of older materials—a reasonable degree of unity and integrity, has by and large been verified. In its different parts, the discourse has turned out to be characterized by a striking conceptual coherence. The principles underlying the various prescriptions and commandments make up a meaningful whole. Although the subject matter, terminology and historical perspective may vary from chapter to chapter, the conceptual framework is everywhere the same. At the same time, the characteristic concepts of the Holiness Code set it apart from other priestly passages in the Pentateuch.[1]

The fruitfulness of the present approach proceeds from the fact that the notions of people and land are indeed central to the thought of this corpus. The people of Israel are its addressees, and it is among them that its ideals are to be realized, while the land is the sacred space within

---

[1] The question of the relationship between Lev 17-26 and the other priestly material in the Hexateuch is a complex one, however. Certain texts, like Num 35:34 and Jos 22:19 are representative of the same conceptual universe as H. They belong to the Holiness School as identified by Knohl, *Sanctuary*.

which the demands and the promises it makes obtain. Thus these notions, and the ideas attached to them, underlie the discourse and give it
its meaning. This concluding chapter will attempt to gather together
some threads and emphasize some of the most important results for the
study of the Holiness Code as a whole.

THE PARAENETIC STRATEGY OF THE HOLINESS CODE

Strictly speaking, the Holiness Code does not present itself as a law
code, nor even as a divine discourse commanding obedience to the law.
Rather, it recounts how such a discourse was addressed, long ago, to the
Israelites delivered from the land of Egypt. Every section of the law is
preceded by the narrative introduction: "And YHWH spoke to Moses
and said...",[2] thus incorporating the following discourse into the history
of Israel as it is told in the Pentateuch. In two passages, the location at
Mount Sinai is explicitly stated,[3] and where the narrative is spun out the
background is that of Israel in the desert.[4] The laws themselves are often
formulated with the realities of the desert camp in mind.[5] Moreover,
several passages make it clear that, for the sons of Israel of the story, the
occupation of the promised land still belongs to the future.[6]

Nevertheless, it would be wrong to describe Lev 17-26 simply as a
narrative informing about past events. The fundamental intention of the
text is to teach the law to its own generation: to imprint it upon their
conscience and to hammer it—or at least its underlying principles—into
their minds. This intention accounts for the "paraenetic tone" often observed by present-day scholars: the commandments are motivated, explained or traced back to their underlying principles. There is more to
the paraenesis than a tone, however. Whereas the function of mere
paraenesis might be understood within the narrative context of Lev 17-
26, i.e. as YHWH's teaching of the law to the generation of the desert,
the structure of the discourse intends to break out of this narrative context in order to speak directly to the real addressees. It is no exaggera-

---

[2] See, e.g., 17:1; 18:1; 19:1.
[3] See 25:1; 26:46.
[4] See 24:10-23.
[5] See, e.g., 17:3-9; 19:21; 24:1-9.
[6] See 19:23; 23:10; 25:2.

tion to speak of a paraenetic strategy, by which the audience are made to realize that these laws, although presented as having been given long ago at Mount Sinai, are addressed to them and need to be put into practice by them.

An important paraenetic technique is that of the intentional anachronism: at several points in the discourse, the fiction of Israel-in-the-desert is abandoned thus revealing something of the contemporary historical reality of the author. Let us recall the following examples:

– although throughout the text the conquest of the land is represented as belonging to the future, the casting out of the earlier occupants is in one passage stated to have already taken place (18:25-27);

– although the Exodus is represented throughout as a recent event, in which the addressees themselves have taken part, one passage speaks of the generation of the Exodus as "ancestors" of a distant past (26:45);

– whereas the Israelites are generally represented as forming an assembly ('ēdāh ; 19:2; 24:14, 16), in one passage they are referred to as the "people of the land" (20:2, 4).

In each of these examples, the historical context of the narrative is briefly suspended and the period of the author and his intended audience peeks through. The Israelites are addressed as if they were living in the land, at a time when the desert period is no more than a memory; or to put it more clearly: it is no longer the Israelites of the Exodus generation that are addressed, but the contemporary audience. This type of anachronism is not the result of clumsiness on the part of the author, as if he had temporarily forgotten the fictional setting of his text, nor of the inexpert combination of different sources. On the contrary, it plays a studied and highly effective role in the paraenetic strategy of the text. By the play of historical perspectives, the author makes his audience realize that these commandments are actually addressed to them. It is they, the Israelites of his own generation, who are called upon to observe the laws of YHWH (see, in particular, pp. 45-47).

Another way in which the tension between the narrated world and the actual historical context is exploited for paraenetic purposes is through the use of paradigms. A prime example is that of the camp in the desert. The camp is in some important aspects a paradigm for the Israelite settlement in the land (see above, pp. 145-148). The principles on which the camp operates will be valid also in the land. As a result, these two notions are at times poorly distinguished: it is not always clear which laws are given with a view to life in the camp and which with a view to the settlement in the land. The confusion seems to be deliberate and its

intention to bring home to the real addressees that all the laws of YHWH
are fully operative in their time.[7]

Yet another method of highlighting the law's relevance for the audience to whom it is actually addressed is the insistence on the solidarity
of the Israelite generations: the demands, the promises and the threats
are valid for the Israelites in the desert, and for their offspring forever
(see above, pp. 120-122).[8] Insofar as the intended audience recognized
that they were the descendants of the Israelites who had come out of
Egypt—a recognition presupposed by the author of the Holiness
Code—this insistence would automatically lead them to understand that
the entire discourse was, in a way, addressed to them.

Taken logically, these various strategies would seem to be mutually
exclusive: the Israelites of the Exodus should be or an image of the later
generation, or a paradigm for them, or their ancestors. In the logic of the
preacher of the law, however, these are simply different techniques by
which he hopes to achieve one and the same goal, namely to bring the
appeal of the law home to his audience.

An additional aim achieved by the peculiar paraenetic shape of the
Holiness Code is the rooting of the authority of the law in the Exodus
event. Indeed, if it weren't for this objective, the author might have dis-
pensed with the narrative fiction altogether. That would have been un-
thinkable, however: the whole *raison d'être* of the law lies in what
YHWH has done for his people when he led them out of slavery in
Egypt. The conception of this event in the Holiness Code is peculiar and
highly developed. It is tied up with an entire ideational complex, which
lends the notions of people and land, and thus the whole discourse, their
significance. The uncovering of this conceptual framework has been the
main object of the preceding chapters.

THE CONCEPTUAL FRAMEWORK OF THE HOLINESS CODE

In the conception of the Holiness Code, the Exodus is the foundational
event not only for Israel in the desert, but for the people throughout their

---

[7] Other examples are the assembly in the desert functioning as a paradigm for the
"people of the land" (see above pp. 45-47); the "sons of Israel" who stand, in a way, for
the actual addressees of the discourse (see above pp. 88-92); and maybe the Tent of
Meeting functioning as a paradigm for the Temple.

[8] This insistence is deeply rooted in the conception of the Israelites as YHWH's
slaves, cf. section 4.1.

generations. What happened when YHWH led the Israelites out of the land of Egypt can at root be described as a change of master: no longer do they belong as slaves to the Egyptians, they have now become slaves of YHWH. In a number of aspects the notion of slavery is taken literally. As YHWH's slaves, the Israelites are beholden to obey all his commandments. Moreover, the principle of hereditary bondage ensures that they will belong to YHWH throughout their generations. In other aspects, however, the metaphorical nature of the notion—the slaves of a god are his servants, his worshippers—comes more clearly to the fore. When YHWH took the Israelites to be his, he did this not in order to become their master but their God (section 4.1, pp. 98-99).

The relationship between God and people is represented as a formal arrangement, a type of contract termed a $b^e r\bar{\imath}t$ ("covenant"), at the core of which lies the understanding that YHWH will dwell among the Israelites and be served by them in his sanctuary. As a direct result, the Israelites are called upon to be holy: since YHWH dwells among them, they need to attune their lives to his holy presence. The spatial nature of this conception is illustrated by the "concentric circles" of holiness around the divine dwelling place: the sanctuary, the priests and the common Israelites are like successive domains of diminishing holiness. The priests, who are closer and draw nearer to YHWH's presence in the sanctuary, need to observe more stringent rules of holiness. By their observance of these rules, and through their presence in the sanctuary, YHWH hallows the priests, who are therefore said to be holy. But the common Israelites, too, are called to holiness. The same principle obtains: the Israelites are hallowed by the holy presence of YHWH among them and by observing the commandments. What is striking is that the commandments allowing the Israelites to attain holiness are not exclusively of a ritual nature, nor even limited to the religious domain. All the different areas of life, religion and ethics, but also economics, politics and social affairs are brought into subjection to the divine will. This seems to be the innovation of the Holiness Code: holiness is made into the rationale of the entire behaviour of the Israelites. The all-englobing nature of the exigencies also implies that no Israelite can ever definitively attain holiness: in the conception of our corpus, holiness is an ideal toward which the Israelites must strive and not an acquired quality (section 4.3, p. 132).

The conceptual universe of the Holiness Code finds characteristic expression in the treatment of the resident alien ($g\bar{e}r$). Not being an Israelite, the resident alien does not directly partake in the calling of the people: he has not been delivered from Egypt, is not YHWH's slave and neither the laws of YHWH nor the exigency of holiness are directly addressed to him. Consequently, he is not obliged to fulfill all the religious requirements incumbent upon the Israelites, such as sacrificing to YHWH and participating in the feasts. Indeed it appears, although the text understandably doesn't stress this point, that he may retain his own religion and at least part of its practices. If he wants to, he may instead adopt Israel's religious practices, in which case he must conform to all the requirements imposed upon the Israelites. Whatever his attitude toward the God of Israel, however, he is to observe the apodictic prohibitions for fear of polluting the land or, ultimately, the sanctuary (section 3.2, pp. 63-70).

This leads us to the notion of the land as it is developed in the Holiness Code. Although the Israelites are represented as camping in the desert, an essential part of YHWH's purpose in leading them out of Egypt was to settle his people on land belonging to him, the land of Canaan. In fact, the land, and the camp which prefigures it in important aspects, is viewed as an extension of the sanctuary. The Israelites, each of whom has received a holding of landed property, are pictured as asylants having found refuge on temple lands. In consequence, they have to honour the divine owner and Lord of the land, through their gifts and through observance of his laws. They must also, as must the resident alien sojourning among them, preserve the purity of the land for fear of polluting the earthly dwelling place of YHWH (Chapter 6, pp. 178-180).

The arrangement between Israel and YHWH comes with high privilege for the people. The proximity of YHWH guarantees them blessing and abundance, peace and prosperity, social, economic and spiritual fulfillment.[9] Two prerogatives are spelled out in particular. Firstly, as slaves of YHWH, the Israelites may not be enslaved to another human being; their personal freedom is a god-given right. Implicit in this affirmation is the conviction that, having been delivered from Egypt to become YHWH's people, the Israelites have attained political independence, without which individual freedom would be a mere mirage. More explicitly, it is stated that the individual Israelites may not, in principle, be enslaved, whether to a fellow Israelite or to a resident alien. Although in practice an Israelite may be forced to sell himself or his family into slavery, such slavery is *de jure* to be regarded as hired labour; and in any

---

[9] See 26:1-13.

event, every fiftieth year, practical reality is to be brought in line with religious principle: all Israelite slaves are to be released. Secondly, the arrangement guarantees each Israelite family a plot of land. Since the land of the Israelites ultimately doesn't belong to them, but to YHWH, it may not, in principle, be sold to a third party. All sale of land is to be regarded as a sale of its produce for a set number of years; every fiftieth year, at the jubilee, the plot that has been alienated will revert to its original owner or to his descendants. The remarkable theological construction by which the entitlement to landed property is anchored in the radical statement that all the land belongs exclusively to YHWH is similar to the paradox, that the Israelites are free because they are YHWH's slaves. They are land-owners because they are resident aliens with YHWH.

On the other hand, the charge of the Israelites comes with a warning. The holy presence of their God in their midst will not tolerate impurity or un-holy behaviour of any kind. Transgression of the commandments must be punished swiftly and severely, and if a crime is perpetrated secretly YHWH himself will see to the extermination of the wrongdoer. Collective, and persistent, disobedience spells even graver consequences. The impurity generated by the transgressions of the Israelites will be projected onto the sanctuary, which in this way will be defiled. The final effect will be the withdrawal of the divinity from his earthly dwelling, for his holiness cannot co-exist with impurity. The departure of YHWH from the midst of his people will cause a reversal of all the blessings attached to the proper functioning of the arrangement between God and people. The results will be famine, disease and menaces of all sorts, and finally the loss of freedom and of the land.[10] And yet, even in the midst of all these catastrophes, should they happen, some hope will remain for Israel. YHWH will not abandon his people: they are his for evermore, and his honour obliges him to continue manifesting himself as their God. Exactly what form this continued sollicitude might take is not stated, however (see above, p. 116 and p. 136).

The concepts which have here been outlined briefly, and are treated at length in the preceding chapters, constitute a coherent structure of ideas, organised around a sacral scheme: a god acquires a group of people, whom he settles around his sanctuary on land belonging to him, so that

---

[10] See 26:14-39.

they may serve him. This conceptual structure is never stated explicitly, and yet it is presupposed throughout. It underlies the whole discourse and lends it its meaning and significance. All the main themes are connected to this basic scheme: the insistence on cult and ritual, the call to holiness, the dignity of the Israelites, the special status of the land, the demands it imposes upon its inhabitants (including the resident alien), the need to obey the commandments, the blessings flowing from their observance, the punishment in the event of disobedience, and YHWH's continuing faithfulness in spite of it.

The basic sacral scheme underlying the Holiness Code finds numerous parallels in Ancient Near Eastern texts. These parallels show that the said conceptual universe is not the free invention of Israelite theologians. The thought world evinced by our corpus is based on the ideology of temple cities and sacred regions generally received in Israel's cultural environment. In spite of some unique traits in the development of the scheme—the most important of which is that in the other instances the group of people liberated to serve the god in his temple are still part of a worldly empire, while our text projects the image of an independent state—a thorough comparison with these parallels will very likely shed more light on the conceptual universe of the Holiness Code. On this point, all that could be done within the scope of the present study was to refer to the study of Weinfeld.[11]

THE HOLINESS CODE AND DEUTERONOMY

The ideational framework of the Holiness Code as it has been described in this work is completely different from the world of ideas underlying Deuteronomy. The central idea in Lev 17-26, commanding all the other themes, is that of the presence of YHWH in the sanctuary. This idea is absent from Deuteronomy, which speaks instead of the place where YHWH has made his Name to dwell. Let us recall some striking divergencies illustrating the distinct theological outlooks of the two corpora. – In H, the word *berīt* refers to the sacral bond between YHWH and Israel instituted at the Exodus and centred upon the notion of YHWH's dwelling in the midst of the Israelites; in Deuteronomy the *berīt* seems

---

[11] Weinfeld, *Justice*; see also J. Joosten, "Le cadre conceptuel du Code de Sainteté", *RHPR* 75 (1995), 385-398, in part. pp. 394-396.

to be viewed on the analogy of a vassal-treaty, it defines a type of personal relationship from which the spatial aspect is absent (pp. 107-120).
– In H, holiness is and remains the calling of the people: they need constantly to attune their lives to the presence of YHWH in the sanctuary; in Deuteronomy holiness is a quality conferred upon Israel once and for all by divine election (p. 96 and pp. 130-133).
– H presents the Israelite camp in the desert as a paradigm for settlement in the land: both the camp and the land are dominated by the presence of YHWH in his sanctuary; in Deuteronomy, the notion of the camp plays a very minor role (p. 138); in fact, according to one passage in Deuteronomy, the desert period was one of anarchy (Chapter 6, note 20).
– In Deuteronomy, the observance of the law is at times presented as a condition for entering into and taking possession of the land; this motif is absent from H (pp. 175-176).
– Whereas in H the land is conceived of as the dwelling-place of YHWH, in Deuteronomy the land's only distinction is that "the eyes of the LORD your God are always upon it", Deut 11:12 (Chapter 6, note 32).
– In H, the land is presented as imposing the application of the law because of the divine presence in its midst; in Deuteronomy, the land is presented as rendering possible the application of the law (pp. 174-175).
– In H, the resident alien is subordinate to laws of ritual purity lest by transgressing them he should pollute the land; in Deuteronomy, the resident alien is not subordinate to purity laws (Chapter 3, note 212; Chapter 6, note 34).

The diverging theological frameworks of the Holiness Code and Deuteronomy should be kept in mind while exegeting passages in either corpus. Identical themes, such as the land or holiness, are developed in a different way owing to the underlying ideas. Even such apparent "Deuteronomisms" as the notion of the covenant or the conditionality of the relationship between YHWH and Israel turn out, on closer inspection, to express very un-Deuteronomic ideas in the framework of the Holiness Code.[12]

For all their importance, divergencies of ideology are not the only characteristics setting the two texts apart. Other divergencies seem to indicate that the social milieu presupposed in the Holiness Code is different from that of Deuteronomy:

---

[12] See, e.g., section 4.2. on the conception of the covenant.

– In H, the usual designation of the people of Israel is $b^e n\bar{e}$ $yi\acute{s}r\bar{a}{}^\prime\bar{e}l$, a term stressing ties of kinship; this designation is rare in the Deuteronomic law code, where we find $yi\acute{s}r\bar{a}{}^\prime\bar{e}l$ instead (Chapter 3, note 7).

– In H, the noun $\acute{}am$ ("people") is used most often to refer to "one's people", i.e. one's (extended) family; in Deuteronomy, this usage is absent: the noun always refers to the people of Israel as a whole (Chapter 3, note 265).

– The internal organization of the people as depicted in H consists of two levels: the assembly and the individual family; the political structure addressed by Deuteronomy is much more differentiated (pp. 87-88).

– In H, no judicial functions are ascribed to the priest, in contrast to Deuteronomy where priests do seem to function in a judicial setting (Chapter 3, note 273).

– As witnessed by many details, the background of H is to be characterized as rural and provincial; Deuteronomy, on the other hand evinces an urban and cosmopolitan background (pp. 154-161).

– In H the practice of writing is never mentioned, whereas the written word plays an important part in several Deuteronomic passages (Chapter 5, note 82).

To these must be added a number of terminological and stylistic divergencies which cannot be explained as reflecting a different theology or social background; they simply show that the Holiness Code stands in a literary tradition different from that of Deuteronomy. Very often these latter characteristics of the Holiness Code are shared by other priestly texts:

– In H, the second person singular is used to address the single Israelite, and the second person plural to address the collective; the use of the second person singular to address the collective, which is standard in Deuteronomy (cf. Deut 6:4 $\check{s}^e ma\acute{}$ $yi\acute{s}r\bar{a}{}^\prime\bar{e}l$), is extremely rare in H (pp. 47-53).

– Allusions to the so-called covenant formula in H are based on its first member, e.g. Lev 22:33: "to be your God"; whereas in Deuteronomy and Deuteronomistic literature they are based on the second member, e.g. Deut 14:2: "to be a people for his own possession" (Chapter 4, note 31).

– The term "the land of Canaan" is used twice in H, but is virtually absent from Deuteronomy (Chapter 5, note 53).

– To designate the foreigner, H uses the term ben $n\bar{e}k\bar{a}r$ whereas Deuteronomy uses $nokr\bar{\imath}$ (p. 75).

– In H, no personal suffixes are joined to the word *gēr* as in Deuteronomy (*gērkā* ; Chapter 3, note 220).
– The Deuteronomic term *bḥr* is absent from H, where the election of Israel is expressed by the priestly term *bdl* (Chapter 4, note 45).
– To stress that a law must be practiced throughout the whole territory of Israel, H uses the expression *bᵉkol mōšᵉbōtēkem*, whereas Deuteronomy uses *bᵉkol gebūlkā* (p. 162).

Taken together, differences of ideology, of social background and of literary tradition make up a strong argument against the view that the Holiness Code stands under the influence of Deuteronomy. Thus it appears that our corpus is neither the priestly answer to Deuteronomy, nor the Deuteronomistic reworking of priestly traditions. Nor does it seem likely that the influence ran in the reverse direction. If similarities with regard to subject matter and overall literary genre exist, as they do, the two corpora should best be explained as independent elaborations of a common theme (the giving of the law in the desert) and motifs (the people, the land), contained in popular Israelite tradition.

This conclusion opposes the tendency, which has recently grown stronger again, to read the Holiness Code in the light of Deuteronomy or of Deuteronomistic theology. Such biased exegesis cannot do justice to the very peculiar presentation of the law one finds in Lev 17-26.

THE HISTORICAL SETTING OF THE HOLINESS CODE

The present work is intended to be an exegetical and not an historical study. Dating the text has not been a primary concern; in fact, in many respects, the exegesis of the Holiness Code has turned out to be viable without inquiring into the historical background of the text, and thus without raising the problem of dating. Nevertheless, questions of date and milieu have been addressed at several points on the conviction that knowledge of the historical background may in its own way assist a better understanding of the text. It has been argued that the Holiness Code can best be understood against the background of a rural milieu in Judah of the pre-exilic period. Within this milieu, kinship and the family would be important factors, while the central authority of the king as exerted from the capital would be all but irrelevant. It has further been suggested that the type of legal exposition incorporated in Lev 17-26 may have emanated from priests connected to the Jerusalem Temple, whose home would be located in this milieu. The image of this type of rural community may be pieced together from information contained in several narrative texts in the Old Testament (see in particular sections 3.3. and 5.4.).

Before recapitulating the main indications favouring a pre-exilic setting of our corpus, it is worthwhile to dwell once more on the extraordinary difficulty facing an exegete wishing to date a text like the Holiness Code solely on the basis of internal indications. To begin with, the text is set in the desert period, and on the whole—except for a few seeming anachronisms which have been discussed above—this fictional context is held to very consistently. Any references to contemporary events or circumstances may therefore be expected to be veiled, and their use for defining the date of the text problematic. Secondly, the Holiness Code certainly incorporates older legislative and paraenetic traditions; indeed, it seems unlikely that any of the laws contained in it were entirely the creation of the author.[13] For this reason, it would be wrong to fasten upon any archaic elements in this earlier material in order to determine the historical background of the final work. Thirdly, it is probable that later additions were made to the text; again these may not be used to date the text as it left the hands of its author. The second and third circumstances make it all but unfeasible to identify isolated phenomena within the text as indications betraying its date.[14] To all this the fact should yet be added that very little is known about the history of Israel, and what is known is constantly being called into question. Relating literary or theological characteristics of the text to a definite period within the history of Israel, in a convincing manner, is therefore made even harder.

The following arguments, however, because they are taken from themes or characteristics which run through the entire text of the Holiness Code, may be judged to override at least some of the methodological strictures listed above.

– If the description of the paraenetic make-up of the text offered above is even approximately adequate, then we must suppose the real addressees of the text to be settled in the land. The fiction of Israel-in-the-desert is

---

[13] Cf M. Noth, *Überlieferungsgeschichte des Pentateuch* (Stuttgart, 1948), 249: "Die Pentateuchquellen haben als Fixierungen und theologische Bearbeitungen der alten Überlieferung eben kaum ein unmittelbares Verhältnis zur jeweiligen Zeitgeschichte; darum ist ihre Datierung so schwierig, aber für ihr Verständnis auch einigermassen belanglos."

meant as a paradigm for the real Israel-in-the-land. Where the real historical situation of the addressees shines through, in the anachronistic passages discussed above, the Israelites are seen to inhabit their own territory: the former inhabitants are out and the Israelites are settled in their stead (Lev 18:25-28); they are the People of the Land, responsible for justice and purity among all its inhabitants (Lev 20:2-5). Of course, the text may have been taken to be authoritative by Israelites living under different circumstances also; but it is difficult to imagine that it came into being in a situation where the people did not occupy land.

– The resident alien (*gēr*)is consistently viewed as a non-Israelite residing on Israelite territory (see section 3.2.),[15] one who might by virtue of his legal status participate in worship of YHWH but was not obliged to do so. Such a definition must have arisen before the exile, when Israel occupied a territory they could call their own. Of course, the use of a term deriving from the pre-exilic period does not by itself determine the date of the text in which it occurs. It might simply belong to the sources used, or to a legislative tradition.[16] On close inspection, however, the theme of the resident alien does seem to bespeak a pre-exilic date for the Holiness Code. The theme is pervasive throughout the corpus. In the specific sense of a non-Israelite residing on Israelite territory, the term *gēr* occurs 18 times, with the mentions spread over every chapter except Lev 21 and Lev 26.[17] The frequent inclusion of the resident alien in the presentation of the laws points to the fact that coming to terms with this type of person was a real preoccupation of the author. Furthermore, the attitude towards the resident alien is closely related to the general conceptual framework underlying the entire discourse. Indeed, the rationale for applying certain laws to the resident alien derives from this framework: he must observe some basic rules for fear of polluting the land and the sanctuary, thus jeopardizing the arrangement by which YHWH dwells in the midst of his people. For these reasons, I think it unlikely that the theme of the resident alien was simply taken over from earlier

---

[14] Cf. C. Houtman, *Der Pentateuch. Die Geschichte seiner Erforschung neben eine Auswertung*, (Kampen, 1994), 432-441.

[15] Where the resident alien appears in the context of the camp, the camp functions as a paradigm of the land, see section 5.1.

[16] The term is used in a traditional sense in the books of Ezekiel, Zecheriah and Malachi.

[17] This high number contrasts with only three occurrences in the Book of the Covenant. In Deuteronomy, the resident alien is often referred to, but in a different way: he is a marginal member of society in need of protection. Thus it seems unlikely that the Holiness Code inherited the problem from either corpus.

tradition.[18] Nor does it seem probable that it was a freely invented theoretical construction of the school which produced this text. It is far more likely that the theme was an item on the agenda owing to a corresponding problem in contemporary society.

– The treatment of the resident alien contains another pointer indicating a pre-exilic date. It is presupposed as a matter of course that the resident alien will be subject to the laws imposed on him by the Israelites: the only question is exactly which laws apply to him and which laws do not. Laws affecting resident aliens extend to such matters as forbidden food, forbidden sexual relationships and the release of Israelite slaves in the jubilee year—prescriptions that would have a real impact on their lives. Moreover, in the case of certain grave transgressions, the death penalty is prescribed. These dispositions indicate that, in the conception of the author, Israel is free to impose their laws in the whole territory occupied by them. This is indeed the impression one gets from other characteristics of the text. Nowhere is foreign domination alluded to, even in a veiled way. The conceptual framework points in the same direction: the notion that the Israelites are slaves of YHWH implies that they have no other master than he, while the application of the Israelite laws in the whole territory is an expression of YHWH's ownership and lordship over the land (see above, pp. 173-174). The circumstances implied in this conception existed only before the exile of Judah: during the exile no territory could be called specifically Israelite, and after the exile the Israelites could not impose their laws in the territory they occupied.

– The notion of YHWH's holy presence in his earthly sanctuary is implicit in every passage of the Holiness Code. It provides the rationale for all the prescriptions and commandments: by observing them, the Israelites can adapt their behaviour and their whole being to the divine presence in whose proximity they live. It also underlies the concept of YHWH's ownership and lordship over the land. The idea that YHWH dwells in his earthly sanctuary fits the early period of the religion of Israel.[19] In Deuteronomy the idea is refined: YHWH does not himself reside in his temple, but he has made his Name to dwell there.[20] After the destruction of Jerusalem and the first Temple, the older view lost its basis in reality: with the House of YHWH destroyed, he could no longer be said to reside there (cf. Ez 1-11, the glory of YHWH leaves the Tem-

---

[18] As suggested by Zimmerli, *Ezekiel*, BKAT, 303.
[19] See, e.g., 1 Sam 4:4; 6:2; 1 Ki 8:10-13. Cf. Clements, *God and Temple*.
[20] See Weinfeld, *Deuteronomy 1-11*, 37-40.

ple). When the Temple was rebuilt by the first returnees, the rebuilding happened under the inspiration of great prophecies (e.g. Hag 1:8; 2:9). However, the doctrine of YHWH's indwelling was never really applied to the Second Temple.[21] These considerations indicate that our text dates from a relatively early period, and in any case from before the destruction of the first Temple in Jerusalem.

To vitiate this train of thought, one might advance the view that the presence of YHWH in his sanctuary is for the Holiness Code not a contemporaneous reality, but a reminiscence of the glorious past (Israel in the desert), or a project for the future.[22] Such a view, however, does not accord with the facts brought to light in the present study. In Lev 17-26, the presence of YHWH among his people is not represented as a reminiscence or a promise. The whole foundation of the discourse is that the Israelites must obey the laws precisely because YHWH *is* present amongst them. The camp in the desert is merely a paradigm for the Israelites of the generation addressed. If YHWH were to be found not to dwell among his people, the greater part of the discourse would fall and its impact would be close to nil.

These conclusions regarding the date of our corpus may seem hopelessly out of step with the mainstream of contemporary research, which tends to date the Holiness Code, together with much other pentateuchal material, in the Persian period. No convincing arguments contradicting a date in the monarchical period are known to me, however.[23] To the contrary, the most convincing approach to the problem of dating, the linguistic method developed by A. Hurvitz, strongly favours the pre-exilic period.[24]

---

[21] Or at least so it appears from the written record; see Clements, *God and Temple*, 123-134. See, however, the divergent opinion expressed by G. I. Davies, "The Presence of God in the Second Temple and Rabbinic Doctrine", in W. Horbury, ed., *Templum amicitiae. Essays on the Second Temple Presented to Ernst Bammel*, JSNTS 48 (Sheffield, 1991), 32-36.

[22] As in Ez 40-48, or in the Temple Scroll from Qumran.

[23] See above in Chapter 1, n. 30.

[24] See the excursus in Chapter 1, pp. 14-15.

SELECTED BIBLIOGRAPHY

Ackroyd, P. A. *Exile and Restoration. A Study of Hebrew Thought in the Sixth Century BC* (London, 1968).

Allen, W. A. "On the Meaning of ΠΡΟΣΗΛΥΤΟΣ in the Septuagint", *Exp* IV 10 (1894), 264-275.

Aloni, J. "The Place of Worship and the Place of Slaughter According to Leviticus 17:3-9", *Shnaton* 7-8 (1983-84), 21-49 [Hebrew].

Alt, A. "Die Ursprünge des israelitischen Rechts", in id., *Kleine Schriften* I (München, 1953), 278-332.

Amit, Y. "The Jubilee Law—An Attempt at Instituting Social Justice", in H. Graf Reventlow and Y. Hoffman, eds., *Justice and Righteousness. Biblical Themes and their Influence*, JSOTS 137 (Sheffield, 1992), 47-59.

Amsler, S. "La motivation de l'éthique dans la Parénèse du Deutéronome", in H. Donner et al., Hsg., *Beiträge zur alttestamentlichen Theologie*, Fs W. Zimmerli (Göttingen, 1977), 11-22.

—, "Les documents de la loi et la formation du Pentateuque", in A. de Pury, éd., *Le Pentateuque en question* (Genève, 1989), 235-257.

Andreasen, N.-E. A. *The Old Testament Sabbath*, SBLDS 7 (Missoula, 1972).

Auerbach, E. "Die babylonische Datierung im Pentateuch und das Alter der Priestercodex", *VT* 2 (1952), 334-342.

Baentsch, B. *Das Heiligkeits-Gesetz* (Erfurt, 1893).

—, *Exodus-Leviticus*, HAT (Göttingen, 1900).

Baltzer, K. *Das Bundesformular*, WMANT 4 (Neukirchen, 1960).

Barbiero, G. *L'asino del nemico. Rinuncia alla vendetta e amore del nemico nella legislazione dell'Antico Testamento (Es 23,4-5; Dt 22,1-4; Lv 19,17-18)*, AnBib 128 (Roma, 1991).

Becker, J. recension of A. Hurvitz, A Linguistic Study of the Relationship between the Priestly Source and the Book of Ezekiel, *Biblica* 64 (1983), 583-586.

Begg, C. T. "The Significance of the *Numeruswechsel* in Deuteronomy. The "Pre-History" of the Question", *ETL* 55 (1979), 116-124.

Berry, G. R. "The Code Found in the Temple", *JBL* 39 (1920), 44-51.

Bertholet, A. *Die Stellung der Israeliten und der Juden zu den Fremden* (Freiburg i. B. & Leipzig, 1896).

—, *Leviticus*, KHCAT (Tübingen, 1901).

Besters, A. "«Israel» et «Fils d'Israel» dans les livres historiques (Genèse-II Rois)", *RB* 74 (1967), 5-23.

Bettenzoli, G. *Geist der Heiligkeit. Traditionsgeschichtliche Untersuchung des QDS-Begriffes im Buch Ezekiel*, Quaderni di Semitistica 8 (Firenze, 1979).

—, "Deuteronomium und Heiligkeitsgesetz", *VT* 34 (1984), 385-398.

Beyerlin, W. "Die Paränese im Bundesbuch und ihre Herkunft", in H. Graf Reventlow, Hsg., *Gottes Wort und Gottes Land*, Fs H.-W. Hertzberg (Göttingen, 1965), 9-29.

Bigger, S. F. "The Family Laws of Leviticus 18 in their Setting", *JBL* 98 (1979), 187-203.

Block, D. I. "'Israel'-'Sons of Israel': A Study in Hebrew Eponymic Usage", *SR* 13 (1984), 301-326.

—, "Israel's House: Reflections on the Use of *byt yśr'l* in the Old Testament in the Light of its Ancient Near Eastern Environment", *JETS* 28 (1985), 257-275.

Blum, E. *Studien zur Komposition des Pentateuchs*, BZAW 189 (Berlin, 1990).

Boecker, H. J. *Redeformen des Rechtslebens im Alten Testament*, WMANT 14 (Neukirchen, 1964[1], 1970[2]).

Braulik, G. "Die dekalogische Redaktion der deuteronomischen Gesetze. Ihre Abhängigkeit von Leviticus 19 am Beispiel von Deuteronomium 22,1-12; 24,10-22;

25,13-16" in G. Braulik, Hsg., *Bundesdokument und Gesetz. Studien zum Deuteronomium*, HBS 4 (Freiburg, 1995), 1-25.

—, "Weitere Beobachtungen zur Beziehung zwischen dem Heiligkeitsgesetz und Deuteronomium 19-25", in T. Veijola, Hsg., *Das Deuteronomium und seine Querbezichungen*, Schriften der Finnischen Exegetischen Gesellschaft 62 (Helsinki & Göttingen, 1996), 23-55.

Brichto, H. C. "Kin, Cult, Land and Afterlife—A Biblical Complex", *HUCA* 44 (1973), 1-54.

—, "On Slaughter and Sacrifice, Blood and Atonement", *HUCA* 47 (1976), 19-55.

Bright, J. "The Apodictic Prohibition: Some Observations", *JBL* 92 (1973), 185-204.

Brueggeman, W. "Amos iv 4-13 and Israel's Covenant Worship", *VT* 15 (1965), 1-15.

—, *The Land* (Philadelphia, 1977).

Bultmann, C. *Der Fremde im antiken Juda. Eine Untersuchung zum sozialen Typenbegriff >ger< und seinem Bedeutungswandel in der alttestamentlichen Gesetzgebung*, FRLANT 153 (Göttingen, 1992).

Cardascia, G. "Droits cunéiformes et droit biblique", *Proceedings of the Sixth World Congress of Jewish Studies—Jerusalem 1973* (Jerusalem, 1977), 63-70.

Cardellini, I. "Stranieri ed «emigrati-residenti» in una sintesi di teologia storico-biblica", *RivBib* 40 (1992), 129-181.

Carroll, R. P. "Textual Strategies and Ideology in the Second Temple Period", in P. R. Davies, ed., *Second Temple Studies 1. The Persian Period*, JSOTS 117 (Sheffield, 1991), 108-124.

Causse, A. *Du groupe ethnique à la communauté religieuse. Le problème sociologique de la religion d'Israel* (Paris, 1937).

Cazelles, H. "La mission d'Esdras", *VT* 4 (1954), 113-140.

—, "Histoire et Institutions dans la Place et la Composition d'Ex 20,22-23,19", in R. Liwak, S. Wagner, Hsg., *Prophetie und geschichtliche Wirklichkeit im Alten Israel*, Fs S. Herrmann (Stuttgart, 1991), 52-64.

Childs, B. S. *Introduction to the Old Testament as Scripture* (London, 1979).

Chirichigno, G. C. *Debt-Slavery in Israel and the Ancient Near East*, JSOTS 141 (Sheffield, 1993).

Chiu, A. "Aspects Related to the "Holiness School" and "Priestly Torah": A Response to Dr Israel Knohl's Presentation", *AJT* 5 (1991), 55-57.

Cholewinski, A. *Heiligkeitsgesetz und Deuteronomium*, AnBib 66 (Rome, 1976).

Clements, R. E. *God and Temple* (Oxford, 1965).

Cooper, A. see Goldstein, B. R.

Cohen, C. "Was the P Document Secret?", *JANES* 1,2 (1969), 39-44.

Cohen, M. "Le «Ger» biblique et son statut socio-religieux", *RHR* 207 (1990), 131-158.

—, "A Diachronic and Synchronic Reconstruction of the Term *Ger* in the Bible", *Proceedings of the Tenth World Congress of Jewish Studies, Division A: The Bible and its World* (Jerusalem, 1990), 11-18 [Hebrew Section].

—, "Ségrégationnisme et intégrationisme comme mobiles sous-jacents à l'antinomie de Dt 14,21 et Lv 17,15-16", *RHPR* 73 (1993), 113-129.

Cortese, E. "L'anno giubilare: profezia della restaurazione? (Studio su Lev. 25)", *RivBib* 18 (1970), 395-409.

—, *La terra di Canaan nella storia sacerdotale del Pentateuco*, Supplementi alla Rivista Biblica 5 (Brescia, 1972).

—, "Levitico 19", in *Evangelizare pauperibus*, Atti della XXIV settimana biblica (Brescia, 1978), 207-217.

—, "L'esegesi di H (Lev. 17-26)", *RivBib* 29 (1981), 129-146.

Cross, F. M. *Canaanite Myth and Hebrew Epic. Essays in the History of the Religion of Israel* (Cambridge MA, 1973).

Crüsemann, F. "Fremdenliebe und Identitätssicherung. Zum Verständnis der »Fremden«-Texte im Alten Testament", *Wort und Dienst* 19 (1987), 11-24.

—, "Le Pentateuque, une Tora. Prolégomènes à l'interprétation de sa forme finale", (trad. S. Amsler), in A. de Pury, éd., *Le Pentateuque en question* (Genève, 1989), 339-360.

—, "Der Exodus als Heiligung. Zur rechtsgeschichtlichen Bedeutung des Heiligkeitsgesetzes", in E. Blum, C. Macholz, E. W. Stegemann, Hsg., *Die Hebräische Bibel und ihre zweifache Nachgeschichte*, Fs für R. Rendtorff zum 65. Geburtstag (Neukirchen, 1990), 117-129.

—, *Die Tora. Theologie und Sozialgeschichte des alttestamentlichen Gesetzes* (München, 1992).

Danell, G. A. *Studies in the Name Israel in the Old Testament* (Uppsala, 1946).

Daube, D. *Studies in Biblical Law* (Cambridge, 1947).

—, *The Exodus Pattern in the Bible*, All Souls Studies 2 (London, 1963).

David, M. "The Manumission of Slaves under Zedekiah (A Contribution to the Laws about Hebrew Slaves)", *OTS* 5 (1948), 63-79.

Davies, G. I. "The Presence of God in the Second Temple and Rabbinic Doctrine", in W. Horbury, ed., *Templum amicitiae. Essays on the Second Temple Presented to Ernst Bammel*, JSNTS 48 (Sheffield, 1991), 32-36.

Day, J. *Molech. A God of Human Sacrifice in the Old Testament*, University of Cambridge Oriental Publications 41 (Cambridge, 1989).

Delitzsch, F. "Pentateuch-kritische Studien. XII. Das Heiligkeitsgesetz", *ZKW* 1 (1880), 617-626.

Dillmann, A. *Numeri, Deuteronomium und Josua*, KEH (Leipzig, 1886).

—, *Die Bücher Exodus und Leviticus*, 3 Aufl. hsg. von V. Ryssel, KEH (Leipzig, 1897).

Doron, P. "Motive Clauses in the Laws of Deuteronomy. Their Forms, Functions and Contents", *HAR* 2 (1978), 61-77.

Driver, S. R. *An Introduction to the Literature of the Old Testament* (Edinburgh, 1913[9]; reprint: New York, 1956).

Eerdmans, B. D. "Ezra and the Priestly Code", *Exp* 7th series, 10 (1910), 302-326.

—, *Alttestamentliche Studien IV. Das Buch Leviticus* (Gießen, 1912).

Ehrlich, A. B. *Randglossen zur hebräischen Bibel, 2. Bd, Leviticus, Numeri, Deuteronomium* (Leipzig, 1909; repr. Hildesheim, 1968).

Elliger, K. "Sinn und Ursprung der priesterlichen Geschichtserzählung", *ZThK* 49 (1952), 121-143. repr. in idem, *Kleine Schriften zum Alten Testament*, Theologische Bücherei, AT 32 (1966), 174-198.

—, "Ich bin der Herr—euer Gott", in *Theologie als Glaubenswagnis*, Fs zum 80. Geburtstag von Karl Heim (Hamburg 1954), 9-34; repr. in K. Elliger, *Kleine Schriften zum Alten Testament*, Theologische Bücherei, AT 32 (München 1966), 211-231.

—, "Das Gesetz Leviticus 18", *ZAW* 67 (1955), 1-25.

—, *Leviticus*, HAT (Tübingen, 1966).

Elliott-Binns, L. E. "Some Problems of the Holiness Code", *ZAW* 67 (1955), 26-40.

Fager, J. A. *Land Tenure and the Biblical Jubilee. Uncovering Hebrew Ethics Through Sociology of Knowledge*, JSOTS 155 (Sheffield, 1993).

Feucht, C. *Untersuchungen zum Heiligkeitsgesetz*, Theologische Arbeiten 20 (Berlin, 1964).

Finkelstein, J. J. *The Ox That Gored*, Transactions of the American Philosophical Society, Vol. 71, Part 2 (Philadelphia, 1981).

Firmage, E. "The Biblical Dietary Laws and the Concept of Holiness", in J. A. Emerton, ed., *Studies in the Pentateuch*, SVT 41 (Leiden, 1990), 177-208.

Fishbane, M. *Biblical Interpretation in Ancient Israel* (Oxford, 1985).

Fohrer, G. *Hauptprobleme des Buches Ezechiel* (Berlin, 1952).

Freedman, D. N. and K. A. Mathews, *The Paleo-Hebrew Leviticus Scroll* (Winona Lake, 1985).

Friedman, R. E. *Who Wrote the Bible?* (London, 1988).

Frymer-Kensky, T. "Law and Philosophy: The Case of Sex in the Bible", *Semeia* 45 (1989), 89-102.

Gabel, J. B. and C. B. Wheeler, "The Redactor's Hand in the Blasphemy Pericope of Leviticus XXIV", *VT* 50 (1980), 227-229.

Galling, K. "Das Gemeindegesetz in Deuteronomium 23", in W. Baumgartner et al., Hsg, Fs A. Bertholet (Tübingen 1950), 176-191.

Gammie, J. G. *Holiness in Israel*, Overtures to Biblical Theology (Minneapolis MN, 1989).

—, "Paraenetic Literature: Toward the Morphology of a Secondary Genre", *Semeia* 50 (1990), 41-77.

Gane, R. "'Bread of the Presence' and Creator-in-Residence", *VT* 42 (1992), 179-203.

Geiger, A. *Urschrift und Uebersetzungen der Bibel in ihren Abhängigkeit von der innern Entwickelung des Judenthums* (Breslau, 1857).

Gemser, B. "The Importance of the Motive Clause in Old Testament Law", in G. W. Anderson et al., eds., *Congress Volume. Copenhagen 1953*, SVT 1 (Leiden, 1953), 50-66.

Gerstenberger, E. S. *Wesen und Herkunft des apodiktischen Rechts*, WMANT 20 (Neukirchen, 1965).

—, "'Er soll dir heilig sein." Priester und Gemeinde nach Lev 21,1-22,9", in F. Crüsemann et al., Hsg., *Was ist der Mensch...? Beiträge zur Anthropologie des Alten Testaments*, Fs H. W. Wolff (München, 1992), 194-210.

—, "»Apodiktisches« Recht »Todes« Recht?", in P. Mommer et al., *Gottes Recht als Lebensraum*, Fs H. J. Boecker (Neukirchen, 1993), 7-20.

Gerstenberger, E. S. *Das 3. Buch Mose. Leviticus*, ATD (Göttingen, 1993).

Gilbert, M. "Le sacré dans l'Ancien Testament", in J. Ries et al., éds., *L'expression du sacré dans les grandes religions. I Proche-orient ancien et traditions bibliques*, Homo Religiosus 1 (Louvain-la-Neuve, 1978), 205-289.

Gilmer, H. W. *The If-You Form in Israelite Law*, SBLDS 15 (Missoula, 1975).

Gispen, W. H. *Het boek Leviticus*, COT (Kampen, 1950).

Görg, M. "Der »Fremde« (*gēr*): ein Fremdwort im Alten Testament?", *BN* 25 (1984), 10-13.

Goldstein, B. R. and A. Cooper, "The Festivals of Israel and Juda and the Literary History of the Pentateuch", *JAOS* 110 (1990), 19-31.

Good, R. M. *The Sheep of His Pasture. A Study of the Hebrew Noun 'Am(m) and Its Semitic Cognates*, HSM 29 (Chico, 1983).

Gorman, F. H. *The Ideology of Ritual, Space, Time and Status in the Priestly Theology*, JSOTS 91 (Sheffield, 1990).

Gowan, D. E. "Reflections on the Motive Clauses in Old Testament Law", in D. Y. Hadidian, ed., Fs M. Barth (Pittsburgh, 1981), 111-127.

Graf, K. H. *Die geschichtlichen Bücher des Alten Testaments* (Leipzig, 1866).

Greenberg, M. "Some Postulates of Biblical Criminal Law", in M. Haran, ed., *Yehezkel Kaufmann Jubilee Volume* (Jerusalem, 1960), 5-28.

—, "More Reflections on Biblical Criminal Law", *Scripta Hierosolymitana* 31, Studies in Bible (Jerusalem, 1986), 1-17.

—, "What are Valid Criteria for Determining Inauthentic Matter in Ezekiel?", in J. Lust, ed., *Ezekiel and his Book*, BEThL 74 (Leuven, 1986), 123-135.

—, "Biblical Attitudes toward Power: Ideal and Reality in Law and Prophets", in E. B. Firmage et al., eds., *Religion and Law. Biblical-Judaic and Islamic Perspectives* (Winona Lake, 1990), 101-112.

Greger, B. "Beobachtungen zum Begriff גר (ger)", *BN* 63 (1992), 30-34.

Grelot, P. "La dernière étape de la rédaction sacerdotale", *VT* 6 (1956), 174-189.

Grintz, J. M. "«Do Not Eat on the Blood» Reconsiderations in Setting and Dating of the Priestly Code", *ASTI* 8 (1972), 78-105.

—, "Archaic Terms in the Priestly Code", *Leshonenu* 39 (1974-75), 5-20, 163-181; 40 (1975-76), 5-32 [Hebrew].

Halbe, J. *Das Privilegrecht Jahwes Ex 34,10-26. Gestalt und Wesen, Herkunft und Wirken in vordeuteronomischen Zeit*, FRLANT 114 (Göttingen, 1975).

—, "Die Reihe der Inzestverbote Lev 18 7-18", *ZAW* 92 (1980), 60-88.

Hallo, W. W. "New Moons and Sabbaths: A Case-Study in the Contrastive Approach", *HUCA* 48 (1977), 1-18.

Halpern, B. "Jerusalem and the Lineages in the Seventh Century BCE: Kinship and the Rise of Individual Moral Liability", in B. Halpern and D. W. Hobson, eds., *Law and Ideology in Monarchic Israel*, JSOTS 124 (Sheffield, 1991), 11-107.

Hamilton, J. M. *Social Justice and Deuteronomy. The Case of Deuteronomy 15*, SBLDS 136 (Atlanta, 1992).

Haran, M. "The Nature of the «'Ohel Mo'ed» in Pentateuchal Sources", *JSS* 5 (1960), 50-65.
—, "Studies in the Account of the Levitical Cities. I Preliminary Considerations", *JBL* 80 (1961), 45-54.
—, "Studies in the Account of the Levitical Cities. II Utopia and Historical Reality", *JBL* 80 (1961), 156-165.
—, "Shiloh and Jerusalem: The Origin of the Priestly Tradition in the Pentateuch", *JBL* 81 (1962), 14-24.
—, Art. Holiness Code, in *Encyclopaedia Judaica* 8 (Jerusalem, 1971).
—, *Ages and Institutions in the Bible* (Tel Aviv, 1972) [Hebrew].
—, *Temples and Temple-Service in Ancient Israel. An Inquiry into the Character of Cult Phenomena and the Historical Setting of the Priestly School* (Oxford, 1978).
—, "The Law-Code of Ezekiel XL-XLVIII and its Relation to the Priestly School", *HUCA* 50 (1979), 45-71
—, "Behind the Scenes of History: Determining the Date of the Priestly Source", *JBL* 100 (1981), 312-333.
Hartley, J. E. *Leviticus*, Word Biblical Commentary 4 (Dallas, 1992).
Heaton, E. W. "Sojourners in Egypt", *Expository Times* 58 (1946), 80-82.
Heider, G. C. *The Cult of Molek. A Reassessment*, JSOTS 43 (Sheffield, 1985).
Heinisch, P. *Das Buch Leviticus*, Die heilige Schrift des AT (Bonn, 1935).
Heltzer, M. *The Rural Community in Ancient Ugarit* (Wiesbaden, 1976).
Hempel, J. *Das Ethos des Alten Testaments*, BZAW 67 (Berlin, 1938).
Hillers, D. R. *Treaty Curses and the Old Testament Prophets*, Biblica et Orientalia 16 (Rome, 1964).
Hoffmann, D. *Die wichtigsten Instanzen gegen die Graf-Wellhausensche Hypothese* (Berlin, 1904).
—, *Das Buch Leviticus übersetzt und erklärt*, Bd 1(Berlin, 1905), Bd 2 (Berlin, 1906).
Hoffman, Y. "Concerning the Language of P and the Date of its Composition", *Te'udah* 4 (1986), 13-22 [Hebrew].
Holzinger, H. *Einleitung in den Hexateuch* (Freiburg i. B., 1893).
Hoonacker, A. Van "Le rapprochement entre le Deutéronome et Malachie", *EThL* 59 (1983), 86-90.
Horst, L. *Leviticus XVII-XXVI und Hezekiel. Ein Beitrag zur Pentateuchkritik* (Colmar, 1881).
Horton, F. L. "Form and Structure in Laws Relating to Women: Lev 18:6-18", *SBL 1973 Seminar Papers, Vol 1* (1973), 20-33.
Houston, W. *Purity and Monotheism. Clean and Unclean Animals in Biblical Law*, JSOTS 140 (1993).
Houten, C. van *The Alien in Israelite Law*, JSOTS 107 (Sheffield, 1991).
Houtman, C. *Der Pentateuch. Die Geschichte seiner Erforschung neben eine Auswertung*, Biblical Exegesis and Theology 9 (Kampen, 1994).
Hulst, A. R. *Wat betekent de naam Israel in het Oude Testament*, Miniaturen 1, Bijlage van Kerk en Israel 16/9 ('s Gravenhage, 1962).
Hurvitz, A. "The Evidence of Language in Dating the Priestly Code. A Linguistic Study in Technical Idioms and Terminology", *RB* 81 (1974), 24-56.
—, *A Linguistic Study of the Relationship between the Priestly Source and the Book of Ezekiel*, Cahiers de la Revue Biblique 20 (Paris, 1982).
—, "The Language of the Priestly Source and its Historical Setting—The Case for an early Date", *Proceedings of the Eighth World Congress of Jewish Studies—Jerusalem 1981* (1983), 83-94.
—, "Dating the Priestly Source in Light of the Historical Study of Biblical Hebrew a Century after Wellhausen", *ZAW* 100 Supplement (1988), 88-100
Jackson, B. S. *Theft in Early Jewish Law* (Oxford, 1972).
—, "The Ceremonial and the Judicial: Biblical Law as Sign and Symbol", *JSOT* 30 (1984), 25-50.
Jagersma, H. *Leviticus 19. Identiteit—Bevrijding—Gemeenschap*, Studia Semitica Neerlandica 14 (Assen, 1972).

Janowski, B. *Sühne als Heilsgeschehen. Studien zur Sühnetheologie der Priesterschrift und zur Wurzel* KPR *im Alten Orient und im Alten Testament,* WMANT 55 (Neukirchen, 1982).

—, "»Ich will in eurer Mitte wohnen« Struktur und Genese der exilischen *Schekina -* Theologie", *JBTh* 2 (1987), 165-193.

Japhet, S. *The Ideology of the Book of Chronicles and its Place in Biblical Thought* (Jerusalem, 1977) [Hebrew].

—, "People and Land in the Restoration Period", in G. Strecker, ed., *Das Land Israel in biblischer Zeit,* Jerusalem-Symposium 1981 (Göttingen, 1983), 103-125.

—, "The Relationship between the Legal Corpora in the Pentateuch in light of Manumission Laws", *Scripta Hierosolymitana* 31 (Jerusalem, 1986), 63-89.

Jenson, P. P. *Graded Holiness. A Key to the Priestly Conception of the World,* JSOTS 106 (Sheffield, 1992).

Jobsen, A. *Krisis en hoop. Een exegetisch-theologisch onderzoek naar de achtergronden en tendensen van de rebelliecyclus in Numeri 11:1-20:13* (Kampen, 1987).

Joosten, J. "Le cadre conceptuel du Code de Sainteté", *RHPR* 75 (1995), 385-398.

Kaufman, S. A. "The Temple Scroll and Higher Criticism", *HUCA* 53 (1981), 29-43.

—, "A Reconstruction of Social Welfare Systems of Ancient Israel", in B. Barrick and J. R. Spencer, eds. *In the Shelter of Elyon,* Fs G. W. Ahlström, JSOTS 31 (Sheffield, 1984), 277-286.

—, "Deuteronomy 15 and Recent Research on the Dating of P", in N. Lohfink, Hsg., *Das Deuteronomium. Entstehung, Gestalt und Botschaft,* BEThL 68 (Leuven, 1985), 273-276.

Kaufmann, Y. (J.) "Probleme der israelitisch-jüdischen Religionsgeschichte", *ZAW* 48 (1930), 23-43.

—, "Probleme der israelitisch-jüdischen Religionsgeschichte. II", *ZAW* 51 (1933), 35-47.

—, *Toledot ha-Emunah ha-Yisra'elit* , vol. 1-4 (Jerusalem, 1937-56) [Hebrew].

—, "Der Kalender und das Alter des Priestercodex", *VT* 4 (1954), 307-313.

—, *The Religion of Israel. From its Beginnings to the Babylonian Exile,* translated and abridged by M. Greenberg (London, 1961).

Kayser, A. *Das vorexilische Buch der Urgeschichte Israels une seine Erweiterungen. Ein Beitrag zur Pentateuch-Kritik* (Strassburg, 1874).

Keller, B. "La terre dans le livre d'Ezéchiel", *RHPR* 55 (1975), 482-490.

Kent, C. F. *Israel's Laws and Legal Precedents* (London, 1907).

Kilian, R. *Literarkritische und formgeschichtliche Untersuchung des Heiligkeits-gesetzes,* BBB 19 (Bonn, 1963).

Klostermann, A. "Ezechiel und das Heiligkeitsgesetz", in idem, *Der Pentateuch. Beiträge zu seinem Verständnis und seiner Entstehungsgeschichte* (Leipzig, 1893), 368-419.

Knierim, R. P. "The Problem of Ancient Israel's Prescriptive Legal Traditions", *Semeia* 45 (1989), 7-25.

Knohl, I. "The Priestly Torah Versus the Holiness School: Sabbath and the Festivals", *HUCA* 58 (1987), 65-117.

—, *The Conception of God and Cult in the Priestly Torah and in the Holiness School,* PhD dissertation, Hebrew University, Jerusalem 1988 [Hebrew].

—, "The Priestly Torah Versus the Holiness School: Ideological Aspects", in *Proceedings of the Tenth World Congress of Jewish Studies. Division A: The Bible and its World* (Jerusalem, 1990), 51-57.

—, "The Law of Sin-Offering of the Holiness School", *Tarbiz* 59 (1989-90), 1-9 [Hebrew].

—, *The Sanctuary of Silence. The Priestly Torah and the Holiness School* (Minneapolis MN, 1995).

Koch, K. "Tempeleinlassliturgien und Dekaloge", in R. Rendtorff und K. Koch, Hsg., Studien zur Theologie der alttestamentlichen Überlieferungen, Fs G. von Rad (Neukirchen, 1961), 45-60.

—, "Der Spruch "Sein Blut bleibe auf seinem Haupt" und die israelitischen Auffassung vom vergossenen Blut", *VT* 12 (1962), 396-416.

Köckert, M. "Gottesvolk und Land. Jahve, Israel und das Land bei den Propheten Amos und Hosea", in A. Meinhold und R. Lux, Hsg., *Gottesvolk*, Fs S. Wagner (Evangelische Veralgsanstalt, 1991), 43-74.

Köhler, L. *Der hebräische Mensch. Eine Skizze. Mit einem Anhang: Die hebräische Rechtsgemeinde* (Tübingen, 1953).

Kornfeld, W. *Studien zum Heiligkeitsgesetz* (Wien, 1952).

—, "QDS und Gottesrecht im Alten Testament", in J. A. Emerton, ed., *Congress Volume. Vienna 1980*, SVT 32 (1981), 1-9.

Kornfeld, W. *Levitikus*, Neue Echter Bibel (Würzburg, 1983).

Korpel, M. C. A. "The Epilogue of the Holiness Code", in J. C. de Moor and W. G. E. Watson, eds., *Verse in Ancient Near Eastern Prose*, AOAT 42 (Neukirchen, 1993), 123-150.

Kraus, H. J. "Das heilige Volk", in idem, *Biblisch-theologische Aufsätze* (Neukirchen-Vluyn, 1972), 37-49.

Küchler, S. *Das Heiligkeitsgesetz. Lev 17-26. Eine literar-kritische Untersuchung* (Königsberg i. Pr., 1929).

Külling, S. R. *Zur Datiering der "Genesis-P-Stücke". Namentlich des Kapitels Genesis XVII* (Kampen, 1964).

Kuenen, A. *An Historico-critical Inquiry into the Origin and Composition of the Hexateuch*, transl. with help of the author by P. H. Wicksteed (London, 1886).

Kuschke, A. "Die Lagervorstellung der priesterschriftlichen Erzählung. Eine überlieferungsgeschichtliche Studie", *ZAW* 63 (1951), 74-105.

Lasserre, G. *Synopse des lois du Pentateuque*, SVT 59 (Leiden, 1994).

Leemans, W. F. "Quelques considérations à propos d'une étude récente du droit du Proche Orient ancien", *BiOr* 48 (1991), 409-437.

Leggett, D. A. *The Levirate and Goel Institutions in the Old Testament. With Special Attention to the Book of Ruth* (Cherry Hill NJ, 1974).

Levenson, J. D. *Theology of the Program of Restoration of Ezekiel 40-48*, HSM 10 (Missoula, 1976).

—, "The Theologies of Commandment in Biblical Israel", *HTR* 73 (1980), 17-33.

—, *The Hebrew Bible, the Old Testament, and Historical Criticism. Jews and Christians in Biblical Studies* (Louisville, 1993).

Levine, B. A. "The Language in the Priestly Source. Some Literary and Historical Observations", *Proceedings of the Eighth World Congress of Jewish Studies—Jerusalem 1981* (1983), 69-82.

—, "The Epilogue to the Holiness Code: A Priestly Statement on the Destiny of Israel", in J. Neusner et al., eds., *Judaic Perspectives on Ancient Israel* (Philadelphia, 1987), 9-34.

—, "The Language of Holiness: Perceptions of the Sacred in the Hebrew Bible", in M. P. O'Connor and D. N. Freedman, eds., *Backgrounds for the Bible* (Winona Lake, 1987), 241-55.

Levinson, B. M., ed., *Theory and Method in Biblical and Cuneiform Law. Revision, Interpolation and Development*, JSOTS 181 (Sheffield, 1994).

Liedke, G. *Gestalt und Bezeichnung alttestamentlicher Rechtssätze*, WMANT 39 (Neukirchen, 1971).

Lipiński, E. "Prohibitive and Related Law Formulations in Biblical Hebrew and in Aramaic", *Proceedings of the Ninth World Congress of Jewish Studies* (Jerusalem, 1988), 25-39.

Loewenstamm, S. E. "Law", in B. Mazar, ed., *The World History of the Jewish People, Vol. 3. Judges* (Tel Aviv, 1971), 231-267.

—, "רכע", *Shnaton* 4 (1980), 94-97 [Hebrew].

—, "רכע", in *Scripta Hierosolymitana* 31 (Jerusalem, 1986), 155-192.

Lohfink, N. *Das Hauptgebot. Eine Untersuchung literarischer Einleitungsfragen zu Dtn 5-11*, AnBib 20 (Rome, 1963).

—, "Dt 26,17-19 und die "Bundesformel"", *ZThK* 91 (1969), 517-553; repr. in idem, *Studien zum Deuteronomium und zur deuteronomistischen Literatur* I, SBAB 8 (Stuttgart, 1990), 211-261.

—, "Die Abänderung der Theologie des priesterlichen Geschichtswerk im Segen des

Heiligkeitsgesetzes. Zu Lev. 26,9.11-13", in H. Gese und H. P. Rüger, Hsg., *Wort und Geschichte*, Fs K. Elliger, AOAT 18 (Neukirchen-Vluyn, 1973), 129-36; repr. in idem, *Studien zum Pentateuch*, SBAB 4 (1988), 157-168.

—, "Die Priesterschrift und die Geschichte", in J. A. Emerton et al., eds., *Congress Volume. Göttingen 1977*, SVT 29 (1978), 189-225.

—, "Kennt das Alte Testament einen Unterschied von »Gebot« und »Gesetz«? Zur bibeltheologischen Einstufung des Dekalogs", *JBTh* 4 (1989), 63-89.

—, "Gibt es eine deuteronomistische Bearbeitung im Bundesbuch?", in C. Brekelmans and J. Lust, eds., *Pentateuchal and Deuteronomistic Studies*, BEThL 94 (Leuven, 1990), 91-113.

—, "Deutéronome et Pentateuque. Etat de la recherche" in P. Haudebert, éd., *Le Pentateuque. Débats et recherches*, Lectio Divina 151 (Paris, 1993), 35-64

Luciani, D. "«Soyez saints, car je suis saint» Un commentaire de Lévitique 19", *NRT* 114 (1992), 212-236.

Lust, J. "Molek and ΑΡΧΩΝ", in E. Lipiński, ed., *Phoenicia and the Bible*, OLA 44 (Leuven, 1991), 193-208.

Luther, B. "Kahal und 'edah als Hilfsmittel der Quellenscheidung im Priestercodex und in der Chronik", *ZAW* 56 (1938), 44-63.

McConville, J. G. and J. G. Millar, *Time and Place in Deuteronomy*, JSOTS 179 (Sheffield, 1994).

Magonet, J. "The Structure and Meaning of Leviticus 19", *HAR* 7 (1983), 151-167.

Mathews, K. A. see Freedman, D. N.

Mathys, H.-P. *Liebe deinen Nächsten wie dich selbst. Untersuchungen zum alttestamentlichen Gebot der Nächstenliebe (Lev 19, 18)*, OBO 71 (Freiburg, 1986).

Mayes, A. D. H. "Deuteronomy 29, Joshua 9, and the place of the Gibeonites in Israel", in N. Lohfink, Hsg., *Das Deuteronomium. Entstehung, Gestalt und Botschaft*, BEThL 68 (Leuven, 1985), 321-325.

Meek, T. J. "The Translation of *Gēr* in the Hexateuch and its bearing on the Documentary Hypothesis", *JBL* 49 (1930), 172-180.

—, "The Origin of Hebrew Law", in idem *Hebrew Origins* (Revised edition, New York, 1950), 49-81.

Meier, W. "»...Fremdlinge die aus Israel gekommen waren...« Eine Notiz in 2 Chronik 30,25f. aus den Sicht der Ausgrabungen im Jüdischen Viertel der Altstadt von Jerusalem", *BN* 15 (1981), 40-43.

Meinhold, A. "Zur Beziehung Gott, Volk, Land im Jobel-Zusammenhang", *BZ* 29 (1985), 245-261.

Milgrom, J. *Studies in Levitical Terminology, I The Encroacher and the Levite. The Term 'Aboda* (Berkeley, 1970).

—, "A Prolegomenon to Leviticus 17:11", *JBL* 90 (1971), 149-156.

—, "The Alleged 'Demythologization and Secularization' in Deuteronomy", *IEJ* 23 (1973), 156-161.

—, "The Priestly Doctrine of Repentance", *RB* 82 (1975), 186-205.

—, "Israel's Sanctuary: The Priestly «Picture of Dorian Gray»", *RB* 83 (1976), 390-399.

—, *Cult and Conscience. The Asham and the Priestly Doctrine of Repentance* (Leiden, 1976).

—, "Profane slaughter and a Formulaic Key to the Composition of Deuteronomy", *HUCA* 47 (1976), 1-17.

—, "The Betrothed Slave-girl, Lev 19 20-22", *ZAW* 89 (1977), 43-50.

—, "Priestly Terminology and the Political and Social Structure of Pre-Monarchic Israel", *JQR* 69 (1978-79), 65-81.

—, "Sancta Contagion and the Altar/City Asylum", in J. A. Emerton, ed., *Congress Volume. Vienna 1980*, SVT 32 (1981), 278-310.

—, "Religious Conversion and the Revolt Model for the Formation of Israel", *JBL* 101 (1982), 169-76.

—, *Studies in Cultic Theology and Terminology* (Leiden, 1983).

—, "Rationale for Cultic Law: The Case of Impurity", *Semeia* 45 (1989), 103-109.

—, "Ethics and Ritual: The Foundations of Biblical Dietary Laws", in E. B. Firmage et al., eds., *Religion and Law. Biblical-Judaic and Islamic Perspectives* (Winona Lake, 1990), 159-191.

—, *Leviticus 1-16*, Anchor Bible (New York, 1991).

Millar, J. G. see McConville, J. G.

Miller, P. D. "The Gift of God. The Deuteronomic Theology of the Land", *Interpretation* 23 (1969), 451-465.

Moor, J. C. de and P. Sanders, "An Ugaritic Expiation Ritual and its Old Testament Parallels", *UF* 23 (1991), 283-300.

Morgenstern, J. "The Decalogue of the Holiness Code", *HUCA* 26 (1955), 1-27.

Neufeld, E. "The Prohibitions against Loans at Interest in Ancient Hebrew Laws", *HUCA* 26 (1955), 355-412.

Niehr, H. *Rechtsprechung in Israel. Untersuchungen zur Geschichte der Gerichtsorganisation im Alten Testament* (Stuttgart 1987).

—, "Grundzüge der Forschung zur Gerichtsorganisation Israels", *BZ* 31 (1987), 206-227.

Nöldeke, Th. *Untersuchungen zur Kritik des Alten Testaments* (Kiel, 1869).

North, R. *Sociology of the Biblical Jubilee*, AnBib 4 (Rome, 1954).

Noth, M. "Die Gesetze im Pentateuch", in idem, *Gesammelte Studien zum Alten Testament*, Theologische Bücherei, AT 6 (München, [3]1966), 9-141.

Noth, M. *Das dritte Buch Mose, Leviticus*, ATD (Göttingen, 1962).

Otto, E. *Wandel der Rechtsbegründungen in der Gesellschafts-geschichte des antiken Israel*, Studia Biblica 3 (Leiden, 1988).

—, *Rechtsgeschichte der Redaktionen im Kodex Ešnunna und im «Bundesbuch». Eine redaktionsgeschichtliche und rechtsvergleichende Studie zu altbabylonischen und altisraelitischen Rechtsüberlieferungen*, OBO 85 (Freiburg & Göttingen, 1989).

—, "Auf dem Wege zu einer altorientalischen Rechtsgeschichte", *BiOr* 48 (1991), 5-13.

—, "Die Geschichte der Talion im Alten Orient und Israel", in D. R. Daniels et al., Hsg., *Ernten, was man sät*, Fs K. Koch (Neukirchen-Vluyn, 1991), 101-130.

—, "Die Bedeutung der altorientalischen Rechtsgeschichte für das Verständnis des Alten Testaments", *ZThK* 88 (1991), 139-168.

—, "Soziale Verantwortung und Reinheit des Landes. Zur Redaktion der kasuistischen Rechtssätze in Deuteronomium 19-25", in R. Liwak und S. Wagner, Hsg., *Prophetie und geschichtliche Wirklichkeit im alten Israel*, Fs S. Herrmann (Stuttgart, 1991), 290-306.

—, "Der Dekalog als Brennspiegel israelitischer Rechtsgeschichte", in J. Hausmann und H.-J. Zobel, Hsg., *Alttestamentlicher Glaube und Biblische Theologie*, Fs H. D. Preuß (Stuttgart, 1992), 59-68.

—, *Theologische Ethik des Alten Testaments*, Theologische Wissenschaft 3,2 (Stuttgart, 1994).

—, "Das Heiligkeitsgesetz Leviticus 17-26 in der Pentateuchredaktion", in P. Mommer, W. Thiel, Hsg., *Altes Testament. Forschung und Wirkung*, Fs H. Graf Reventlow (Frankfurt a. M., 1994), 65-80.

—, "Rechtsreformen in Deuteronomium XXII-XXVI und im mittelassyrischen Kodex der Tafel A (KAV 1)", in J. A. Emerton, ed., *Congress Volume. Paris 1992*, SVT 61 (Leiden, 1995), 239-273.

—, "Gesetzesfortschreibung und Pentateuchredaktion", *ZAW* 107 (1995), 373-392.

Otto, R. *Das Heilige. Über das Irrationale in der Idee des Göttlichen und sein Verhältnis zum Rationalen* (Breslau, 1921[6]).

Paran, M. *Forms of the Priestly Style in the Pentateuch. Patterns, Linguistic Usages, Syntactic Structures* (Jerusalem, 1989) [Hebrew].

Paton, L. B. "The Original Form of Leviticus xvii.-xix.", *JBL* 16 (1897), 31-77.

—, "The Original Form of Leviticus xxi., xxii.", *JBL* 17 (1898), 149-175.

—, "The Original Form of Leviticus xxiii., xxv.", *JBL* 18 (1899), 35-60.

Patrick, D. *Old Testament Law* (London, 1985).

Paul, S. M. *Studies in the Book of the Covenant in Light of Cuneiform and Biblical Law*, SVT 18 (Leiden, 1970).

Perlitt, L. "»Ein einzig Volk von Brüdern.« Zur deuteronomischen Herkunft der biblischen Bezeichnung »Bruder«", in D. Lührmann und G. Strecker, Hsg., *Kirche*, Fs G. Bornkamm (Tübingen, 1980), 27-52.

—, "Motive und Schichten der Landtheologie im Deuteronomium", in G. Strecker, Hsg., *Das Land Israel in biblischer Zeit*, Jerusalem-Symposium 1981 (Göttingen, 1983), 46-58.

Péter-Contesse, R. *Lévitique 1-16*, CAT (Genève, 1993).

Phillips, A. *Ancient Israel's Criminal Law. A New Approach to The Decalogue* (Oxford, 1970).

—, "Uncovering the Father's Skirt", *VT* 30 (1980), 38-43.

van der Ploeg, J. "Studies in Hebrew Law", *CBQ* 12 (1950), 248-259; 416-427; *CBQ* 13 (1951), 28-43; 164-171; 296-307.

Polzin, R. *Late Biblical Hebrew. Toward an Historical Typology of Biblical Hebrew Prose*, HSM 12 (Missoula, 1976).

Pons, J. "La référence au séjour en Egypte et à la sortie d'Egypte dans les codes de lois de l'Ancien Testament", *ETR* 63 (1988), 169-182.

Preuss, H. D. Art. Heiligkeitsgesetz, in TRE 14 (Berlin, 1985), 713-718.

Rabast, K. *Das apodiktische Recht im Deuteronomium und im Heiligkeitsgesetz* (Berlin-Hermsdorf, 1948)

Rad, G. von *Das Gottesvolk im Deuteronomium*, BWANT 47 (Stuttgart, 1929).

—, *Die Priesterschrift im Hexateuch*, BWANT 65 (Stuttgart, 1934).

—, "Verheißenes Land und Jahwes Land im Hexateuch", *ZDPV* 66 (1943), 191-204; repr. in idem, *Gesammelte Studien zum Alten Testament*, Theologische Bücherei, AT 8 (München, 1961), 87-100.

—, *Deuteronomium-Studien*, FRLANT 58 (Göttingen, 1947) repr. in idem, *Gesammelte Studien II*, Theologische Bücherei, AT 48 (München, 1973), 109-153.

—, "»Gerechtigkeit« und »Leben« in der Kultsprache der Psalmen", in W. Baumgartner et al., Hsg., Fs A. Bertholet (Tübingen, 1950), 418-437.

Rendsburg, G. "Late Biblical Hebrew and the Date of 'P'", *JANES* 12 (1980), 65-80.

Rendtorff, R. *Das Alte Testament. Eine Einführung* (Neukirchen-Vluyn, 1983).

—, *Die "Bundesformel". Eine exegetisch-theologische Untersuchung*, SBS 160 (Stuttgart, 1995).

Reventlow, H. Graf *Das Heiligkeitsgesetz formgeschichtlich untersucht*, WMANT 6 (Neukirchen, 1961).

—, "Kultisches Recht im Alten Testament", *ZThK* 60 (1963), 267-304.

Ringgren, H. "The Prophetical Conception of Holiness", *Uppsala Universitets Årsskrift* 1948:12 (1948), 3-30.

Robertson Smith, W. *Lectures on the Religion of the Semites* (Edinburgh, 1889).

Robinson, G. *The Origin and Development of the Old Testament Sabbath*, Beiträge zur biblischen Exegese und Theologie 21 (Frankfurt am Main, 1988).

—, "Das Jobel-Jahr", in D. R. Daniels et al., Hsg., *Ernten, was man sät*, Fs K. Koch (Neukirchen-Vluyn, 1991), 471-494.

Rofé, A. *Introduction to Deuteronomy* (Jerusalem, 1988) [Hebrew].

Rooker, M. *Biblical Hebrew in Transition. The Language of the Book of Ezekiel*, JSOTS 90 (Sheffield, 1990).

Rost, L. "Die Bezeichnungen für Land und Volk im Alten Testament", A. Alt et al., Hsg., Fs O. Procksch (Leipzig, 1934), 125-148.

—, *Die Vorstufen von Kirche und Synagoge im Alten Testament. Eine wortgeschichtliche Untersuchung*, BWANT 76 (Stuttgart, 1938).

Rücker, H. *Die Begründungen der Weisungen Jahwes im Pentateuch*, Erfurter Theologische Studien 30 (Leipzig, 1973).

Saebø, M. "Priestertheologie und Priesterschrift", in J. A. Emerton, ed., *Congress Volume. Vienna 1980*, SVT 32 (1981), 357-374.

Sailhammer, J. H. *The Pentateuch as Narrative. A Biblical-Theological Commentary* (Grand Rapids, 1992).

P. Sanders, see Moor, J. C. de

Schmidt, K. L. "Israels Stellung zu den Fremden und Beisassen und Israels Wissen um seine Fremdling- und Beisassenschaft", *Judaica* 1 (1945-46), 269-296.

Schneider, H. *Das Buch Leviticus*, Echter-Bibel (Würzburg, 1958).

Schottroff, W. "Zum alttestamentlichen Recht", *VF* 22 (1977), 3-29.

Schüngel-Straumann, H. *Tod und Leben in der Gesetzesliteratur des Pentateuch unter besonderer Berücksichtigung der Terminologie von "töten"* , Diss. Rheinische Friedrich-Wilhelm-Universität, Bonn, 1969.

Schulz, H. *Das Todesrecht im Alten Testament. Studien zur Rechtsform der Mot-Jumat-Sätze*, BZAW 114 (Berlin, 1969).

Schwartz, B. J. recension of R. Sonsino, Motive Clauses in Biblical Law, *JSS* 28 (1983), 161-163.

—, "A Literary Study of the Slave-Girl Pericope—Leviticus 19:20-22", *Scripta Hierosolymitana* 31 (Jerusalem, 1986), 241-255.

—, *Selected Chapters of the Holiness Code*, PhD dissertation, Hebrew University, Jerusalem 1987 [Hebrew].

—, "The Prohibition Concerning the 'Eating' of Blood in Leviticus 17", in G. A. Anderson and S. M. Olyan, eds., *Priesthood and Cult in Ancient Israel*, JSOTS 125 (Sheffield, 1991), 34-66.

Smelik, K. A. D. "Moloch, Molekh or Molk-Sacrifice? A Reassessment of the Evidence Concerning the Hebrew term Molekh", *SJOT* 9 (1995), 133-142.

Smend, R. *Die Bundesformel* (Zürich, 1963); repr. in idem, *Die Mitte des Alten Testaments. Gesammelte Studien Band* 1 (München, 1986), 11-39.

—, *Die Entstehung des Alten Testaments* (Stuttgart, 1978).

Smith, M. *Palestinian Parties and Politics that Shaped the Old Testament* (New York & London, 1971).

Snaith, N. H. *Leviticus and Numbers*, Century Bible (London, 1967).

Sonsino, R. *Motive Clauses in Biblical Law. Biblical Forms and Near Eastern Parallels*, SBLDS 45 (Chico, 1980).

Soss, N. M. "Old Testament Law and Economic Society", *Journal of the History of Ideas* 34 (1973), 323-344.

Speiser, E. A. "Leviticus and the Critics", in M. Haran, ed., *Yehezkel Kaufmann Jubilee Volume* (Jerusalem, 1960), 29-45; repr. in idem, *Oriental and Biblical Studies. Collected Writings of E. A. Speiser*, edited by J. J. Finkelstein and M. Greenberg (Philadelphia, 1967), 123-142.

—, ""People" and "Nation" of Israel", in idem, *Oriental and Biblical Studies. Collected Writings of E. A. Speiser*, edited by J. J. Finkelstein and M. Greenberg (Philadelphia, 1967), 160-170.

Spina, F. A. "Israelites as Gērîm, 'Sojourners,' in Social and Historical Context", in C. L. Meyers and M. O'Connor, eds., *The Word of the Lord Shall Go Forth*, Fs. D. N. Freedman (Winona Lake, 1983), 321-335.

Sulzberger, M. "The Status of Labor in Ancient Israel", *JQR* NS 13 (1922-23), 245-302, 397-459.

Talmon, S. "Der jüdische עם הארץ in historischer Perspektive", in idem, *Gesellschaft und Literatur in den hebräischen Bibel* (Neukirchen-Vluyn, 1988), 80-91.

Thiel, W. "Erwägungen zum Alter des Heiligkeitsgesetzes", *ZAW* 81 (1969), 40-73.

—, recension of A. Cholewinski, Heiligkeitsgesetz und Deuteronomium, *ThLZ* 103 (1978), 258-260.

Thompson, R. J. *Moses and the Law in a Century of Criticism since Graf*, SVT 19 (Leiden, 1970).

Toorn, K. van der "La pureté rituelle au proche-orient ancien", *RHR* 206 (1989), 339-356.

Tosato, A. "The Law of Leviticus 18:18: a Reexamination", *CBQ* 46 (1984), 199-214.

Valeton, J. J. P. "Bedeutung und Stellung des Wortes בר ית im Priestercodex", *ZAW* 12 (1892), 1-22.

Vaux, R. de *Les institutions de l'Ancien Testament*, vol. I (Paris, 1958), vol. II (Paris, 1960).

Vink, J. G. "The Date and Origin of the Priestly Code in the Old Testament", *OTS* 15 (1969), 1-144.

Wacholder, B. Z. "The Calendar of Sabbatical Cycles during the Second Temple and the

Early Rabbinic Period", *HUCA* 44 (1973), 153-196.

Wagner, V. *Rechtssätze in gebundener Sprache und Rechtssatzreihen im israelitischen Recht. Ein Beitrag zur Gattungsforschung*, BZAW 127 (Berlin, 1972).

—, "Zur Existenz des sogenannten »Heiligkeitsgesetzes«", *ZAW* 86 (1974), 307-316.

Walton, J. H. *Ancient Israelite Literature in its Cultural Context. A Survey of Parallels Between Biblical and Ancient Near Eastern Texts* (Grand Rapids, 1989).

Watts, J. W. "Public Readings and Pentateuchal Law", *VT* 45 (1995), 540-557.

Weber, M. *Gesammelte Aufsätze zur Religionssoziologie. III Das antike Judentum* (Tübingen, 1921).

Weimar, P. "Struktur und Komposition der priesterschriftlichen Geschichtsdarstellung", *BN* 23 (1984), 81-134; *BN* 24 (1984), 138-162.

Weinberg, J. P. *The Citizen-Temple Community*, transl. by D. L. Smith-Christopher, JSOTS 151 (Sheffield, 1992).

—, "Die Mentalität der jerusalemischen Bürger-Tempel-Gemeinde des 6.-4. Jh. v. u. Z.", *Transeuphratène* 5 (1992), 133-141.

Weinfeld, M. *Deuteronomy and the Deuteronomic School* (Oxford, 1972).

—, "Burning Babies in Ancient Israel", *UF* 10 (1978), 411-413.

—, "Literary Creativity", in A. Malamat, ed., *The World History of the Jewish People, Vol. 4,2. The Age of the Monarchies: Culture and Society* (Jerusalem, 1979), 27-70.

—, "Julius Wellhausen's Understanding of the Law of Ancient Irael and its Fallacies", *Shnaton* 4 (1980), 62-93 [Hebrew].

—, "Sabbath, Temple and the Enthronement of the Lord—The problem of the Sitz im Leben of Gen 1:1-2:3", in *Mélanges bibliques et orientaux en l'honneur de M. Henri Cazelles*, AOAT 212 (Neukirchen, 1981), 501-512.

—, "The Extent of the Promised Land—The Status of Transjordan", in G. Strecker, Hsg., *Das Land Israel in biblischer Zeit*, Jerusalem-Symposium 1981 (Göttingen, 1983), 59-75.

—, *Justice and Righteousness in Israel and the Nations. Equality and Freedom in Ancient Israel in Light of Social Justice in the Ancient Near East* (Jerusalem, 1985) [Hebrew].

—, "Sabbatical Year and Jubilee in the Pentateuchal Laws and their Ancient Near Eastern Background", in T. Veijola, ed., *The Law in the Bible and its Environment*, Publications of the Finnish Exegetic Society 51 (Göttingen, 1990), 39-62.

—, *Deuteronomy 1-11*, Anchor Bible (New York, 1991).

Weingreen, J. "The Case of the Blasphemer (Lev xxiv 10ff.)", *VT* 22 (1972), 118-123.

Welker, M. "Security of Expectations: Reformulating the Theology of Law and Gospel", *Journal of Religion* 66 (1986), 237-260.

Wellhausen, J. *Die Composition des Hexateuchs und der historischen Bücher des Alten Testaments* (Berlin, 1899³).

—, *Prolegomena zur Geschichte Israels* (Berlin, 1886³).

Wenham, G. J. *The Book of Leviticus*, NICOT (Grand Rapids, 1979).

—, "The Old Testament Attitude to Homosexuality", *Expository Times* 102 (1991), 359-363.

Westbrook, R. "Biblical and Cuneiform Law Codes", *RB* 92 (1985), 247-264.

—, *Studies in Biblical and Cuneiform Law*, Cahiers de la Revue Biblique 26 (Paris, 1988).

—, "Adultery in Ancient Near Eastern Law", *RB* 97 (1990), 542-580.

—, *Property and Family in Biblical Law*, JSOTS 113 (Sheffield, 1991).

Wiener, H. M. *Studies in Biblical Law* (London, 1904).

Wildberger, H. "Israel und sein Land", *EvTh* 16 (1956), 404-422.

Wold, D. J. "The *Kareth* Penalty in P: Rationale and Cases", *SBL 1979 Seminar Papers*, Vol. 1 (Missoula, 1979), 1-45.

Wright, C. J. H. *God's People in God's Land. Family, Land and Property in the Old Testament* (Grand Rapids, 1990).

Wurster, P. "Zur Charakteristik und Geschichte des Priestercodex und Heiligkeitsgesetzes", *ZAW* 4 (1884), 112-133.

Zevit, Z. "Converging Lines of Evidence Bearing on the Date of P", *ZAW* 94 (1982), 481-511.

Zimmerli, W. "Ich bin Jahwe", in *Geschichte und Altes Testament.* Beiträge zur historischen Theologie 16. Albrecht Alt zum 70 Geburtstag dargebracht (Tübingen, 1953), 179-209; repr. in idem, *Gottes Offenbarung. Gesammelte Aufsätze*, Theologische Bücherei, AT 19 (München ,1963), 11-40.

—, "Die Eigenart der prophetischen Rede des Ezechiel. Ein Beitrag zum Problem an Hand von Ez. 14 1-11", *ZAW* 66 (1954), 1-26.

—, "Israel im Buche Ezechiel", *VT* 8 (1958), 75-90.

—, "Sinaibund und Abrahambund. Ein Beitrag zum Verständnis der Priesterschrift", *ThZ* 16 (1960), 268-80; repr. in idem, *Gottes Offenbarung. Gesammelte Aufsätze*, Theologische Bücherei, AT 19 (München, 1963), 205-216.

—, "Heiligkeit nach dem sogenannten Heiligkeitsgesetz", *VT* 30 (1980), 493-512.

Zipor, M. A. "Notes sur les chapitres XIX à XXII du Lévitique dans la bible d'Alexandrie", *EThL* 67 (1991), 328-337.

Zunz, L. "Bibelkritisches", *ZDMG* 27 (1873), 669-689.

INDEX OF PASSAGES DISCUSSED

SUPPLEMENTS TO VETUS TESTAMENTUM

2. POPE, M.H. *El in the Ugaritic texts.* 1955. ISBN 90 04 04000 5
3. *Wisdom in Israel and in the Ancient Near East.* Presented to Harold Henry Rowley by the Editorial Board of Vetus Testamentum in celebration of his 65th birthday, 24 March 1955. Edited by M. NOTH and D. WINTON THOMAS. 2nd reprint of the first (1955) ed. 1969. ISBN 90 04 02326 7
4. *Volume du Congrès* [International pour l'étude de l'Ancien Testament]. Strasbourg 1956. 1957. ISBN 90 04 02327 5
8. BERNHARDT, K.-H. *Das Problem der alt-orientalischen Königsideologie im Alten Testament.* Unter besonderer Berücksichtigung der Geschichte der Psalmenexegese darge-stellt und kritisch gewürdigt. 1961. ISBN 90 04 02331 3
9. *Congress Volume,* Bonn 1962. 1963. ISBN 90 04 02332 1
11. DONNER, H. *Israel unter den Völkern.* Die Stellung der klassischen Propheten des 8. Jahrhunderts v. Chr. zur Aussenpolitik der Könige von Israel und Juda. 1964. ISBN 90 04 02334 8
12. REIDER, J. *An Index to Aquila.* Completed and revised by N. Turner. 1966. ISBN 90 04 02335 6
13. ROTH, W.M.W. *Numerical sayings in the Old Testament.* A form-critical study. 1965. ISBN 90 04 02336 4
14. ORLINSKY, H.M. *Studies on the second part of the Book of Isaiah.* — The so-called 'Servant of the Lord' and 'Suffering Servant' in Second Isaiah. — Snaith, N.H. Isaiah 40-66. A study of the teaching of the Second Isaiah and its consequences. Repr. with additions and corrections. 1977. ISBN 90 04 05437 5
15. *Volume du Congrès* [International pour l'étude de l'Ancien Testament]. Genève 1965. 1966. ISBN 90 04 02337 2
17. *Congress Volume,* Rome 1968. 1969. ISBN 90 04 02339 9
19. THOMPSON, R.J. *Moses and the Law in a century of criticism since Graf.* 1970. ISBN 90 04 02341 0
20. REDFORD, D.B. *A study of the biblical story of Joseph.* 1970. ISBN 90 04 02342 9
21. AHLSTRÖM, G.W. *Joel and the temple cult of Jerusalem.* 1971. ISBN 90 04 02620 7
22. *Congress Volume,* Uppsala 1971. 1972. ISBN 90 04 03521 4
23. *Studies in the religion of ancient Israel.* 1972. ISBN 90 04 03525 7
24. SCHOORS, A. *I am God your Saviour.* A form-critical study of the main genres in Is. xl-lv. 1973. ISBN 90 04 03792 2
25. ALLEN, L.C. *The Greek Chronicles.* The relation of the Septuagint I and II Chroni-cles to the Massoretic text. Part 1. The translator's craft. 1974. ISBN 90 04 03913 9
26. *Studies on prophecy.* A collection of twelve papers. 1974. ISBN 90 04 03877 9
27. ALLEN, L.C. *The Greek Chronicles.* Part 2. Textual criticism. 1974. ISBN 90 04 03933 3
28. *Congress Volume,* Edinburgh 1974. 1975. ISBN 90 04 04321 7
29. *Congress Volume,* Göttingen 1977. 1978. ISBN 90 04 05835 4
30. EMERTON, J.A. (ed.). *Studies in the historical books of the Old Testament.* 1979. ISBN 90 04 06017 0
31. MEREDINO, R.P. *Der Erste und der Letzte.* Eine Untersuchung von Jes 40-48. 1981. ISBN 90 04 06199 1
32. EMERTON, J.A. (ed.). *Congress Vienna 1980.* 1981. ISBN 90 04 06514 8
33. KOENIG, J. *L'herméneutique analogique du Judaïsme antique d'après les témoins textuels d'Isaïe.* 1982. ISBN 90 04 06762 0

34. BARSTAD, H.M. *The religious polemics of Amos*. Studies in the preachings of Amos ii 7B-8, iv 1-13, v 1-27, vi 4-7, viii 14. 1984. ISBN 90 04 07017 6

35. KRAŠOVEC, J. *Antithetic structure in Biblical Hebrew poetry*. 1984. ISBN 90 04 07244 6

36. EMERTON, J.A. (ed.). *Congress Volume*, Salamanca 1983. 1985. ISBN 90 04 07281 0

37. LEMCHE, N.P. *Early Israel*. Anthropological and historical studies on the Israelite society before the monarchy. 1985. ISBN 90 04 07853 3

38. NIELSEN, K. *Incense in Ancient Israel*. 1986. ISBN 90 04 07702 2

39. PARDEE, D. *Ugaritic and Hebrew poetic parallelism*. A trial cut. 1988. ISBN 90 04 08368 5

40. EMERTON, J.A. (ed.). *Congress Volume*, Jerusalem 1986. 1988. ISBN 90 04 08499 1

41. EMERTON, J.A. (ed.). *Studies in the Pentateuch*. 1990. ISBN 90 04 09195 5

42. McKENZIE, S.L. *The trouble with Kings*. The composition of the Book of Kings in the Deuteronomistic History. 1991. ISBN 90 04 09402 4

43. EMERTON, J.A. (ed.). *Congress Volume*, Leuven 1989. 1991. ISBN 90 04 09398 2

44. HAAK, R.D. *Habakkuk*. 1992. ISBN 90 04 09506 3

45. BEYERLIN, W. *Im Licht der Traditionen*. Psalm LXVII und CXV. Ein Entwicklungs-zusammenhang. 1992. ISBN 90 04 09635 3

46. MEIER, S.A. *Speaking of Speaking*. Marking direct discourse in the Hebrew Bible. 1992. ISBN 90 04 09602 7

47. KESSLER, R. *Staat und Gesellschaft im vorexilischen Juda*. Vom 8. Jahrhundert bis zum Exil. 1992. ISBN 90 04 09646 9

48. AUFFRET, P. *Voyez de vos yeux*. Étude structurelle de vingt psaumes, dont le psaume 119. 1993. ISBN 90 04 09707 4

49. GARCÍA MARTÍNEZ, F., A. HILHORST AND C.J. LABUSCHAGNE (eds.). *The Scriptures and the Scrolls*. Studies in honour of A.S. van der Woude on the occasion of his 65th birthday. 1992. ISBN 90 04 09746 5

50. LEMAIRE, A. AND B. OTZEN (eds.). *History and Traditions of Early Israel*. Studies presented to Eduard Nielsen, May 8th, 1993. 1993. ISBN 90 04 09851 8

51. GORDON, R.P. *Studies in the Targum to the Twelve Prophets*. From Nahum to Malachi. 1994. ISBN 90 04 09987 5

52. HUGENBERGER, G.P. *Marriage as a Covenant*. A Study of Biblical Law and Ethics Governing Marriage Developed from the Perspective of Malachi. 1994. ISBN 90 04 09977 8

53. GARCÍA MARTÍNEZ, F., A. HILHORST, J.T.A.G.M. VAN RUITEN, A.S. VAN DER WOUDE. *Studies in Deuteronomy*. In Honour of C.J. Labuschagne on the Occasion of His 65th Birthday. 1994. ISBN 90 04 10052 0

54. FERNANDÉZ MARCOS, N. *Septuagint and Old Latin in the Book of Kings*. 1994. ISBN 90 04 10043 1

55. SMITH, M.S. *The Ugaritic Baal Cycle*. *Volume 1*. Introduction with text, translation and commentary of KTU 1.1-1.2. 1994. ISBN 90 04 09995 6

56. DUGUID, I.M. *Ezekiel and the Leaders of Israel*. 1994. ISBN 90 04 10074 1

57. MARX, A. *Les offrandes végétales dans l'Ancien Testament*. Du tribut d'hommage au repas eschatologique. 1994. ISBN 90 04 10136 5

58. SCHÄFER-LICHTENBERGER, C. *Josua und Salomo*. Eine Studie zu Autorität und Legitimität des Nachfolgers im Alten Testament. 1995. ISBN 90 04 10064 4

59. LASSERRE, G. *Synopse des lois du Pentateuque*. 1994. ISBN 90 04 10202 7

60. DOGNIEZ, C. *Bibliography of the Septuagint – Bibliographie de la Septante (1970-1993)*. Avec une préface de Pierre-Maurice Bogaert. 1995. ISBN 90 04 10192 6

61. EMERTON, J.A. (ed.). *Congress Volume*, Paris 1992. 1995. ISBN 90 04 10259 0

62. SMITH, P.A. *Rhetoric and Redaction in Trito-Isaiah.* The Structure, Growth and Authorship of Isaiah 56-66. 1995. ISBN 90 04 10306 6

63. O'CONNELL, R.H. *The Rhetoric of the Book of Judges.* 1996. ISBN 90 04 10104 7

64. HARLAND, P. J. *The Value of Human Life.* A Study of the Story of the Flood (Genesis 6-9). 1996. ISBN 90 04 10534 4

65. ROLAND PAGE JR., H. *The Myth of Cosmic Rebellion.* A Study of its Reflexes in Ugaritic and Biblical Literature. 1996. ISBN 90 04 10563 8

66. EMERTON, J.A. (ed.). *Congress Volume.* Cambridge 1995. 1997.
    ISBN 90 04 106871

67. JOOSTEN, J. *People and Land in the Holiness Code.* An Exegetical Study of the Ideational Framework of the Law in Leviticus 17–26. 1996. ISBN 90 04 10557 3